Y0-BVQ-437

REGIONAL ECONOMIC POLICY

STUDIES IN OPERATIONAL REGIONAL SCIENCE

Folmer, H., Regional Economic Policy. 1986. ISBN 90-247-3308-1.

Regional Economic Policy

Measurement of its Effect

by

Hendrik Folmer

1986 **MARTINUS NIJHOFF PUBLISHERS**
a member of the KLUWER ACADEMIC PUBLISHERS GROUP
DORDRECHT / BOSTON / LANCASTER

Distributors

for the United States and Canada: Kluwer Academic Publishers, 190 Old Derby Street, Hingham, MA 02043, USA
for the UK and Ireland: Kluwer Academic Publishers, MTP Press Limited, Falcon House, Queen Square, Lancaster LA1 1RN, UK
for all other countries: Kluwer Academic Publishers Group, Distribution Center, P.O. Box 322, 3300 AH Dordrecht, The Netherlands

Library of Congress Cataloging in Publication Data

ISBN 90-247-3308-1

PREFACE

Impact analysis of economic policy is a subject which is gaining increasing interest in both theoretical and applied economic research. Two main reasons for the growing interest can be distinguished. First, the situation of the government's finances is making it more than ever necessary to assess critically the effects of the instruments used to pursue public policy goals. Secondly, because of the economic stagnation government will be increasingly appealed to for support.

Impact analysis, however, is hampered by three major problems: methodological deficiencies, lack of econometric approaches which have been adapted to the specific conditions of this kind of analysis and data availability. The present book deals with these problems in the context of regional economic policy. However, the main findings are broadly applicable in various other fields.

This book is primarily oriented towards those who have a practical interest. Therefore, attention is mostly paid to the practical aspects of the methodology and the measurements methods. Furthermore, the methodological and econometric parts are supplemented by two extensive case studies.

Three people have contributed constructive criticisms and suggestions on some chapters of the book: Peter Nijkamp, Theo Dijkstra and Manfred Fischer. I am very grateful for their support. They, of course, share no blame for any deficiences in the present form of the book. I also gratefully acknowledge the assistance of Harry Barkema and Marja Schuring with the computations. Moreover, I want to thank Fokke de Jong for his improvement of the English. Finally, thanks are due to Maidra Lukkien-Bernadina, Alie Wolterman and Margreet Miedema for their typing and editioral assistance without which this book would not have come to fruition.

Finally, I do hope that this publication will provide stimulii for a broadening and deepening of economic policy analysis.

Groningen, June 1985   Hendrik Folmer

CONTENTS

PART II: **ECONOMETRIC METHODS**

EPILOGUE

1. INTRODUCTION

1.1 The purpose of this study

During the first three decades after the Second World War, the economies of most Western countries expanded rapidly. This growth was accompanied by greater governmental involvement with increasing shares for public expenditure. The expansion did not only occur in the traditional domains of activity such as defence, infrastructure investment and general administration, but also in areas such as subsidies to private enterprises and, especially, social welfare programs.[1] Finally, the government involvement expanded in the form of increased regulation of various activities. The expanding public expenditures had far-reaching consequences for the economy in the form of increasing taxes, public sector lending, government employment, gross household incomes, etc.

For several reasons, such as the outbreak of the oil crisis, the collapse of the exchange rate system and the commodity and wage booms, the 1970s and 1980s have witnessed severe stagflation. This imbalance has seriously affected various aspects of the economy, not in the least the public sector. The size of its spending and the involvement of the public sector with the private sector in general have come under closer scrutiny. Even more so, the public sector is increasingly mentioned as an independent, contributing cause to weaker economic performance, witness the well-known theories of supply-side and monetary economists (see, among others, Hailstones, 1982). On the other hand, in the opinion of various other economists the government still has to play a firm role in the economic process (see, among others, Hahn, 1980, 1982).

The huge implications of its involvement and the confusion about its results have led to a growing interest in a systematic evaluation of the role of the government in the economic process. In this study attention

---

[1] The increase of social welfare programs is generally considered as the main cause of the observed overall expansion of general government expenditure (see, among others, OECD, 1978).

is paid to one of its aspects, viz. **economic policy**. The importance of policy evaluation is recognized by both official governmental authorities and by theoretical economists. For instance, in his opening address to the 22nd European Congress of the Regional Science Association at Groningen the Dutch Minister of Economic Affairs stated (Terlouw, 1982):

> A government should always consider the effects of its policies, including regional policies. The situation of the government's finances is now making it more than ever necessary to assess critically the goals pursued so far and the tools used to attain them. You will not be surprised to hear that we are facing big practical problems in our evaluation of the effectiveness of policies. Nevertheless, it is a subject which requires ever closer attention.

The importance from a theoretical point of view is clearly expressed by, among others, Marschak (1969):

> The economist is asked to predict how some specified changes in the environment will affect economic variables. Of particular interest are those changes of the environment that are deliberately designed and are called 'policies', and those economic variables that are a given policy-maker's decision- criteria.

As will be motivated in the sequel, only one aspect of policy evalua-tion will be considered here, viz. measurement of effects of economic policy (also to be denoted as "impact analysis"). The "big practical problems" referred to by the Dutch Minister of Economic Affairs, however, also apply to impact analysis. They can be divided into three, closely related categories: methodological problems, adaptation of econometric approaches and data availability.

It should be marked in passing that methodology is understood here to be occupied with the construction of a conceptual model of the problem at hand and with the selection of an appropriate method to investigate the conceptual model empirically (see, amongst others, Riley, 1963). With respect to the construction of a conceptual model the following aspects of the problem are under discussion:

-Delimitation of the research problem at hand;

-Identification and operational definition of the relevant variables in the research problem;

-Specification of the relationships between the variables;

-Definition of the elements (individuals, firms, regions, etc.) to which the characteristics and relationships refer;

Econometric methods on the other hand are concerned with the **quantification** of the relationships between the variables of the conceptual model.

Although considerable progress has been made with respect to their general development, relatively little attention has been paid to the **adaptation** of the methodology of economics and of econometric methods to the specific conditions of impact analysis of economic policy. Therefore, an attempt is made in this study to formulate a methodology of impact analysis and to adapt some econometric methods to the present measurement problem. It should be marked that special attention will be paid here to the analysis of impacts of **packages** of instruments of economic policy. Policy packages are increasingly being applied in order to reinforce the effects of separate instruments or to counterbalance negative effects of particular instruments. The incorporation of policy packages into an econometric model poses a problem because a policy package is not defined in operational terms.

With respect to the third practical problem mentioned above, viz. data availability, two situations can be distinguished. First, essential information may be missing with respect to a subset of explanatory variables in terms of which the impact variable is to be described. The missing information may seriously hamper adequate impact analysis. As will be argued below, the set of explanatory variables is made up by a subset of policy variables and a subset of non-policy variables. In this study a measurement method (viz. two-stage time series analysis) will be presented which can be applied if observations on the impact variable and the policy instruments are available (which is often the case in practice), though there are no observations available on the non-policy variables.

In the second situation information on all relevant explanatory variables is available in the form of a macro-economic multivariate time series, but the **number** of observations is too small for adequate econometric analysis. Moreover, micro data on e.g. firms which accepted investment subsidies are not available or can only be obtained at high costs. (Additional disadvantages of the use of micro data for impact analysis will be outlined in chapter 3). It is argued in this study that in such circumstances it is worthwhile to consider the use of **spatio-temporal** data. Such data consists of a time series of observations on a set of regions. If this kind of data is used relatively few observations over time are needed for adequate econometric analysis. The analysis of spatio-temporal data has the following additional advantages. First, insight into the effects of policy can often be obtained at an early stage. This makes it possible to redesign policy programs relatively fast, if necessary. Secondly, effects of policy could be discerned which might be diluted in macro data. Spatio-temporal data can be seen as an intermediate form between macro data and micro data, which usually gives the most detailed information on effects of policy.

A prerequisite for the analysis of spatio-temporal data is that economic policy is regionally and temporally differentiated. This requirement is met by those forms of regional economic policy which vary over both space and time. Various forms of macro-economic policy, however, are also spatio-temporal of nature. For instance, investment policy, which intends to stimulate investments at the macro-economic level, frequently favors certain regions more than other regions. Moreover, this kind of policy usually also varies over time. It is with this kind of spatially and temporally differentiated economic policy, which is denoted here as "regional economic policy", that we will be concerned in the sequel. The linear structural equation approach with latent variables (abbreviated as the "LISREL approach") will be adapted to analyze this kind of data.

It should be observed that in order to promote the coherence of this study the two-stage time series analysis measurement approach will also be discussed in the framework of regional economic policy. Its applicability with respect to this kind of policy, however, is limited to the analysis of time series of observations on a single region (i.e. spatio-temporal data with the number of regions equal to one).

This section ends with the following remarks. First, the use of spatio-temporal data has also disadvantages. The main is that the quality of the data is sometimes rather poor. In particular, spatio-temporal data is usually to be obtained from such authorities as a central bureau of statistics. This implies that the researcher has no control over the variables on which information is gathered. Moreover, there is often a delay in the publication of the data (see chapter 9 for an example). Another disadvantage is that the delimitation of the spatial units to which the data refers cannot be influenced by the researcher. Consequently, the spatial units may not be the most appropriate for the impact analysis, neither from a statistical nor from a policy-making point of view. In this study it will be shown that the advantages of the use of spatio-temporal data outweigh the disadvantages. Secondly, in order to avoid too ambitious a project only effects on **regional** policy objectives, such as regional investments, employment, etc. are considered in this study. No attempts are made to measure effects on the national economy nor to estimate international effects. Thirdly, no attention is paid to budget effects. In particular, no systematic cost-benefit analysis is entertained where benefits such as increases in tax payments from assisted firms, savings in unemployment payments, etc. are compared with costs in the form of the financing of the policy programs. Neither are opportunity costs considered. These costs are made up by the alternative uses that could have been made of the funds applied to a given policy program. It is obvious that measurement of national and international effects and cost benefit analysis usually require more complex methodologies and econometric approaches, than are needed to analyze effects on some key variables of regional economies.

1.2 Main causes of spatial inequality and justification of regional economic policy

The purpose of this section is to give some elementary background information on spatial inequality and regional economic policy. As mentioned in the preceding section, this study deals primarily with methodological aspects and econometric methods of impact analysis. In this regard, theoretical aspects of regional economic development and policy will incidentally be touched upon. Therefore, some general theoretical background information is given here.

It is well-known that economic activities and developments are unequally distributed in space. This unequal spatial distribution is generally referred to as "spatial economic inequality". It may manifest itself in such contrasts as low versus high unemployment, income per capita, concentration of investments, population density, economic growth, good environmental quality versus pollution, etc. Throughout the literature several causes of spatial inequality have been identified and described (see, among others, Hoover, 1975). They can be briefly summarized under the following headings:

-The quality and exploitation of natural resources, which determines the productive capacity of a region to a certain extent. Not only does this factor influence the sectors of agriculture, fishing, mining and forestry, but, also, inter alia, location conditions for industrial activities.

-The size and structure of the population, which influences consumption patterns and the supply of labor.

-Agglomeration advantages, such as scale factors, the presence of strong intersectoral relationships and, on the other hand, agglomeration disadvantages in the form of the congestion of many activities.

-The stage of economic development. In stages of economic growth relatively many new activities usually originate in the so-called less developed regions, whereas in periods of stagnation or recession there is often a slow-down. Furthermore, many firms in less developed regions are often more vulnerable to economic stagnation than those in developed regions. This may lead to a reduction of activities in the lagging regions in the case of stagnation.

-The stage of technological development, which influences the kinds of goods produced as well as the organization and the location of the production process.

-Political factors, in the form of general and regional policy. It should be observed that not only economic policy is relevant in this regard, but also various forms of non-economic policy.

-Institutional factors, such as the degree of regional autonomy, historical development, etc.

-Physical location factors, in the form of the availability of harbors, airports, the quality of road and railway networks, the availability of industrial sites, etc.

-Socio-cultural facilities such as the degree of urbanization, the availability of educational and research centres, etc.

Spatial economic inequality and regional development have been key-issues in regional economic policy in many countries since World War II. Globally speaking, there exist two reasons for government intervention (see also Stilwell, 1972, Richardson, 1979). First, there is the goal of **equity**, which requires such a spatial distribution of economic activities that the inhabitants of all regions have more or less equal opportunities to reach a desired level of welfare. Secondly, there is the goal of national **efficiency**, which requires the optimal use of production capacity in order to promote national welfare. Both goals may be compatible, but they may also conflict. [1])

Regional economic policy is tending to grow in importance in many countries. Not only does this apply to the amounts of money spent, but also to the kinds of activities affected. (For detailed information on the Dutch case, among others, Bartels and van Duyn, 1981.) In spite of more intensive regional economic policy there are various indications that spatial economic inequality has increased instead of decreased in many countries, especially during the last decade. This is, inter alia, the case in the Netherlands (see, among others, FNEI, 1981). Furthermore, spatial economic inequality is likely to increase during the eighties, and perhaps even in the more remote future, inter alia, because of the economic stagnation many countries have

---

[1]) For identification of the cases where a conflict between these goals may exist, an elaboration on the nature of the trade-off between equity and efficiency, suggestions for regional policy that help to minimize the effects of the conflict, and cases where these two goals are compatable see, among others, Richardson (1979).

been facing (see the list of causes mentioned above). Consequently, the need for effective regional economic policy in the future is probably to be very strong.

As in the case of economic policy in general, regional economic policy has huge financial implications and there is much confusion about its results. Moreover, in the context of impact analysis of this kind of policy similar methodological problems occur as in the case of economic policy in general. Finally, the analysis of spatio-temporal data requires special adaptations of econometric methods. These considerations form the rationale for this study.

1.3 Outline of the study

In the present section the various chapters of this study are briefly introduced.

Part I, consisting of the chapters 2 and 3, deals with general methodological aspects. Chapter 2 is concerned with the conceptual model of impact analysis. First, a definition of regional economic policy and an overview and classification of the most important instruments in market economies are given. Then a frame of reference for the concept of effects of an instrument of regional economic policy is constructed. The causal context is briefly described and the concept of a regional profile is introduced to cope with the multi-effective character of regional economic policy. Next, a distinction between direct and indirect effects is made and the notion of a n-th order effect is introduced. These notions are required because the measurement method to be used often depends on the type of effect to be measured, in addition to the type of instrument under consideration. A related problem to be dealt with in this context is the openness of regional systems. Finally, the concept latent variable is introduced so as to be able to incorporate policy packages explicitly into the measurement model. Besides, latent variables may be used to represent other kinds of "packages" of variables and they have important advantages with respect to the analysis of spatio-temporal data.

In chapter 3 a frame of reference for the measurement methods to be discussed in this study, viz. the LISREL and the two-stage time serious approaches, is constructed by reviewing various operational measurement methods. Two basic types of approaches are distinguished: micro and spatial analyses. The former consist of experimental, quasi-experimental and non-experimental approaches. In the second type data on micro research elements such as firms, households, etc. are aggregated and analyzed at the level of a given spatial unit. The following types of spatial models have more or less frequently been used in practice and will be discussed:

-Models with explanatory policy variables only;

-Single equation models with explanatory non-policy variable only;

-Single equation models with both policy and non-policy variables as explanatory variables;

-Simultaneous equation models.

This chapter also includes an overview of the kinds of effects of the types of instruments distinguished in chapter 2 and their most appropriate measurement methods.

Part II, comprising the chapters 4-8, deals with econometric methods. In chapter 4, the linear structural equation approach with latent variables is introduced. This method is capable to handle latent and observable variables simultaneously. First, the structure and the basic characteristics of this class of models are described. Next, identification is discussed and attention is paid to three kinds of estimators of LISREL models: initial estimators, maximum likelihood and unweighted least squares. Then judgement of LISREL models is described.

In chapter 5 spatio-temporal LISREL models are considered. The specific feature to which the general LISREL approach has to be adapted here is that of spatial and temporal correlation of the residuals. First, the nature and detection of this kind of correlation is extensively described. Next, the estimation of LISREL models on the basis of spatio-temporal data is dealt with.

The spatio-temporal LISREL measurement model of effects of regional economic policy is paid attention to in chapter 6. The basic principles of the measurement model are described first. Next, point estimators of effects are derived from the parameter matrices of the spatio-temporal LISREL model. Attention will also be paid to interval estimators. Finally, the conditions under which the LISREL measurement procedure can be applied are reviewed.

The second measurement method mentioned above, i.e., two-stage time series analysis, is the subject of chapter 7. First, the structure of this class of measurement models is described. Then the fitting procedure, consisting of the stages of identification, estimation and model judgement are dealt with. In this chapter attention is also paid to the manner of taking spatial spill-over effects into account and to the conditions under which the present measurement procedure can be used.

Chapter 8 is of a rather miscellaneous nature. First, the bootstrap and the jackknife are introduced as distribution-free methods to assess the variability of the estimators applied in the framework of the LISREL and two-stage time series measurement approaches. Next, attention is paid to the selection of an appropriate model candidate out of a set of alternatives and to some simple devices to get insight into the accuracy of data-instigated models.

Part III, consisting of the chapters 9 and 10 is made up by an application of each of the measurement approaches discussed in Part II. In chapter 9 the spatio-temporal LISREL approach is applied to measure effects of Dutch regional industrialization policy (investment premiums and accelerated fiscal depreciation) for the period 1974-1976.

In chapter 10 two-stage time series analysis is used to estimate effects of extra employment programs on the development of unemployment in the province of Groningen for the period 1972-1976.

In the epilogue, consisting of the final chapter 11 attention is paid to some remaining problems, which could be of interest for future research.

PART I: METHODOLOGY

2 A CONCEPTUAL FRAMEWORK

2.1 Introduction

The purpose of this chapter is to construct a conceptual framework which will form the vocabulary of subsequent chapters. The first problem in this regard is the definition and the delimitation of regional economic policy. It will be dealt with in section 2.2. Furthermore, the conceptual model (see section 1.1) of regional economic policy and measurement of its effects will be outlined in that section. As policy evaluation and measurement of effects of policy are frequently mixed up, a distinction between both activities will be made in section 2.3.

From the discussion of its nature it follows that regional economic policy may take different forms. The concept of policy instrument is introduced in section 2.4 to differentiate between these forms. The most important instruments in market economies will also be classified and enumerated in this section. In section 2.5 the notion of effect (or impact) of a policy instrument is discussed. In this regard the causal context of an effect in a non-experimental setting is extensively described. Moreover, the notion of a regional profile is introduced so as to deal with the multi-effective nature of policy instruments. Finally, the concepts direct, indirect and n-th order effects are introduced because the measurement method to be used is dependent on, inter alia, the kind of effect under consideration. As regional economic policy may not only affect the profile of a region where it has been implemented but also the profiles of other regions, attention is paid to the openness of regional systems in section 2.6.

The last concept to be dealt with is that of a latent variable. It plays an important role in the analysis of effects of policy packages, which are paid special attention to in this study. Furthermore, it is a key concept in the LISREL approach, which is one of the main measurement methods to be developed and applied in this study. It is dealth with in section 2.7.

2.2 Definition of regional economic policy

By economic policy forms of economic behavior are indicated which are "directed towards the maximalisation of the ordinary ophelimity functions" (Tinbergen, 1977). In this study the notion of economic policy will refer to governments. Although economic policy in general can quite well be delimitated by this definition, it is too broad in the context of regional economic policy. For instance, if regional economic policy is defined as all those acts of the national, the regional or the local governments that affect economic characteristics of one or more regions, then all economic policy and also substantial parts of non-economic policy are regional economic policy. Therefore it is limited here to those acts of the central, regional or local governments which are consciously **aimed** at influencing the economic situation of one or more regions.

The following remarks are in order here. First, according to this definition regional economic policy may also take the form of interventions in other societal subsystems than the economic subsystem. For instance, a regional economy may be stimulated by means of creating educational or recreational facilities. Secondly, regional economic policy may be **stimulative** or **restrictive**. The first kind is usually applied in less developed, peripheral regions dominated by agriculture, and in declining industrial or mining regions. The second kind is mostly applied in congested regions, where high concentrations of people and economic activities cause high economic, social and environmental costs (see also Stilwell, 1972).[1] Secondly, Tinbergen (1966, 1977) distinguishes between **qualitative** and **quantitative** economic policy. This distinction also applies to regional economic policy. The first type refers to changes of certain aspects of the economic structure, e.g., the construction of a highway which connects a relatively inaccesible region with the economic core regions. Quantitative economic policy refers to changes, within the qualitative framework of the

1) It should be noted that the more the freedom of enterprise is valued, and the more open an economy is, the less restrictive (regional) economic policy usually is.

given structure, in the values of instruments of policy, e.g., changes in investment premiums. It should be noted that mixtures of qualitative and quantitative policy occur in practice. An example of a mixture is the opening of a region by a toll-highway, if the use of the high-way system was previously free of charge. It should be marked that both stimulative and restrictive as well as qualitative and quantitative policy are considered in this study.

In the conceptual model of regional economic policy the following types of variables can be distinguished:
- The **goal** variables. These variables are relevant to the regional well-being. As mentioned in chapter 1, two main goals of regional economic policy can be distinguished in most Western economies, viz. the goals of equity and efficiency.

From the policy goals, the more concrete and operational policy **objectives** are derived, such as a desired volume of employment, a certain income distribution, a given quality of the environment, etc. A numerical value of some policy objective will be denoted as a **target** here. It should be marked that impact assessment occurs primarily in terms of objectives and only incidentally in terms of policy goals.
- The **instruments** of policy (also to be denoted as "policy variables"). These are variables under the command of the government by means of which the policy goals and instruments are pursued. An instrument of regional economic policy consists of a specific set of possible governmental acts, aimed at influencing regional economies, which are internally cohesive, and externally distinguishable, with respect to other governmental acts in the same field. When several instruments are simultaneously applied so as to reinforce each other or to counterbalance each other's negative effects we will speak of a policy **package.**
- **Non-policy** variables. The policy objectives are usually not only influenced by policy variables but also by variables which are not under the command of the government. Frequently, the effects of these non-policy variables are more important than the effects of the policy variables.

- **Additional impact** variables. Not only may regional economic policy affect policy objectives but also other types of variables. This set of additional impact variables consists of all those variables which for the policy problem under study do not belong to the set of policy objectives or policy instruments but which are being affected by policy. It should be observed that the policy objectives and the additional impact variables together are denoted as "impact variables".

- **External** variables, which are considered to be external to the policy problem under study, although they may have impacts on the various types of variables distinguished above. Moreover, external variables themselves may be affected by either kind of the above-mentioned variables. It is assumed that the impacts of, respectively, on the external variables may be neglected for the measurement problem under consideration, or that they are given or that they can be taken into account outside of the measurement framework, e.g. because they are constant throughout time or throughout a set of regions. The reasons why certain types of variables are treated as external variables in a given study usually relate to time and financial restrictions. As mentioned in chapter 1, impact variables at the national and international levels belong to the external variables in this study. (Other categories of external variables will be specified in the sequel.)

The conceptual framework outlined above can be represented by means of the stimulus-response model presented in Figure 2.1 (see also Folmer and Nijkamp, 1985).

The following remarks are in order here. First, feedback mechanisms have been neglected in Figure 2.1; however, they can easily be introduced (see chapter 9 for an example). Secondly, the various types of variables mentioned above have to be defined explicitly in concrete studies. Thirdly, some aspects of the conceptual framework outlined above will be described in greater detail in the sequel of this chapter.

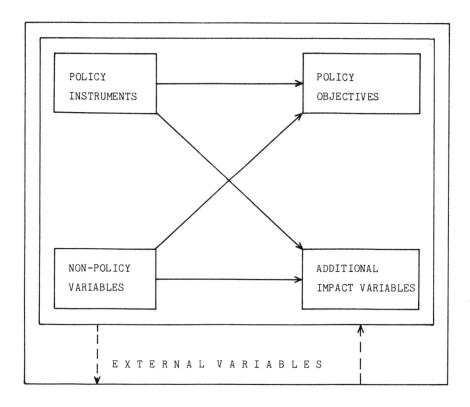

FIGURE 2.1 A stimulus response model for regional impact assess
ment.

2.3. Policy evaluation and impact assessment

In this section the subject of this study is clarified further by
describing the difference between impact assessment and policy evaluation
which impact assessment is often mixed up with. Preliminarily, the formal
difference is that the latter is concerned with the mutual relationships
between policy goals, policy objectives and policy variables. The former, on
the other hand, is only concerned with changes in the impact variables

caused by the policy variables. The rationales of policy objectives and goal variables are treated as given and are not under discussion in impact analysis. Below the difference between policy evaluation and impact analysis will be described in greater detail. In this regard it is necessary to make a distinction between **ex ante** and **ex post** impact assessment. The former takes place before and the latter during or after a process of policy implementation.

Policy evaluation can now be described as an iterative process consisting of the following steps:

(i)   Identification and classification of policy goals;

(ii)   Generation of policy objectives from the policy goals;

(iii)   Identification of a collective preference indicator from the individual preference indicators of the agents involved in a given regional economic policy problem;

(iv)   Deduction of the targets of the policy objectives from the collective preference indicator;

(v)   Identification of qualitative and quantitative instruments of policy;

(vi)   Ex ante assessment of effects and costs of the identified instruments;

(vii)   Determination of the policy interventions; [1]

(viii) Ex post measurement of effects and costs;

(ix)   Adjustment of the preceding steps on the basis of the ex post measurement results.

The process of policy evaluation is summarized in Figure 2.2. It should be noted that only some major feedback loops are presented in this figure.

---

[1] In the case of qualitative instruments this step consists of the decisions whether or not the intervention is to be made and in the case of quantitative instruments it consists of the determination of the quantitative values of the instruments.

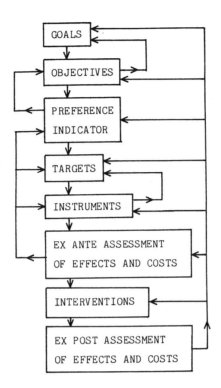

FIGURE 2.2 Schematic representation of policy evaluation

The following remarks are in order here. First three types of ex ante impact assessments can be distinguished:
- Simulation of various policy alternatives (see among others, Naylor, 1971, Orcutt et al., 1980, Haveman and Hollenbeck, 1980, Danziger et al., 1980 and Eliasson, 1980).
- Optimization of a welfare function or optimal control (see among others, Pindyck, 1973, Klein, 1977, and Buiter and Owen, 1979).
- The fixed target method, where the quantitative values of the instruments are determined, given the targets and the model parameters (cf. Tinbergen, 1956).

Secondly, ex ante assessment requires a priori information about effects of policy. This applies in particular to the fixed target method and to optimal control. This information is usually derived from a priori reasoning or ex post studies in similar fields or regional systems.

From this discussion it is clear that, however important, impact assessment is only part of the comprehensive process of policy evaluation. Because of its importance in the process of policy evaluation impact assessment has been chosen as the subject of this study. However, even the whole topic of impact assessment, both ex ante and ex post, would be too ambiguous a project. For that reason, attention is only paid to ex post assessment. Moreover, as was mentioned in chapter 1, not even all aspects of ex post assessment are considered.

In the remainder of this chapter the conceptual framework for this limited kind of ex post impact assessment will be worked out.

2.4 Classification of policy instruments

From the previous discussion it is clear that one of the key concepts in impact assessment is that of instrument of policy. In this section a typology of instruments of regional economic policy, based on the degree of control exerted by the government, will be developed. As will be shown in chapter 3, the degree of control inherent in an instrument is of great importance with respect to the most appropriate measurement approach and the representation of the instrument in the measurement model.

Another purpose of this section is to describe the most important instruments in market economies, in particular in the Netherlands to which the case studies in the chapters 9 and 10 refer. The classification and description of the policy instruments will be made on the basis of the most important theories of regional economic development.

2.4.1 Control and influencing instruments

The criterion to classify instruments in this study is that of the degree of **control**. Regional economic policy in market economies ranges from attempts at influencing to actions aimed at gaining full control of the behavior of certain types of agents in a regional system. Consequently, two types of instruments will be distinguished here: control instruments and influencing instruments. In the case of the former, relevant aspects of the behavior of an agent (including governmental organizations) or a project are under the command of the government. In the latter case the **relative attractiveness** of one or more options of the set of possible actions of an agent is changed. From these definitions it follows that a control instrument will actually be applied once the government has decided to apply it. In the case of an influencing instrument, however, the actual application is dependent on the voluntary participation of the agents. In principle there is no application of the instrument of policy at all if no agent responds to the policy stimulus.

The following examples may help to clarify the difference between the types of instruments distinguished above. The relocation of a governmental organization, regionally differentiated aid to companies in trouble and regional employment programs are interventions where certain aspects of the behavior of the agents (i.e the governmental organization, the company in trouble) and the projects which make up the program are under the command of the government. Hence, these instruments are control instruments. In the case of e.g. investments premiums the relative attractivities of the location conditions of the regions in the system are changed so as to influence location decisions of firms. However, the firms are basically free in their decisions and behavior. Therefore, this is an example of an instrument of the influencing type.

It should be noted that a given instrument may be of the influencing type for one category of agents and of the control type for another category. For example, the establishment of a state-owned company in a given region is of the control type from the point of view of the company concerned. However, it is of the influencing type in as far as it is intended to create favorable socio-cultural and economic location conditions for private enterprises.

2.4.2 Some theories of regional economic development

In this section the most important instruments in market economies will be described on the basis of the kinds of policy interventions advocated by some well-known theories of regional economic development.

-**The neo-classical growth theory** is primilarily oriented to the supply side. The fact that economic growth is also determined by demand is relatively neglected. The growth rate of a regional economy is determined by the accumulation of capital, increase in labor supply and technical progress. Furthermore, regional growth can also be reached by intersectoral shifts. Because of substitutability between production factors and flexible prices of these factors, productive overcapacity can only exist for a short term, both at the national and regional level (see also Armstrong and Taylor, 1978).

In this theory, spatial inequality is caused by impedients which hamper the interregional mobility of the production factors. Therefore, regional economic policy should correct the imperfections of the market mechanism and stimulate interregional mobility by instruments of the **influencing** type, such as investment and migration subsidies, improvement of the physical infrastructure, etc.

- In contrast to the neo-classical theory, **export base theory** emphasises demand factors. A region ought to specialize on those commodities for which it has comparative cost advantages and the regional specialization will lead to export. Economic growth is highly dependent on the flexiblity and mobility of production factors. This flexibility and mobility could be stimulated by means of the same instruments as advocated by the neo-classical theory. Moreover, whereas in the neo-classical theory application of instruments of the control type should be avoided so as not to interfere with the working of the market mechanism, application of this kind of instruments, such as governmental aid to and state-participation in private enterprises, is quite legitimate in export-base theory. Those sectors should be favored by regional policy where the effect of an initial stimulus is strengthened by a significant multiplier effect (see amongst others, Lloyd and Dicken, 1979).

- In the **location theory** spatial economic inequality is caused by differences in location factors. According to the earliest versions, these factors are transportation and communication costs. Therefore, regional economic policy should focus on physical infrastructural investments such as road and railwaysystems, etc. (For further details, see, amongst, Lloyd and Dicken, 1979.)

Later versions also stressed the importance of socio-cultural location conditions, such as educational facilities, medical care, etc. (cf. Hirschman, 1958). Consequently, the provision of this kind of location factors also forms an important instrument of regional economic policy in this theory.

- The **growth pole theory** has been developed especially by Perroux (1955) and Boudeville (1966). It views regional economic development as a process connected to some 'industries motrices'. Because of input-output relationships, other sectors in the surroundings of the growth pole will benefit from developments of the 'industries motrices'.

Whereas the growth pole theory stresses the positive spill-over effects, the related **cumulative causation theory** emphasizes negative, centripetal backwash effects. According to Myrdal (1957), economic development is a cumulative process in the regions with agglomeration advantages, which will lead to a growing discrepancy between developed and less developed regions.

In both the growth pole theory and the cumulative causation theory the most important instrument of regional economic policy is the creation and development of industrial complexes in backward regions. According to the former a small number of well-spread complexes, containing some 'industries motrices', would suffice. The latter favours a greater number of relatively small complexes.

- The **life-cycle theory** views the production of goods as a process with several stages: innovation, maturity and decline (see among others, Engström, 1970, Pred, 1967). Both the stage of innovation and that of actual production has its own, most favourable location. For the stage of innovation many direct personal contacts are required. Therefore, the most favorable location for innovation is in big cities. The stage of actual production may take place in the more peripheral regions. Consequently, these peripheral regions are vulnerable, because in the case of saturation, the production activities are finished or take place at a lower level, whereas new innovation activities occur in regions with big cities. According to this theory, regional economic policy should concentrate on creating favorable conditions for the stage of innovation in less developed regions, for instance, by establishing educational and research centres.

- In the **power theories** spatial inequality is ascribed to political and economic power. Holland (1976,1979) stresses that prices are not flexible because production and trade are to a high degree controlled by the mesostructure, which consists of multi-regional and multi-national corporations. In the first decades after World War II, the corporations of the mesostructure established subsidiary branches in peripheral regions in the Western countries, especially in those regions with a large supply of cheap labour. When the wages in these region rose and grew inflexible because of the strong position of the unions, the comparative advantage of low wages disappeared. Moreover, less need was felt for investments in less developed regions because of the migration of labor from these regions to developed regions. In the late sixties and early seventies multinational firms started moving their production units to Third World Countries. This process was favored by diminishing transportation costs.

According to Holland, the neglect of power and of the international aspect of location decisions leads to the failure of regional economic policy in the Western countries. In order to be effective the government should have a high degree of control over location decisions which, possibly, might take the form of nationalisation of key industries.

Another kind of power theory has been developed by Friedmann (1979). In Friedmann's view spatial inequality is caused by the disturbed balance between the functional and the territorial bases of social transformation (i.e. between city and countryside). This has led to the concentration of economic and political power in the urbanized centres. The rulers are eager to continue the status quo. This goal is pursued by means of regional economic policy, which is used to prevent the revolution of the oppressed regions. Therefore, in the view of Friedmann, the problem of spatial inequality can only be solved by a revolution which redistributes economic power and restores the balance between functional and territorial integration.

Most Western economies, including the Dutch, follow a mixture of the theories described above, with the exception of the Friedmann version of the power theories. This means that in these economies a large variety of instruments of both the influencing and the control type are applied. The former, however, are the most important in as far as location decisions of **private** firms are concerned. The managements of privately owned companies take essential decisions such as how much of what to produce, why, how and where. A government will try to influence these essential decisions for reasons of public interest. If control instruments are used with respect to privately owned companies they consist mainly of **participations** or of **prohibitions**. Compulsion is pratically unknown as far as private location decisions are concerned. It should be noted that even state-owned companies have a high degree of independent decision-making and that if control instruments are used with regard to state-owned companies they are usually of the prohibitive type. (An exception in the Netherlands in the relocation of the headquarters of the Postal Service.)

Finally, in the areas of the non-market activities of the government itself the instruments are of the control type (e.g. the relocation of governmental organizations, extra employment programs, etc.).

2.4.3 Overview and classification of Dutch instruments

In the preceding section, the instruments advocated by the most important theories of regional economic development have been briefly described. In this section an overview of the instruments, as applied in the Netherlands to which the case studies in Part II apply, is given. Moreover, they will be classified according to the criterion for the degree of control.

The following instruments have more or less frequently been used in the Netherlands (see also Oosterhaven and Folmer, 1983): [1]

(a) Relocation or establishment of governmental organizations or of state-owned companies.

(b) Regionally biased, direct, financial aid to companies in trouble in the form of subsidies and loans.

(c) Participation in privately owned companies, e.g. by regional development companies.

(d) Provision of work, especially in periods of recession by regionally differentiated, employment programs.

(e) House building projects.

(f) Investments in economic, social and physical infrastructure in order to influence the locational conditions of a region. The investments consist of such projects as the construction of industrial sites, harbors, roads and the provision of socio-cultural and recreational facilities.

(g) Subsidies on capital, for instance, premiums on gross investments, fiscal accelerated depreciation, fiscal investment deducation, and subsidies on land-use.

(h) Subsidies on labor.

(i) Mobility stimulating measures such as migration subsidies for migrants and enterprises.

---

[1] Some of the instruments were also aimed at non-economic policy goals, such as a more equal spread of the population, environmental quality, etc.

(j) Subsidies on transportation and energy use.

(k) Government expenditure policy.

(l) Allowances of several types.

The following remarks are in order here. First, various well-known instruments such as direct and indirect taxes are not included here because they are not specifically aimed at influencing regional economies. Secondly, an instrument may be simultaneously aimed at several policy objectives. For instance, house building projects may be aimed at improving the social location profile of a region and at the provision of work to combat short term unemployment. Thirdly, as mentioned above, instruments may be combined to policy packages. In chapter 9 for instance, it will be shown that investment premiums and fiscal accelerated depreciation have been applied as a policy package in the Netherlands. Fourthly, classification of the instruments according to the degree of control gives the following results. The instruments (g) - (j) are of the influencing type, whereas the instruments (a) - (f) and (k) may be of the control type for one category of agents and of the influencing type for another category. Instrument (l) is mainly of the control type, although it may also influence the location conditions of a region in general.

2.5 The causal context and the multi-effective nature of regional economic policy

In this section the notion of 'effect' of regional economic policy will be analyzed. [1] First, in section 2.5.1., the causal relationship between an independent causal policy variable and a dependent impact variable will be

---

[1] Sometimes the notion of 'effectivity' instead of 'effect' is used. The former will be understood here to imply the existence of a norm by which a change in an impact variable is judged. The notion of effectivity belongs to the vocabulary of policy evaluation but not to that of impact analysis as defined above. Therefore, it will not be used in the sequel.

described. Next, in section 2.5.2., the multi-effective nature of regional economic policy will be dealt with.

2.5.1 The causal framework

As a starting point the classical notion of causality, given by Basman (1963), is taken:

> Assume that the mechanism under investigation can be isolated from all systematic, i.e., non-random external influences; assume that the mechanism can be started over repeatedly from any definite initial condition. If, everytime the mechanism is started up from approximately the same initial conditions, it tends to run through approximately the same sequence of events, then the mechanism is said to be causal.

With regard to this definition the following remarks are important. First causality analysis aims at identifying the direction of influence between two variables. This means that when one speaks of x as a cause of y, one has in mind a **unidirectional** relationship from x to y and not merely covariation. In addition to the direction, there is usually interest in the magnitude of a causal relationship. Secondly, in non-experimental sciences as economics the mechanism can usually not be "started over repeatedly from any definite initial condition". Moreover, in these sciences only **covariation** between variables can be established. Finally, one can never infer the causal ordering of two or more variables if only the values of the correlations or the partial correlations are known. Therefore, the causal ordering, i.e. the direction of the relationship has to be based on postulates and on logic derived from theory (see, among others, Blalock, 1971). Thirdly, at a first thought this definition may raise a nasty problem in economics because of the fact that dependent economic variables, including impact variables, are usually influenced by a large number of causal variables. This would imply that "the mechanism under investigation" has to be isolated from a large number of variables. However, as pointed out by Haavelmo, the number of **important** variables is usually rather small in economics. Haavelmo (1944) puts it like this:

> Do we actually need to consider an enormous number of factors to explain decisions to produce, to consume, etc.? I think our experience is rather to the contrary. Whenever we try, a priori, to specify what we should think to be important factors, our imagination is usually exhausted rather quickly; and when we attempt to apply our theory to actual data (e.g. by using certain regression methods), we often find even a great many of the factors in our priori list turn out to have practically no factual influence'.

Guiding principles for the selection of the relevant variables are usually given by theory (Feigl, 1956, Zellner, 1978). It specifies in the first place the variables to be included in a causal relationship. Furthermore, as mentioned above, it indicates what variable is the impact variable and what variables are the independent causal variables. If a theory is not well-developed, so that the theoretical information needed to specify a causal relationship is not available, the role of theory is taken over by ad hoc reasoning and intuition (see, among others, Riley, 1963, Segers, 1977).

Some remarks will be made now, which are intended to clarify the description of causality. First, the definition given above leads to the following well-known conditions for the existence of causality (see, among others, Wold, 1954, Nijkamp and Rietveld, 1981):

- Lack of spuriousness. A relationship between two variables is called spurious, if both variables are influenced by a third variable without influencing each other (see als Simon, 1954);

- Predictability. This characteristic follows directly from the definition given above (see also Feigl, 1956, Basman, 1963, Zellner, 1978).

- The relationship between the causal and impact variable is non-reflexive, asymetric and transitive.

- The covariation between two variables, for which a causal relationship holds, is unequal to zero. This last condition makes the assumption of a causal relationship empirically verifiable (see also, Simon, 1954, Zellner, 1978).

Secondly, from a **conceptual** point of view it has been argued that inherent in the concept of causality is the notion of **time**, i.e. the impact variable does not precede the causal variable in time (see, among others, Wold, 1954, Strotz and Wold, 1960, 1963). Consequently, the time-specific relationship between a causal and impact variable is asymmetric and transitive which is expressed in a triangular recursive model structure. However, at an **emprirical** level these characteristics may get lost and interdependencies between variables may arise because of aggregation over individuals or over time (Bentzel and Hansen, 1955). It should be noted that interdependencies between variables lead to non-recursive model structures.

Thirdly, a dependent variable may in its turn be the cause of a third variable, and so on. In this way a causal **chain** can be envisaged. In the case of only one dependent variable such a chain is considered to have length one, and, in general, in the case of n causally related dependent variables, it is said to be of length n.

With the notions given above, it is possible to define the effect, say β_{ij}, of a causal variable x_j on a dependent variable y_i. In the context of the LISREL and two-stage time series measurement approaches to be developed below, a definition in terms of marginal changes, holding the other causal variables of y_i constant, is adequate [1]. Formally:

$$\beta_{ij} = \frac{\Delta y_i}{\Delta x_j} \tag{2.1}$$

---

[1] As pointed out by Nijkamp and Rietveld (1981) a definition in terms of elasticities has advantages, especially in connection with non-linear models.

The following remarks are in order here. First, definition (2.1) applies to both policy instruments and non-policy variables. Secondly, the notion of effect can also be defined in terms of a partial derivative (if it exists). Thirdly, in some cases, for instance, when effects of a mix of several variables are studied, the ceteris paribus condition may not be valid. (Extensive information on the effects of a mix of variables, in particular of a policy package, can be found in chapter 6.). Fourthly, in the case of linear models, when β_{ij} does not depend on the values of the causal and the dependent variables, an effect can be derived from the (estimated) model coefficients (see chapter 6 for an extensive description in the case of the LISREL approach).[1] Fifthly, in the terminology of causal analysis the policy instruments are causal variables with respect to the impact variables in as far as effects of policy are studied. The impact variables, however, may also be causal variables with respect to the instruments. This is the case when the values of the impact variables give rise to policy interventions. Finally, some effects of regional economic policy are being realized over a **short** term and other effects over a **long** term. For example, some effects of a relocation of a governmental organizations are realized before the organizations has actually been relocated (such as employment effects caused by the construction of offices), whereas it may take several years before infrastructural projects lead to an increase of private investments. So, it is very important to take the time-dependent nature of an effect into account. In order to make this explicit we will speak of an effect during a given period.

In the next sections the notion of effect of an instrument of regional economic policy will be elaborated further.

[1] For the case of non-linear models see, among others, Nijkamp and Rietveld (1981).

2.5.2 The regional profile

As mentioned above, an instrument of regional economic policy is usually **multi-effective.** That is, it influences several characteristics of a region, often of both an economic and a non-economic nature. For example, industrialization policy may have consequences for employment, and for environmental characteristics of a region in the form of increased polution. It is obvious that adequate measurement should take into account all possible policy effects on both economic and non-economic variables. For this purpose the notion of a **regional profile** is introduced. It is defined as a vector representation of a set of elements that characterize a region (Nijkamp, 1977). The regional profile can be thought of as being composed of four basic components: the economic, social, spatial-physical and environmental subprofiles (see Nijkamp, 1977). Each of these subprofiles comprises a set of elements. For example, the economic subprofile consists of such elements as demand for regional output, investments, unemployment, export and import, etc.

With the notion of a regional profile a regional system can be adequately described as follows. Let the vector $v_{r,t}$ with elements $v_{j,r,t}$ ($j = 1, 2, \ldots, J$), denote the regional profile of a region r at time t and the vector $s_{r,t}$, with elements $s_{i,r,t}$ ($i = 1, 2, \ldots, I$) the policy variables. If we assume for the moment that the regional system is **closed**[1], so that there exist no relationships with other regions, region r at time t can formally be described as follows (see also Nijkamp, 1977):[2]

$$v_{r,t} = f_1(v_{r,t}, v_{r,t-1}, \ldots, v_{r,t-T}, t) + f_2(s_{r,t}, s_{r,t-1}, \ldots, s_{r,t-T}^{*}, t),$$

$$t \in N, \qquad (2.2)$$

[1] This assumption will be dropped in section 2.6

[2] The discrete-time representation has been chosen here because it is most common in practical economic research.

$$v_{r,t} = f_1(v_{r,t}, v_{r,t-1}, \ldots, v_{r,t-T}, t) + f_2(s_{r,t}, s_{r,t-1}, \ldots, s_{r,t-T^*}, t),$$

$$t \in N, \qquad (2.2)$$

where

f_1 is a vector-valued function of the interaction between profile elements;

f_2 is the so-called direct impact function representing effects of instruments of policy on profile elements;

N is the set of positive integers.

If the functions f_1 and f_2 are linear, (2.2) can be written as:

$$v_{r,t} = F_1 \begin{bmatrix} v_{r,t} \\ v_{r,t-1} \\ \vdots \\ v_{r,t-T} \end{bmatrix} + F_2 \begin{bmatrix} s_{r,t} \\ s_{r,t-1} \\ \vdots \\ s_{r,t-T^*} \end{bmatrix}, \quad t \in N \qquad (2.3)$$

where F_1 is a J x TJ matrix of interaction coefficients and F_2 a J x T*I
matrix of impact coefficients.

2.5.3 Direct, indirect and n-th order effects

In chapter 3 it will be shown that the measurement procedure of effects
of a policy variable is highly dependent on the situation whether or not
intermediate variables between the policy variable exist, as well as on the
kind of such intermediate variables. If there exist **no** intermediate variables between a policy variable and an impact variables we will speak of a
direct effect. An **indirect** effect, on the other hand, arises via intermediate variables. As an illustration of these definitions, consider the
causal chain between the policy variable investment subsides (SU), and the
impact variables investments (IN) and employment (EM). This chain is represented in Figure 2.3

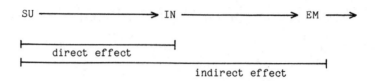

FIGURE 2.3 Schematic representation of direct and indirect effects.

In this example the effect of SU on EM is called indirect, since these variables are related via IN. The effect of SU on IN is called direct, because there are no intermediate variables. Whether a relation between two variables is classified as direct or indirect is dependent on the model or theory at hand (see also Simon, 1954). The direct effects of policy variables can be derived from the direct impact functions f_2 or F_2 given in (2.2) and (2.3), respectively. In order to calculate indirect effects, however, both the direct impact function and the interaction function between profile elements are required. (Further details will be given in chapter 6.)

From a methodological point of view it is also important to introduce the notion of a n-th order effect. It is defined as follows. Assume the existence of a causal chain between an instrument and a profile element under study. If the profile element appears only once in the causal chain we will speak of a first order effect. If the profile element itself is one of the intermediate variables (i.e., as a lagged dependent variable) the effect will be called a n-th (n ϵ N) order effect if it appears n times in the causal chain.[1]

---

[1] The lagged dependent variable may be a spatially or a temporally lagged variable. In the former case the effect on an impact variable in a given region arises via the impact variable in another region (see also chapter 5).

Figure 2.3 may be helpful to clarify these concepts. In this figure SU, IN, and EM are defined in the same way as in Figure 2.1, although ordered in time. The effect of SU on EM is under consideration.

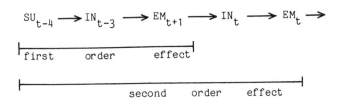

FIGURE 2.4 Schematic representation of first and second order effects.

In Figure 2.4 the effect of SU_{t-4} on EM_{t-3} is a first-order effect because it is the first occuring impact of SU on EM. The effect on EM_t is a second-order effect because it arises via EM_{t-3}.

From this exposition it becomes clear that the class of policy impacts is usually made up by direct and indirect effects as well as effects of several orders. In order to get a detailed insight into the working of a policy instrument it is important to break down the effect on a given impact variable into its constituting elements. However, this has important consequences for the structure of the measurement model. In particular, the causal chain between the instrument and the ultimate policy objective has to be modeled adequately. This problem will be dealt with in detail in chapter 3 and especially in chapter 6.

This section concludes with the remark that all the variables in a causal chain originated by a policy instrument belong to the set of impact variables which, as mentioned above, may consist of both policy objectives and additional impact variables.

2.6 Interregional effects of regional economic policy

Regional economic systems are known to be open systems. This means that a policy intervention in one region may have effects on profile elements in other regions. Therefore, **interregional** effects should be taken into account in addition to intraregional effects.

When the assumption of a closed regional system is dropped, the equations (2.2) and (2.3) are no longer valid. If the number of regions is equal to R the equations (2.2) and (2.3) should be reformulated as:

$$v_{r,t} = \tilde{f}_1(v_{r,t}, Wv_t, v_{r,t-1}, Wv_{t-1}, \ldots, v_{r,t-T}, Wv_{t-T}, t) +$$

$$+ \tilde{f}_2(s_{r,t}, \tilde{W}s_{t-1}, s_{r,t-1}, \tilde{W}s_{t-1} \ldots, s_{r,t-T*}, \tilde{W}s_{t-T*}, t), \quad t \in N \qquad (2.4)$$

and

$$v_{r,t} = \tilde{F}_1 \begin{bmatrix} v_r \\ Wv_t \\ \vdots \\ v_{r,t-T} \\ Wv_{t-T} \end{bmatrix} + \tilde{F}_2 \begin{bmatrix} s_{r,t} \\ \tilde{W}s_t \\ \vdots \\ s_{r,t-T} \\ \tilde{W}s_{t-T} \end{bmatrix} \qquad t \in N \qquad (2.5)$$

where:

v_t is the compound vector representing the regional profiles of the regions other than region r;

s_t is the compound vector of policy variables in regions other than region r;

W is a $J \times (R-1)J$ matrix of spatial contiguity weights between region r and the other regions in the spatial system with respect to the profile elements and relating to such matters as population density, distance, etc. (see also chapter 5);

$\tilde{W}$ is a I x (R-1)I matrix of spatial contiguity weights with respect to the instruments of policy;

$\tilde{f}_1$ and f_2 are interaction and direct impact functions, respectively with respect to the system of regions;

$\tilde{F}_1$ and $\tilde{F}_2$ are J x T(R-1)J and I x T* (R-1)I matrices of interaction and impact coefficients, where T and T* denote the total number of time lags.[1]

The openness of regional systems has important consequences for the measurement methods because both intra- and interregional effects should be taken into account. This implies that **interregional** models, which make it possible to incorporate interregional linkages into the model structure, should be used instead of multiregional models, which only describe intraregional relationships (see, among others, Fischer and Folmer, 1983). Furthermore, single region models should be modified in such a way that spatial spill-over effects can be taken into account. In the chapters 5 and 7 we will return to these aspects.

2.7 Latent variables [2]

In chapter 6 it will be shown that latent variables are appropriate to measure effects of policy packages. Furthermore, in the chapters 4 and 5 it will be argued that latent variables are also suitable to represent other

---

[1] For the sake of simplicity the time lags in $v_{r,t}$ and v_t are assumed to be equal. The same applies to $s_{r,t}$ and s_t.

[2] This section has been inspired by Fischer (1982).

types of variables which consist of mixes of variables. Therefore, in this section the basic features of latent variables will be briefly described.

Following, among others, Carnap (1936, 1937, 1956), Hempel (1958), Spector (1966) and Stegmüller (1970) the variables of empirical sciences can be divided into two classes:

-The class of **observable** variables;

-The class of **theoretical** or latent variables.

Observable variables, such as age and income, possess direct empirical meanings derived from experience. Latent variables on the other hand refer to those phenomena that are supposed to exist but cannot be observed directly. [1] The reason for not being observable is either that those phenomena do not correspond directly to anything that is likely to be measured, or that observations of the phenoma concerned are contaminated with measurement errors (for further details see, among others, McCorguodale and Weehl, 1956 and Hempel, 1958). Examples of latent variables are 'welfare', quality of life', 'economic expectation', 'permanent in-come','socio-economic status', etc.

A latent variable can be uni- or multi-dimensional, which depends on the number of viewpoints from which it is defined theoretically. An example of a multi-dimensional latent variable is 'welfare'. A distinction is usually made between the economic, social and psychic dimensions of welfare. Carnap (1936) has shown that latent variables cannot be replaced by expressions consisting of observable variables. However, latent variables are given empirical meanings by means of **correspondence statements** or operational definitions. Such a statement connects a latent variable with a set of observable variables. However, the theoretical terms are given merely partial specifications. [2]

[1] It should be noted that observability is not an absolute category, but a matter of degree only.

[2] The partial interpretation view offers the possibility of changing correspondence statements in response to new empirical findings or theoretical developments (see Hempel, 1958, 1970, Blalock, 1971).

On the other hand, theoretical terms have operational implications for relationships among observable variables. In particular, they indicate which observable variables are highly correlated because they are indicators of a given latent variable.

In an empirical-analytical theory two kinds of statements can be distinguished:
- **Theoretical** statements, which contain only latent variables;
- **Correspondence** statements, which contain both latent and observable variables.

The set of statements of the first kind is usually called the main theory and the set of correspondence statements the measurement theory. It is highly desirable to use a method to investigate a given theory empirically which is capable of dealing with both the main and the measurement theories **simultaneously**. This follows directly from the relationships between both kinds of variables. As mentioned above, latent variables can only be observed by means of observable variables so that relationships among the former can only be estimated by means of the latter. On the other hand, relationships between observable variables, which are indicators of latent variables, only represent partial relationships between the corresponding latent variables (see, among others, Stegmüller (1970) and Hempel (1970) for further details). In chapter 4 it will be described how both theories are simultaneously dealt with in the LISREL approach.

2.8 Conclusions

In this chapter a conceptual framework has been constructed which forms the vocabulary of subsequent chapters. Regional economic policy has been delimited and the conceptual model of impact analysis of this kind of policy has been presented. The instruments of regional economic policy have been inventarized and classified on the basis of the degree of control exerted by the government.

The causal context of an effect of an instrument has been described and the notion of a regional profile has been introduced to define direct, and n-th order effects. Furthermore, intra- and interregional effects have been dealt with. Finally, the notion of a latent variable, which will be used to represent policy packages and other mixes of variables, has been described.

3   OVERVIEW AND METHODOLOGICAL ASPECTS OF VARIOUS OPERATIONAL MEASUREMENT APPROACHES

3.1   Introduction

The purpose of this chapter is to depict the advantages and disadvantages of the LISREL and two-stage time series measurement approaches by reviewing the various methods which have been used to measure effects of regional economic policy. An important aspect with regard to which the various measurement approaches may differ is the representation of policy variables in the model. Therefore, attention is also paid to this issue.

The various measurement approaches can be divided into micro and spatial approaches. In the former the data is of the lowest level of aggregation and refers to firms, households, etc. Three kinds of micro studies are usually distinguished (see, among others, Campbell and Stanley, 1966):[1]

-Experimental approaches;

-Quasi-experimental approaches;

-Non-experimental approaches.

In spatial approaches the data obtained by some micro study has been spatially aggregated and the behavior of spatial units is investigated. It should be observed that in addition to aggregation to spatial units the data is usually also aggregated to sectors. The following types of spatial approaches can be distinguished:[2]

-Models with policy variables only;

-Single equation models with non-policy variable only;

[1] The distinction between quasi-experimental and non-experimental research could also be applied to the spatial approaches to be discussed below. In order to avoid confusion, however, this terminology will only be used here in relation to micro studies and not to spatial approaches. With respect to the latter it is clear from the context whether a quasi-experimental or a non-experimental measurement framework is meant.

[2] It should be observed that several types of models mentioned here can be applied to data from micro studies as well. The applications to spatial and spatio-temporal data, however, usually require adaptations to the specific features of these kinds of data.

-Single equation models with both policy and non-policy variables;
-Simultaneous equation models.

The organization of this chapter is as follows. In section 3.2 attention will be paid to the representation of policy variables in a measurement
model. The various micro- and spatial measurement approaches will be
described and evaluated in the sections 3.3 and 3.4, respectively. Finally,
in section 3.5, attention will be paid to the methodological problem which
approaches are most appropriate to measure the various kinds of effects of
instruments of the influencing type and of instruments of the control type
(distinguished in section 2.3).

3.2 Representation of policy variables in a measurement model

It is a well-known fact that information needed for regional studies is
sometimes rather poor. The situation with respect to regional economic
policy is often even worse. Two main reasons for this can be distinguished.
First, information about regional economic policy is often intertwined with
information which does not refer to it. For example, in the case of public
investments, it is often difficult to determine which expenditures relate to
regional policy and which do not. Secondly, information about regional
policy is sometimes secret, as in the case of financial aid to companies[1].
The lack of information may lead to the exclusion of some relevant explanatory variables from the investigation. Measurement methods using such a
selected set of variables, however, usually gives biased results (see inter
alia chapter 7 for further details). Therefore, it is of great importance
to include the policy variables explicitly into the model. Some ways to
represent policy variables are described below.

The crudest way to incorporate a policy variable into a measurement
is by simply distinguishing between situations where policy

---

[1] This is a problem which also frequently occurs in impact studies of other
kinds of economic policy.

interventions take place (to be denoted as **policy-on** situations) and situations without policy interventions (to be denoted as **policy-off** situations). The distinction between policy-on and policy-off situations can be handled formally by means of **dummy** variables. However, the use of dummy variables has two disadvantages:

-First, effects caused by changes in omitted non-policy variables, which happen to coincide with the changes between policy-on and policy-off periods, are easily attributed to policy.

-Secondly, the simple distinction between policy-on and policy-off situations does not reveal the **intensity** of policy, which may lead to inadequate assessment of effects of policy.

From these remarks one can conclude that, in general, a more refined representation of policy variables than by means of the policy-on policy-off distinction is preferable. If detailed information about regional economic policy is available, it may be possible to present the data in the form of a **volume** measure or a measure of **intensity**. The former consists of the use that **has** actually been made of policy, whereas the latter represents the use that **can** be made of it. In the former case one can think of, e.g., the actual expenditures on investment subsidies in a given region, and in the latter case of the prevailing percentage of investment subsidies.

In the case of an instrument intended to **influence** decisions of private economic agents the volume measure is not adequate. An example may clarify this. Suppose one wants to investigate the effect of investment premiums on investments. In this case a volume measure, which represents the actual amounts spent by the government, is a consequence of investments. It comprises both the subsidies given to those who (inter alia) based their investment decisions on the investment premiums and the subsidies given to those whose decisions were not influenced by the premiums but were based on other considerations.[1] In other words, the level of the impact variable

---

[1] This is a consequence of the fact that subsidies are usually based on actual investments and not on the rationale of investment decisions.

partly codetermines the volume measure. Another objection to the use of volume measures in the case of instruments of the influencing type stems from the fact that these measures may be partly dependent on the business cycle. Continuing the example, it is well-known that investments occur more frequently in times of economic growth than in periods of stagnation. Consequently, the volume measure would indicate that a more intensive use of the premiums has been made in the former kind of periods than in the latter, regardless whether the increase has been caused by policy rather than by the state of the business cycle. The upshot of this paragraph is that in case of instruments of the influencing type measures of intensity should be used instead of volume measures.

In the case of instruments of the control type only volume measures are usually available. With respect to this type of instruments, however, a volume measure is adequate because it does not reflect combined effects of the policy variables and of non-policy variables. Moreover, effects of non-policy variables, such as the state of the business cycle, can easily be handled (see chapter 10 for an example).

This section ends with the following remarks. First, in some cases the instruments may not only influence the policy objectives, but the objectives may also directly influence the instruments. For instance, the amounts spent on extra employment programs are usually influenced by the rate of unemployment which these programs are intended to combat. In order to study the interaction between the objective and the policy variables simultaneous equation models are required. Secondly, in policy impact studies lagged policy variables are frequently needed (see also section 6.2). When the time lag is not adequately taken into account, the estimators of the policy effects may be biased. An example may help to clarify this problem. In the case of investment premiums several periods may elapse before the investments induced by the premiums in a given period are realized. In the meantime the premiums may change. If the appropriate time lag is not taken into account the investments in various periods may be related to the wrong percentages of premiums. Finally, in some studies (for instance, Paelinck, 1971, 1973; NEI, 1972) several instruments of policy were combined a priori by the researcher to a weighted index. Two objections can be raised against this approach. First, in order to get as detailed an insight into the effects of policy as possible it is desirable to obtain both the effects of the policy package and of the individual instruments. Therefore, all the relevant instruments should be explicitly included into the analysis. Secondly, a priori construction of an index by the researcher has the disadvantage that weights may be determined in an arbitrary way. In chapter 6 it will be shown that both problems inherent in the analysis of policy packages can appriopriately be handled by means of the LISREL approach.

3.3 Micro approaches

As mentioned in the introduction, the behavior of agents (such as firms, households), at which policy has been directly aimed, is investigated in micro studies. Three types of micro studies have been distinguished above: experimental research, quasi-experimental studies and non-experimental research. The first type will be discussed in section 3.3.1; the latter two in section 3.3.2.

3.3.1. Controlled experimentation

This type of micro approaches has been used relatively little in impact studies of economic policy. There seems to be a growing interest in this kind of policy research, however, and therefore it is briefly described here.

According to Festinger and Katz (1954), the essence of laboratory experimentation lies in "... observing the effect on a dependent variable of the manipulation of an independent variable under controlled conditions". In this extreme form controlled experimentation has hardly ever been applied in economic policy research. Instead, more moderate variants have been used.

These moderate approaches operate (or could operate) along the following lines. Groups with different histories of the independent policy variable are selected and in these groups differences with respect to the impact variable are analyzed. Conversely, groups are selected on the basis of differences in the policy variable and then difference with respect to the impact variable are investigated. In both cases the selection is supplemented by matching as many of the relevant independent variables as possible so as to control the effects of other variables than the policy variable. In practice, only a limited number of variables can be matched. Therefore, the matching is usually supplemented by a technique called "control through measurement". This means that a relevant variable, which cannot be used for matching, is taken into account by gathering information about it from the respondents. The relationship between the impact and policy variable is tested within each of the groups obtained on the basis of the information about this relevant variable. Finally, the possible disturbing influences of uncontrolled variables are taken into account by randomly selecting samples from the matched groups. (For further details see, among others, Riley, 1963.)

From this exposition it is clear that the main advantage of controlled experiments lies in the high degree to which the causal relations between policy instrument and impact variable are isolated from disturbing influences of other variables. However, there are various difficulties inherent in the use of controlled experiments in policy research. First, the problem of matching may be difficult or impossible in many situations. The reason for this is that participation in the experiment is usually voluntary so that the groups of participants and non-participants are incomparable by definition. In regional impact studies the problem of matching is worsened by the fact that both the experimental and control groups have to be located in the same region or at least in similar regions, which may seriously limit the number of members in both groups. Secondly, the results are restricted to the experiences of the groups involved in the experiment. In particular, the duration of the experiment may impose serious restrictions. So, the specific results of the experiment may be difficult to generalize to other situations. Finally, the experimental setting may have disturbing effects on the participants which may lead to less reliable outcomes of the experiment.

In spite of these difficulties, controlled experiments have been applied in various situations. For instance, Smith (1979) studied the provision of public goods; Hall (1975) analyzed the effects of income taxes on the supply of labor and Rasmussen (1980) investigated the impacts of housing policies.

3.3.2 Quasi-experimental and non-experimental research

Quasi-experimental research consists of surveys among agents who are expected to have been affected by policy. Two types of surveys can be distinguished: **interviews** and **self-administration of questionaires**. A comparison of both types can be found in, among others, Riley (1963) and Segers (1977).

Surveys may provide detailed information on the various factors influencing decision-making processes and especially on the relative weights of policy instruments. The information obtained via surveys may relate to direct and indirect effects of policy. As an example of the latter, consider the case that investment subsidies have led to the establishment of an important industrial enterprise in a given region. In order to assess indirect effects of the subsidies for other firms in the region (via the establishment of the important enterprise) a survey could be held among these firms with respect to the importance of the newly-located enterprise for their economies.

From this brief exposition it follows that well-designed surveys may give detailed information about the decision processes of the respondents, in particular, of their perceptions of the importance of relevant factors. Furthermore, surveys may provide information to make comparisons between different situations, e.g. before and after the move of a firm. Finally, information about such matters as time lags between decisions with regard to and realisations of e.g. investments can be obtained.

The survey approach as a measurement method, however, may suffer from the drawbacks that surveys in general may suffer from. These can be grouped under the headings: lack of respondent orientation, and in the case of interviews, errors on account of communication barriers and of perception disturbances of the respondent, and measurement errors due to the interviewer. (For detailed information on these drawbacks see, inter alia, Cannel and Kahn, 1953, 1968, Segers, 1977). These drawbacks may result in a **gap** between the actual effects and the effects as reported by the respondents. For example, the respondents could under-estimate the effect of prevailing investment subsidies so as to promote higher subsidies in the future. Another example is the ex post rationalization of the proper factors underlying the decision made. The present problem may be mitigated by incorporating questions into the questionnaire which only **indirectly** relate to the policy variables and by confronting respondents with hypothetical situations. (For further details see, among others, Oppenheim, 1966, and Segers, 1977). Another limitation is that surveys can usually only provide information on effects on variables associated with the respondents investigated. That is, only effects on variables relevant for the respondents for the time period, for which the survey has been formulated, can be estimated. In order to estimate **subsequent** effects new surveys have to be undertaken.[1] Because surveys of the present kind are usually very costly and time-consuming they are organized only incidentally in practice. Not only is the range of surveys limited in the future, but also in the past. It is often very difficult to obtain reliable data on the past because of the "loss of memory" of organizations as a consequence of new management, destruction of information, etc. A final limitation to be mentioned here is the high rate of non-response in surveys nowadays (see among others, Segers,

---

[1] Of great importance in this regard are panel studies where the same sample is investigated in subseqent periods. Such studies make it possible to trace long term policy effects in a given sample.

1977). This might partly be due to the large number of surveys certain catagories of respondents are facing. This problem might be mitigated by organizing relatively few, well-designed surveys of which the results could be used for several purposes.

The survey method has been applied to a variety of problems in many countries. For instance, Baumont (1979) investigated the impacts of migration incentives; Calame (1980) studied effects of wage subsidy programs; Poolman and Wever (1978), Marquand (1980) and Krist (1980) investigated the impacts of investment subsidies on the location decisions of firms.

The third kind of micro approaches consists of non-experimental research. Whereas the researcher has control over the influences of the causal variables on the impact variable in experimental research and over the data collection in quasi-experimental research, no control is exerted by him in non-experimental research. It is restricted to the observation of the impact variable in different situations, such as before and after a policy intervention or in different regions. In non-experimental research no attempts are made to separate effects of policy variables from effects of non-policy variables. Therefore, its use is restricted to situations where the latter types of effects do not exist or can be taken into account in other ways. This is inter alia the case in situations where direct effects of instruments of the control type are under study. For instance, the direct employment effects of the construction of an infrastructural project for a firm can be derived from the construction costs in a straightforward way.

3.4 Spatial approaches

3.4.1 Introduction

The data used in spatial approaches is obtained from micro units in surveys conducted by authorities, such as a central office of statistics. The surveys are usually relatively simple and relate to key issues, such as investments, number of persons employed, etc. In contrast to the surveys dealt with in section 3.3, the information asked for does usually **not** directly relate to regional economic policy. Therefore, there is less danger of answers which have been biased to influence future policy. It is obvious that when no information on policy is gathered from the micro units it has to be obtained elsewhere, for instance, at the ministry responsible for the policy. An important feature of many surveys organized by public authorities, such as a ministry or a central bureau of statistics, is that they are repeated periodically. This means that information to estimate effects of policy becomes available for much longer periods than in the case of the micro studies discussed in the preceding section, which are usually organized only incidentally.

In the introduction a typology of spatial approaches was given. This typology is based on the pragmatic criterion of the use in practical research. In the sequel the various types will be discussed subsequentially.

3.4.2 Approaches with explanatory variables of the policy type only

The present kind of approaches consists of the comparison of a set of impact variables in policy-on situations with policy-off situations, and of ascribing the differences **solely** to policy[1]. This means that it is assumed that possible effects of non-policy variables can be neglected[2].

This type of approach can be used in situations with prior knowledge about the absence of the effects of non-policy variables or when effects of these variables can be completely isolated from effects of policy (e.g., in

---

[1] In contrast to the other types of spatial approaches, the present type rarely makes use of a mathematical representation of the problem at hand.

[2] Concerning the degree of control over the influences of variables or over the data collection exerted by the researcher the present approach is similar to the non-experimental micro approach discussed in section 3.3.2.

the cases of direct effects of the building of new towns (Tuppen, 1979) and the relocation of government offices).

In many situations in practice, however, these conditions are not fulfilled. For those cases methods should be used which make it possible to control non-policy variables. This leads to the other categories of spatial studies.

3.4.3 Single equation models with explanatory variables of the non-policy type only

This class of methods is based on the comparison of the actual policy-on situation with the hypothetical policy-off situation where the latter is **extrapolated** on the basis of the non-policy variables only. As in the former case, the gap between the two situations is defined as the effect of policy. Several variants of this class of models can be distinguished.

-The simplest variant is the extrapolation on the basis of a **univariate time series** of the impact variable for the policy-off situation in a single region. It rests on the assumption that the autonomous development of the impact variable in both the policy-on and the policy-off period is the same. This assumption may be violated, especially when a development from a short policy-off period is extrapolated over a long policy-on period. A schematic representation of this approach can be found in Figure 3.1.

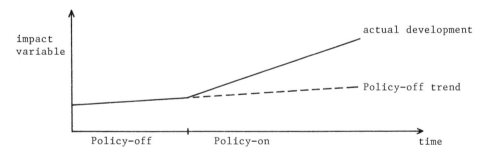

FIGURE 3.1. Schematic representation of the trend extrapolation method.

The extrapolation may be made by means of such sophisticated methods as seasonal autoregressive integrated moving average approaches (see chapter 7 for a detailed description). It may also be based on more simple methods such as relating the development of the impact variable in a policy region to the development of the impact variable in non-policy regions or to the development of related variables in the same region which have not been affected by policy.

If there is evidence of adequate extrapolation of the impact variable, the present method is a simple and easy device to estimate policy effects. It has been used by Frost (1975) to study effects on regional employment and by Hart (1971) and Begg et al. (1976) to measure effects on investments.

-The basic feature of the second variant is that the impact variable is extrapolated by means of a **multivariate time series** model of the impact variable and its determining non-policy variables. This implies that changes in the values of the non-policy variables in the policy-on period can be taken into account which may give a more adequate extrapolation than by means of the preceding univariate method.

An example of this approach can be found in Recker (1977), who estimated the impacts of regional policy on employment and investments in the regions of the Federal Republic of Germany.

-Spatial **cross-section analysis** has been used in the Netherlands by Vanhove (1962) and van Duyn (1975). They estimated the equation of the first-order difference of industrial employment over policy-on periods by ordinary least squares on the basis of cross-section data for all provinces.[1] The

[1] This approach does not allow of the estimation of the total effect of policy because positive residuals in some regions are offset by negative ones in other regions. This is because the average of the ordinary least squares residuals is zero. Moreover, a quantitative estimate of the policy effect cannot be obtained from the absolute values of the residuals. Insight into the degree of succes could be derived from a ranking of the estimated residuals by size.

had experienced different degrees of intensity of policy. The regional
values of the estimated residuals were used as indicators for the effects of
policy. In particular, in the case of a positive residual for a province
which had benefitted from regional policy it was concluded that the effects
of regional policy were positive.

Impact analysis by means of the present multivariate time series
analysis and cross-section analysis approaches encounters the following
methodological problems. First, because of the usual lack of regional data
the set of explanatory variables may be incomplete. Consequently, the gap
between the actual and the extrapolated policy-off situation may also be
influenced by the missing non-policy variables. In the case of the cross-
section method this means that the estimated residuals represent non-policy
variables as well. The inclusion of both policy and non-policy variables
could reduce this problem. Secondly, even if the set of non-policy variables
in the model is complete, the omission of policy variables, which both have
a direct effect on the impact variable and are correlated with the explanatory non-policy variables, leads to biased estimators of the regression
coefficients and thus of the effects of policy. (See, among others, Theil,
1957).

-The next variant to be discussed here is **shift-share analysis.** It is based
on the decomposition of the value of a regional impact variable into a
national-structural component and a specific regional component, which
includes the effects of policy. Formally:

$$y_{r,t} = \sum_i y_{i,r,0} \frac{y_{i,t}}{y_{i,0}} + d_{r,t} \tag{3.1a}$$

where:

$y_{r,t}$ is the value of the impact variable y in region r in period t;

$y_{i,r,0}$ is the value of y in sector i in region r in base period 0;

$y_{i,t'}$ is the national value of y in period t', t' = 0,t

$d_{r,t}$ is the regional contribution to $y_{r,t'}$, in particular the effect of policy.

Let us denote the first (structural) term in (3.1.a) as $z_{r,t}$. This structural term is used to extrapolate the policy-off situation. The regional component $d_{r,t}$ is obtained by subtracting $z_{r,t}$ from the observed value $y_{r,t}$. If the regional component is **solely** attributable to policy, $d_{r,t}$ is equal to zero in the policy-off period. If this is not the case a trend is fitted for the policy-off period, extrapolated into the policy-on period and used to correct the national-structural term. Let us denote the moment of transition from policy-off to policy-on as T. Some obvious trends are:

$$f(t) = y_{r,t} - z_{r,t} \qquad , \quad t < T \qquad\qquad (3.2)$$

and

$$h(t) = \frac{y_{r,t}}{z_{r,t}} \qquad , \quad t < T, \qquad\qquad (3.3)$$

Model (3.1) is then modified as follows:

$$y'_{r,t} = z_{r,t} + \hat{f}(t) + d_{r,t}, \quad t > T \qquad\qquad (3.1b)$$

or

$$y_{r,t} = z_{r,t} \hat{h}(t) + d_{r,t} \quad , \quad t > T \qquad\qquad (3.1c)$$

where $\hat{h}(t)$ and $\hat{g}(t)$ are the trends extrapolated into the policy-on period.

If the relationship between the non-policy variables and the impact variable in the policy-on period is the same as in the policy-off period and if there are no disturbing influences of additional variables in the policy-on period, $d_{r,t}$ may give a correct indication of the policy effect. However, there are some serious problems which seriously hamper in the use of shift-share analysis in impact analysis and which are briefly mentioned here.[1]

[1] For some general comments on shift-share analyais, see Richardson (1978) and Schofield (1979).

First, both the national structural and the regional components may have been influenced by regional policy. Consequently, shift-share analysis may give an incorrect estimate of the effect of policy. (see also Ashcroft, 1979). Secondly, in small regions national growth may differ considerably from regional growth (Dessant and Smart, 1977). In that case the national-structural term in (3.1a)-(3.1c) may be invalid.

Shift-share analysis has been applied to a variety of problems. For instance, Moore and Rhodes (1973, 1974) and Ohlsson (1980) analyzed employment effects; Ashcroft (1979) and Moore and Rhodes (1973, 1974) investigated impacts on investments; MacKay (1979) studied impacts on the movement of firms.

-The last variant of single equation approaches with non-policy variables only to be discussed here is **analysis of variance.** The impact model reads as follows (cf. Buck and Atkins, 1976):

$$g_{ir} \, w_{ir} = \alpha_i d_i \, w_{ir} + \beta_r d_r \, w_{ir} + u_{ir} \, w_{ir} \tag{3.4}$$

where:

g_{ir} is growth of the impact variable in sector i in region r in a certain period;

w_{ir} is the weight of sector i in region r;

d_i is a sectoral dummy variable (value 1 for sector i and 0 elsewhere);

d_r is a regional dummy variable (value 1 for region r and 0 elsewhere);

u_{ir} is a random residual term;

α_i and β_r are unknown coefficients which have to be estimated.

The regional (policy) component for region r' is

$$\beta_{r'} - \sum_{\substack{r \\ r \neq r'}} \tilde{w}_r \, \beta_r \tag{3.5}$$

where

$\tilde{w}_r$ is the weight of region r in the nation.

It has been pointed out by Ashcroft (1979) that (3.4) only gives the systematic effect of policy and that non-systematic effects are absorbed by the residual term. [1] Furthermore, the application of this approach in small regions leads to the same problem as the application of shift-share analysis in such regions.

A case study by means of the present approach with regard to employment impacts can be found in Buck and Atkins (1976).

3.4.4 Single equation models with both policy and non-policy variables as explanatory variables

In the present section, two kinds of situations will be considered. In the first, information·on important non-policy variables is missing but is taken indirectly into account. In the second, information on all relevant variables is available.

-The method to be used in the first situation will be called **two-stage time series analysis**. It will be described in detail in chapter 7. In this place only some general remarks will be made, which allow of a crude comparison with the time series methods discussed in the preceding section.

In order to apply two-stage time series analysis, a univariate time series of the impact variable for the pre-intervention period and a multivariate time series of the impact variable and the various instruments of policy for the policy-on period must be available. The first step in the measurement procedure is to model the pre-intervention series. Of considerable applicability is the class of **multiplicative seasonal autoregressive integrated moving average models** (abbreviated as SARIMA-models) as developed by, among others, Box and Jenkins (1976). The second

---

[1] This is a rather peculiar observation because the essence of econometric analysis, including impact analysis, is to estimate systematic effects of the policy variables and to leave non-systematic effects represented by the variance of the residual term unexplained.

step consists of removing the effects of the non-policy variables, estimated on the basis of the pre-intervention series, from the second series by means of a transformation of the latter series. This removal is succesful if the relationships between the impact variable and the non-policy variables in the intervention period are the same as in the pre-intervention period. Under the conditions of the independence of the policy instruments of the non-policy variables and an additive model structure, the effects of policy on the impact variable can be estimated by standard techniques from the transformed multivariate time series.

The following remark is in order here. As mentioned above, one is likely to get biased estimators when important explanatory variables are missing. By taking the omitted variables indirectly into account, as in the way described above, however, the problem of biased estimators can be avoided.

For an application of the present measurement approach see chapter 10.

-When information on both policy and non-policy variables is available, standard approaches with both types of explanatory variables explicitly included (i.e., a multivariate time series analysis approach to a single region, a multi-regional or interregional cross-section approach, or a spatio-temporal approach to a system of regions) can be used to estimate effects of the instruments of policy.

Examples can be found in, among others, Shaffer (1979), Ashcroft and Taylor, (1977, 1979), Bowers and Gunawerdena (1978).

This section ends with the following remark. With single equation methods only **direct** effects of instruments on an impact variable can be estimated. In addition, single equation methods as such do not allow of the estimation of the effects of an instrument on several profile components. For both purposes, either several single equation models are required or simultaneous equation methods have to be used. In the next section we will turn to the latter.

3.4.5 Simultaneous equation models

In this section attention will be paid to two classes of simultaneous equation models: **general simultaneous equation models** and **input-output models**. The latter record transactions between economic activities, which are classified into production and demand sectors. The former are **not** restricted to relationships between demand and production variables. They can also describe mutual relationships between e.g. investments and their determinants, such as production, socio-cultural and physical location factors, etc. So, the applicability of this class of models is much larger than that of input-output models. In section 3.4.5.1 general simultaneous equation models are discussed; in section 3.4.5.2 input-output models.

3.4.5.1 General simultaneous equation models

In this section, only some general remarks are made which allow of the comparison of this approach with the single equation approaches discussed above. Various other aspects of measuring effects of policy by means of simultaneous equation models will be discussed in detail in chapter 6.

The structural form of the conventional general simultaneous equation measurement model reads as follows:

$$A_0 \, y_t = \sum_{i=1}^{p} A_i \, y_{t-i} + \sum_{j=0}^{q} B_j \, x_{t-j} + \sum_{k=0}^{m} C_k \, z_{t-k} + \varepsilon_t \qquad (3.6)$$

where:

y_t is a g-vector with current endogenous variables;

y_{t-i} is a g-vector with lagged endogenous variables in period t-i;

x_{t-j} is a m-vector with exogenous non-policy variables in period t-j;

z_{t-k} is a n-vector with exogenous policy variables in period t-k; [1]

ε_t is a g-vector with random disturbances;

A_i is a gxg matrix with unknown coefficients corresponding to y_{t-i};

[1] In chapter 6 it will be argued that the policy variables should be specified as endogenous variables.

B_j is a gxm matrix with unknown coefficients corresponding to x_{t-j};
C_k is a gxn matrix with unknown coefficients corresponding to z_{t-k}.

It should be noted that (3.6) is a single region model. In the case of multi-regional and interregional models, (3.6) has to be modified. This will be extensively dealt with in chapter 5.

As mentioned above, single equation approaches are not appropriate to decompose policy effects which arise along causal chains of length longer than one and to estimate effects on several impact variables simultaneously. Both aspects, however, can be handled in the framework of simultaneous equation models in the following way (see also Folmer, 1980).

-In order to estimate the direct effects of an instrument of policy on several impact variables, all these impact variables should be incorporated into the model as current **endogenous** variables (i.e. should be included in the vector y_t). Each impact variable should be specified as a function of the instruments of policy and of the other relevant explanatory variables.

-In order to decompose indirect effects of an instrument on a given impact variable, both the ultimate impact variable and each of the intermediate variables in the causal chain between the impact variable and the instrument of policy should be specified as current endogenous variables. Thus, a causal chain is represented by a **system** of equations where each causal variable is among the explanatory variables of the variable it directly affects. For example, in terms of Figure 2.1, both IN and EM are endogenous variables. Furthermore, SU is an explanatory variable of IN (and not of EM if there is no direct impact of SU on EM) and IN is an explanatory variable of EM. The indirect effect of SU on EM along the causal chain SU→IN→EM equals the product of the coefficients in that chain. (For further details see chapter 6).

Applications of the use of simultaneous equation models in impact studies can be found in, among others, Centraal Planbureau (1973), van Delft et al (1977), Berentsen (1978), Bolton (1980), Glickman (1980), Courbis (1979), Ballard et al (1980) and in chapter 9.

3.4.5.2 Input-output models

As mentioned above, this type of model records transactions between the production and demand sectors as well as between the production sub-sectors. Therefore, input-output models can be used to calculate the effects of policy variables which originate from **demand** and **production** variables. Depending on the degree of sectoral disaggregation, effects for different sectors can be assessed. Furthermore, if an interregional input-output model is available, interregional effects can be calculated.

A (common) version of the interregional input-output model for J sectors and R regions, which can be used to measure effects of regional economic policy, reads as follows (cf. Folmer and Oosterhaven, 1985):

$$(I - A) \; \Delta x = \Delta f \qquad\qquad\qquad (3.7)$$

where:

I is the RJ x RJ identity matrix;

A is the RJ x RJ matrix of intermediate input coefficients;

Δx is the RJ vector with changes in gross production;

Δf is the RJ vector with changes in exogenous final demand.

Model (3.7) can be generalized in various ways. For example, income growth of resident workers (cf. Miernyk et al. 1967, Tiebout, 1969) can be specified as an endogenous variable. Moreover, the pure input-output model can be embedded in a demo-economic model framework (for further details see Batey, 1984, Batey and Madden, 1983, Madden and Batey, 1983, Folmer and Oosterhaven, 1985).

From (3.7) it is obvious that if a policy intervention can be specified in terms of changes in exogenous final demand or input coefficients, the impacts can be obtained straightforwardly if an adequate input-output model is available. However, when specifications in such terms are not possible, as in the case of direct effects of subsidies on investments, input-output analysis is not appropriate.

It should be marked that although input-output analysis is a very useful method to analyze effects of a number of frequently used instruments, its employment is seriously limited by the scarcity of data, especially with respect to interregional linkages. For the same reason, the relations in input-output models are usually not quantified by means of conventional econometric methods.

Examples of the input-output measurement approach can be found in Leontief et al. (1965) where the effects of possible arms cuts are studied; in Moore and Rhodes (1976), where the impacts of labor subsidies are investigated and in Oosterhaven (1981), where the effects of the relocation of a governmental organization and of a land reclamation project are analysed.

3.5 Instruments of regional economic policy and measurement approaches of their impacts

In this section it will be indicated what method or combination of methods should be applied to measure effects of the two types of instruments distinguished in chapter 2, i.e. instruments of the control type and instruments of the influencing type. As mentioned above, the choice of the method(s) is dependent on various conditions, such as the financial and time budgets, the data available, and the impact variables one is interested in. In this respect the following remarks are in order. First, in order to facilitate the exposition, the effects on only one impact variable will be considered here, viz. the creation of **employment,** which is often the ultimate policy objective of regional economic policy. (See Oosterhaven and Folmer, 1983, for the case of the Netherlands.) Estimation of effects on other impact variables can usually be performed in similar ways. Secondly, the restrictions resulting from the financial and time budgets and from the data available will be taken into account by describing both an "ideal" procedure, which may require detailed information or be time consuming, and an alternative with contrasting features.

To begin with, a simple situation is considered, viz. the estimation of **direct** effects of **control** instruments. In this situation it is often possible to remove the effects of non-policy variables so that the direct effect of this type of instrument can be obtained by spatial models with explanatory variables of the policy type only or by non-experimental micro approaches. For instance, the total direct effect resulting from the reloca-tion of a governmental organization can be obtained by calculating the number of jobs involved in the construction of the offices, the total number of jobs relocated, the number of employees, who migrate with their organiza-tion and the number of jobs obtained by native unemployed. It should be observed, however, that in the case of state participation in firms and of financial aid to companies in trouble, the number of jobs concerned gives the maximum effect, since both the creation of this new employment and the number of jobs saved from vanishing might also have taken place without the aid provided.

Indirect effects of instruments of the control type, which arise via demand or production variables, e.g., via investments in buildings for the relocated governmental organization, can be calculated by means of input-output analysis, provided that an appropriate, operational input-output model is available.[1] By means of this approach detailed information on the various kinds of effects can be obtained. If an appropriate input-output model is not available but a univariate pre-intervention series of the impact variable and a multivariate time series of the impact variable and the policy variables are available, two stage time series analysis may be used to estimate the total effect on employment in a given region. The following remarks are in order here. First, the total effect estimated by means of the two-stage time series analysis approach is made up by the sum of the direct and indirect effects. Moreover, the effects which stem from the influencing aspect of the instrument are also included. Secondly, when it is possible to calculate the direct effects separately, this should be done as a check on the results of the two-stage time series analysis approach. Finally, two-stage time series analysis gives less detailed infor-mation on the effects than input-output analysis. However, intermediate forms between input-output analysis and two-stage time series analysis, such as general simultaneous equation models, are sometimes possible. (See for an example, Folmer and Oosterhaven, 1983.)

---

[1] It is obvious that various direct effects of instruments of the control type can also be obtained by means of input-output analysis.

As mentioned in chapter 2, instruments of the control type may be of the influencing type for certain categories of agents. Measurement of this kind of effects is discussed in the framework of effects of instruments of the influencing type in general.

The only instrument of the **influencing** type of those listed in chapter 2, which has **direct** effects on employment is that of employment subsidies. Its effects can be measured by means of a **survey** among firms which make use of the subsidies concerned. If a survey is not possible, a **single equation spatial model** with regional employment (or unemployment) as dependent variable and employment subsidies as one of the explanatory variables can be used. Furthermore, this spatial approach can be applied as a check on the outcomes of a survey (see also Marquand (1980) and Moore and Rhodes (1976b, 1977) who state that the reliability of impact studies can be improved when micro and spatial approaches are used in combination).

Indirect effects of employment subsidies (e.g., effects on employment via new locations) are of the same kind as the effects of the other instruments of the influencing type and are discussed in the next paragraph.

First-order effects of instruments of the influencing type can be measured by means of surveys. When the effects, in terms of new establishments are known, **second-order** and **higher-order** effects, which arise via demand or production variables, can be calculated by means of input-output analysis. An alternative to the combination of the micro and input-output approaches, which is considerably less cumbersome, is the use of **simultaneous equation models**. Because most instruments of the influencing type have indirect effects (usually via investments) on employment one equation is to give the effect of the instrument on investments and another the effect of investments on employment.

3.6 Conclusions

In this chapter various measurement approaches of effects of regional economic policy have been described and evaluated. The evaluation has resulted in a set of methodological requirements which can be summarized as follows (see also Folmer, 1980, 1981):

-Effects of policy variables should be disentangled from effects of non-policy variables. If effects of non-policy variable are present and if it is not possible to take these effects into account outside the measurement framework the policy variables should be explicitly included in the measurement model. The crudest way to represent the policy variables is by means of dummy variables. If more detailed information than the simple distinction between policy-on and policy-off situations is available, it is desirable to use this detailed information. In the case of instruments of the influencing type measures of intensity should be used and in the case of instruments of the control type volume measures are appropriate.

-The multi-effective nature of an instrument should be taken into account.

-In addition to intraregional effects, interregional, national and international effects are of importance.

-Both direct and indirect effects, as well as short-, medium-, and long-term effects should be calculated.

-It is desirable to compare effects of different instruments of regional economic policy.

These requirements will form guidelines in the design of the measurement approaches, which will be discussed in subsequent chapters.

From the overview given in this section one may conclude that appropriate measurement methods of effects of the various instruments of regional economic policy are available. It has also been made clear, that the choice of a measurement approach is dependent on such circumstances as the kinds of effects to be measured, the data available and the time and financial budgets. Two-stage time series analysis and general simultaneous equation models have been found to give sufficient information needed for the evaluation and design of regional economic policy in a variety of situations. Moreover, they are often the only possible approaches given the time-, budget- and data restrictions. These features and the fact that these two approaches, compared to various other measurement methods discussed above, are relatively unknown, may be seen as a preliminary justification of the attention to be paid to them in subsequent chapters.

PART II: ECONOMETRIC METHODS

4. LINEAR STRUCTURAL EQUATION MODELS WITH LATENT VARIABLES

4.1 Introduction

In the preceding chapter it has been shown that effects of policy packages can often be handled by using latent variables. Furthermore, the advantages of simultaneously dealing with the main theory (i.e. the set of relationships between latent variables only) and the measurement theory (i.e. the set of relationships which contains both latent and observable variables) within one model framework have been described.

In this chapter the class of linear structural equation models with latent variables (abbreviated as LISREL models), which possesses this advantage, is introduced. In order to deal simultaneously with both the measurement and the main theory a LISREL model is made up of two related submodels:

-A **latent variables measurement model** [1], which represents the relationships between the latent variables and their observable indicators.
-A **structural model**, representing the relationships between the latent
variables.

The organization of this chapter is as follows. In section 4.2, the structure of LISREL models is described in detail. The problem of identification of LISREL models and the way it is dealt with in the computer program LISREL V, which has been developed to estimate this class of models, is described in section 4.3. The types of estimators used in LISREL V, are discussed in section 4.4. These estimators are: the so-called "initial estimator", maximum likelihood and unweighted least squares. In section 4.5 attention is paid to the estimation of the residuals, which are needed when spatio-temporal correlation is dealt with (chapter 5). The

---

[1]It should be noted that the model consisting of the relationships between the latent variables and the observable indicators will be referred to as the "latent variables measurement model". The model intended
to measure effects of economic policy will be referred to as "measurement model", without the addition "latent variables".

last section 4.6 is devoted to model judgement. After an overview of the judgement statistics given by the LISREL V-program, diagnostic checking of the fit of data instigated models is described. Next, hypothesis testing proper is dealt with. In this chapter hypothesis testing is only considered in situations where the observed variables are multinormally distributed. Situations, where the distribution of the observables deviates from normality or is unknown, are paid attention to in chapter 8. In that chapter LISREL models will be dealt with in the framework of the bootstrap and jackknife estimation procedures.

This introductory section concludes with the following remarks. First, the LISREL approach has been developed by, among others, Jöreskog (1973a, 1973b, 1977a), Goldberger (1972), Goldberger and Duncan (1973) and Jöreskog and Sörbom (1981). This chapter is partly based on these references. Secondly, it is important to stress the linear-additive nature of LISREL models here. However, when non-linear or non-additive relationships occur they can often be transformed into linear-additive ones. After such a transformation, the LISREL approach can be applied in the usual way. Furthermore, if transformations are not possible or not wanted, the range of the variables is often small enough to allow for a linear approximation. Thirdly, the extension of LISREL V, i.e. LISREL VI (cf. Jöreskog and Sörbom, 1984 forthcoming) contains five estimators: instrumental variables, two-stage least squares, maximum likelihood, unweighted least squares, and generalized least squares. It should be noted that the first two estimators are also contained in LISREL V in the initial estimator (see section 4.4).

4.2. The structure

In this section attention is first paid to the basic structure of LISREL models (i.e. to the latent variables measurement models and the structural model) and next to the various submodels contained in the general model framework. The third subject of this section is the description of the structure of the various theoretical parameter matrices and the corresponding sample matrices.

4.2.1. <u>The latent variables measurement models and the structural model</u>

Let $y = (y_1, y_2, \ldots, y_p)^T$ and $x = (x_1, x_2, \ldots x_q)^T$ be vectors of observable endogenous and exogenous variables, respectively.[1] Furthermore, let $\eta = (\eta_1, \eta_2, \ldots, \eta_m)^T$ be a vector of latent endogenous variables and $\xi = (\xi_1, \xi_2, \ldots, \xi_n)^T$ a vector of latent exogenous variables. Finally, $\varepsilon = (\varepsilon_1, \varepsilon_2, \ldots \varepsilon_p)^T$ and $\delta = \delta_1, \delta_2, \ldots, \delta_q)^T$ are defined as vectors of measurement errors of y and x, respectively. The relationships between the observed and latent variables are given in the latent variables measurement models (4.1) and (4.2):

$$y = \Lambda_y \eta + \varepsilon \tag{4.1}$$

and:

$$x = \Lambda_x \xi + \delta \tag{4.2}$$

where Λ_y and Λ_x are (p x m) and (q x n) matrices of regression coefficients (also called factor loadings).

The structural model consists of a set of relationships among the latent variables:

$$\eta = \tilde{B}\eta + \Gamma\xi + \zeta \tag{4.3}$$

or

$$B\eta = \Gamma\xi + \zeta \tag{4.4}$$

where:

$\tilde{B}$ is a m x m coefficient matrix with β_{ij} representing the effect of the j-th endogenous variable on the i-th endogenous variable;

Γ is a m x n coefficient matrix with γ_{ij} representing the effect of the j-th exogenous variable on the i-th endogenous variable;

ζ is a random vector of residuals;

$B = I - \tilde{B}$, where I is the identity matrix.

In connection with model (4.1) – (4.4), the following notation is introduced. The covariance matrices of ε and δ, which need not be diagonal in LISREL, will be denoted by Θ_ε(p x p) and Θ_δ(q x q) and the covariance matrices of ξ and ζ by Φ(n x n) and ψ(m x m).

[1] The upperscript "T" denotes the transposed vector or matrix.

The following remarks are in order here. First, for reasons of simplicity but without loss of generality, it is assumed that B is non-singular. Thus, dependent equations are assumed to have been removed from the system of equations. Secondly, it is possible to estimate intercept terms of the equations (4.1) – (4.4). Such parameters may be of interest in the comparison of different, mutually exclusive, sets of regions. In the present kind of studies, however, attention will only be paid to the analyses of single samples. In such analysis, the intercept terms hardly provide any information. Therefore, the assumption is made here, that both the observed and the latent variables are centralized. Formally:

$$E(y) = 0; \quad E(x) = 0; \quad E(\eta) = 0; \quad E(\xi) = 0 \qquad (4.5)$$

Thirdly, the following standard assumptions are made:

$$E(\varepsilon) = 0; \quad E(\delta) = 0; \quad E(\zeta) = 0$$

$$E(\eta\varepsilon^T) = 0; \quad E(\xi\delta^T) = 0; \quad E(\eta\delta^T) = 0; \quad E(\xi\varepsilon^T) = 0; \quad E(\varepsilon\delta^T) = 0 \qquad (4.6)$$

$$E(\zeta\xi^T) = 0; \quad E(\zeta\delta^T) = 0; \quad E(\zeta\varepsilon^T) = 0$$

In (4.5) and (4.6) "0" denotes a vector or matrix of apropriate order.

Fourthly, multiple observable variables for a latent variable are often preferable and necessary so as to provide a tool for identification (see, among others, Goldberger, 1972, 1973). Besides, one single observable variable may be an indicator of more than one latent variable. Finally, as described by, among others, Theil (1971), the problem of multicollinearity arises as a consequence of the occurance of (highly) correlated explanatory variables. It usually leads to the increase of the estimated variances of the estimators of the coefficients of the collinear explanatory variables, so that one may be led to drop variables incorrectly from an equation. By means of the possibility to handle observable and latent variables simultaneously within one model framework, as in the LISREL case, the consequences of multicollinearity can be mitigated. This can be seen as follows. Collinear explanatory variables, which are indicators of a given latent variable, are **dependent** variables in one of the latent variables measurement models (4.1) and (4.2) and therefore are not removed from one of these models because of their collinear nature. Furthermore, in the structural model the latent variables appear instead of their corresponding observable variables. So, collinear variables are neither removed from the structural model in spite of the fact that they are collinear.

4.2.2 Submodels

Model (4.1) - (4.) is a general framework in which several specific models are contained. The most common of these models are first- and second- order factor analysis models, structural equation models for directly observable variables and various types of regression models. The specifications for the various models mentioned above are given below.

-Suppose the following specifications are made: $B = 0$, $\Gamma = 0$, $\Lambda_y = 0$, $\Theta_\varepsilon = 0$, $\psi = 0$, where "0" denotes a zero matrix of appropriate order. Then the well known factor analysis model is obtained:

$$x = \Lambda_x \xi + \delta \qquad (4.7)$$

-If only the x-variables are removed from the model, i.e. $\Lambda_x = 0$, $\Theta_\delta = 0$, we have:

$$y = \Lambda_y \eta + \varepsilon \qquad (4.8)$$

$$(I-\tilde{B}) \eta = \Gamma \xi + \zeta \qquad (4.9)$$

or

$$\eta = (I-\tilde{B})^{-1} (\Gamma \xi + \zeta) \qquad (4.10)$$

Putting $\tilde{B} = 0$ and substituting (4.10) in (4.8) gives:

$$y = \Lambda_y (\Gamma \xi + \zeta) + \varepsilon \qquad (4.11)$$

Model (4.11) is a second-order factor analysis model. (see, for details, among others, Jöreskog, 1969, 1974).

-Remove all latent variables from the model by specifying identity relationships between y and η and between x and ξ. This is done by defining Λ_x and Λ_y as identity matrices and Θ_ε and Θ_δ as zero matrices. This results in:

$$By = \Gamma x + \zeta \qquad (4.12)$$

which is a simultaneous equation model with observables only.

-If (4.12) is written as

$$y = \tilde{B}y + \Gamma x + \zeta \qquad (4.12a)$$

and $\tilde{B}$ is specified as a zero matrix then the "classical" linear model is obtained:

$$y = \Gamma x + \zeta \qquad (4.13)$$

If (4.13) consists of one equation only, we have the standard linear
model.

-If only the latent exogenous variables are removed from the general model
i.e., $\xi \equiv x$, so that $\Lambda_x = I$, the identity matrix, and $\Theta_\delta = 0$, we get:

$$y = \Lambda_y \eta + \varepsilon \tag{4.14}$$

$$B\eta = \Gamma x + \zeta \tag{4.15}$$

A special case of model (4.14), (4,15) is the so-called **fixed-x**
model. In that case the conditional distribution of the y variables for
given x is studied. This type of model is frequently met in traditional
econometrics (see, for instance, Johnston, 1972). It should be noted that
in both the fixed-x and the random-x case $\Phi = S_{xx}$, where S_{xx} is the sample
covariance matrix of the x-variables.

4.2.3   The theoretical and the sample matrices

When the topics of identification estimation and judgement of LISREL
models are discussed, the theoretical covariance matrix and the corresponding sample matrix play essential roles. As will be explained below, the
sample covariance matrix should preferably be analyzed. The sample covariance matrix of $z = (y^T, x^T)^T$ will be denoted as S and the theoretical
covariance matrix as Σ.

Let us first pay attention to the structure of Σ. The matrix Σ can be
expressed in terms of the eight model matrices Λ_y, Λ_x, B, Γ, Φ, ψ, Θ_ε and
Θ_δ. This can be seen as follows. Because B^{-1} exists, equation (4.4) can be
written as:

$$\eta = B^{-1}\Gamma\xi + B^{-1}\zeta \tag{4.16}$$

Substitution of (4.16) in (4.1) gives

$$y = \Lambda_y (B^{-1}\Gamma\xi + B^{-1}\zeta) + \varepsilon \tag{4.17}$$

Calculation of the covariance matrix of y, i.e. $E(yy^T)$, using (4.17) and
the assumptions (4.6) gives:

$$E(yy^T) = E(\Lambda_y(B^{-1}\Gamma\xi + B^{-1}\zeta) + \varepsilon)(\Lambda_y(B^{-1}\Gamma\xi + B^{-1}\zeta) + \varepsilon)^T$$

$$= \Lambda_y(B^{-1}\Gamma\Phi\Gamma^T(B^{-1})^T)^T + B^{-1}\psi(B^{-1})^T)\Lambda_y^T + \Theta_\varepsilon \tag{4.18}$$

In similar ways $E(xx^T)$ and $E(yx^T)$ are calculated. This gives:

$$\Sigma = \begin{bmatrix} \Lambda_y B^{-1}(\Gamma\Phi\Gamma^T + \psi)(B^{-1})^T \Lambda_y^T + \Theta_\varepsilon & \Lambda_y B^{-1}\Gamma\Phi\Lambda_x^T \\ \\ \Lambda_x \Phi\Gamma^T(B^{-1})^T \Lambda_y^T & \Lambda_x \Phi\Lambda_x^T + \Theta_\delta \end{bmatrix} \qquad (4.19)$$

On the basis of prior information (expectations, theoretical consi-derations, etc.), the elements in the parameter matrices, and thus in Σ, may be regarded either as free, fixed or constrained (see among others, Johnston, 1972). A constrained parameter is unknown but assumed to be equal to one or more other parameters.[1] All independent, free and con-strained parameters contained in the matrices Λ_x, Λ_y, B, Γ, Φ, ψ, Θ_ε and Θ_δ will be denoted by the vector π. It is obvious that a specific struc-ture of π, i.e. a specific configuration of free, fixed and constrained parameters, determines a specific structure of Σ.[2] Moreover, the deter-mination of the value of π forms the core of the estimation problem.

Let us now turn to the **sample** covariancematrix S. Let Z be a M x (p+q) matrix of M observations of the y and x vectors and $\bar{z} = (\bar{y}^T, \bar{x}^T)^T$ the sample mean vector. Then:

$$S = \frac{1}{M-1}(Z^T Z - M\bar{z}\bar{z}^T) \qquad (4.20)$$

When there are ordinal or nominal variables among the observable var-iables (4.20) cannot be used in general. In the case of ordinal or nominal x-variables (4.20) can be employed when the x-variables are fixed. When there are **ordinal** variables among the y-variables or among the x-var-iables, which may not be considered as fixed, the LISREL V program can estimate and analyze the matrices of polychoric, tetrachoric and polyser-ial correlation coefficients. In all three cases the ordinal z variable is regarded as a crude measurement of an underlying unobservable continuous

---

1) In addition to these constraints various other equality and inequality constraints on various parameters, such as variances, correlations, factor loadings and structural coefficients, as well as ordered inequa-lities can be imposed, although the LISREL V computer program does not explicitly allow of such constraints (see Rindskopf, 1983, 1984).

2) It should be noted that when Σ must explicitly be expressed as a func-tion of π, we will write $\Sigma(\pi)$; otherwise the argument will be omitted.

variable, say z*, which is assumed to be standard normally distributed. The polychoric correlation coefficient is the correlation between two underlying z* variables.[1] The tetrachoric correlation coefficient is a special case when both observables are dichotomous. The correlation between a z* variable and a normally distributed observed variable is called the polyserial correlation coefficient. By way of the observable variables the various correlations mentioned above are estimated. (For details see, among others, Olsson, 1979, Olsson et al, 1981 and Muthén, 1978, 1979, 1981).

When there are **nominal** variables among the y-variables or nominal x-variables, which should not be considered to be fixed, the sample can be split up in several groups on the basis of the nominal variables. Data from the various groups can be analyzed simultaneously. Because in measurement studies of effects of economic policy no basic objections to the use of fixed x-variables exist and nominal y variables are not frequently met, we will not pay attention to multi-group analysis here. For information about this issue the reader is referred to, among others, Jöreskog and Sörbom (1981), Sörbom (1978, 1981).

It should be noted that not only the sample covariance matrix can be analyzed by the LISREL V program. The sample matrix of **moments about zero** and the sample **correlation** matrix can also be used to estimate their theoretical counterparts. The sample matrix of moments about zero, defined as:

$$\frac{1}{M} Z^T Z \qquad (4.21)$$

has to be used when intercept terms and means of the latent variables are required.

When the measurement scales are very different the correlation matrix could be analyzed for numerical expediency. Then each variable is expressed in units of its standard deviation. The correlation matrix is defined as:

1) In the case of a large number of distinct categories the ordinal variable is treated as a continuous variable.

$$D^{-1} \, S \, D^{-1} \qquad (4.22)$$

with

$$D = (\text{diag } S)^{1/2}, \qquad (4.23)$$

i.e. a diagonal matrix of standard deviations.

Now that the most important features and assumptions of LISREL models have been described, we can pay attention to the identification problem in connection with this type of models.

4.3 Identification

The rationale behind the specification of econometric models in general, and thus also of LISREL models, is that a certain specific structure of parameters has generated the observations under consideration. The major objective of the analysis of the data gathered is to estimate the unknown parameters and to test certain restrictions on them. Estimation of LISREL models is done by fitting the theoretical covariance matrix Σ to the covariance matrix S of the observable variables z.[1] The estimation procedure is based on the assumption that the distribution of the observed variables of LISREL models is adequately described by the moments of first and second order. Because the variables are assumed to be centralized (see section 4.2.1), the distribution of z is characterized by the independent parameters in Σ. Therefore estimation of LISREL models is done by fitting Σ to S.

In order to be able to draw inferences for the vector π from the variance-covariance matrix of the observable variables, the structure of Σ has to be such as to allow a unique solution of π from Σ. Thus, the vector π has to be uniquely determined by Σ; in other words, the model has to be identified. With these notions it can easily be understood that if two or more different π's yield the same Σ, the model under consideration is not identified. However, if a **single** parameter has the same value in all π's that generate the same Σ, the parameter is identified. If all

1) The discussion of identification and estimation is in terms of the covariance matrix though it also applies to the matrix of moments about zero and the correlation matrix.

the parameters of the model are identified, the whole model is identified.[1)]

A necessary condition for identification is that the number of distinct elements in Σ is at least as large as the number of independent parameters to be estimated. Let this latter number be h. There are

$\frac{(p+q)(p+q+1)}{2}$ equations in h unknowns. Therefore, a necessary condition for identification is that:

$$h \leqslant \frac{(p+q)(p+q+1)}{2} \qquad (4.24)$$

A second necessary condition for identification is that each individual parameter can be separated from the other parameters. This condition is often difficult to test. Furthermore, it is not a sufficient condition. However, the LISREL V program gives hints about identification problems. It calculates an estimate of the matrix of second-order derivatives of the fitting function used to estimate the model. (The fitting functions used in the LISREL V program will be described in section 4.4). The estimate of the matrix of second-order derivatives is obtained by substituting the value of π, for which the first-order derivatives of the fitting function with respect to the unknown parameters are equal to zero, into the matrix of second-order derivatives.

If the log-likelihood function of the random sample is used as a fitting function, the negative of the expected value of the matrix of second-order derivatives is the **information matrix,** denoted as $J(\pi)$, with elements:

$$J_{ij}(\pi) = - E_{\pi} \left[\frac{\partial^2}{\partial \pi_i \partial \pi_j} \log p(z; \pi) \right] \qquad (4.25)$$

where $p(z; \pi)$ is the likelihood function.

Under certain regularity conditions, which are fulfilled when the observed variables are normally distributed, (cf. Rao, 1965) the following condition holds:

$$J_{ij}(\pi) = E_{\pi} \left[\frac{\partial}{\partial \pi_i} \log p(z; \pi) \cdot \frac{\partial}{\partial \pi_j} \log p(z; \pi) \right] \qquad (4.26)$$

---

1) It should be noted that identifiability of a parameter is a necessary but not a sufficient condition for consistent estimation (see Gabrielsen, 1978).

In the sequel, the expected value of the matrix of second-order derivatives of the fitting function will be denoted as 'information matrix'.

Rothenberg (1971) has shown that under quite weak regularity conditions local identifiability is equivalent to non-singularity of the information matrix. The LISREL program evaluates the information matrix at the minimum of the fitting function. If the estimated information matrix is singular, this usually means that the model is not identified (see also Silvey, 1970. (For a criticism of this pragmatic data-instigated criterion see Bentler, 1982). Furthermore, the rank of the matrix indicates which parameters are not identified (Jöreskog, 1981). These parameters are indicated by the LISREL V program.

Another way of checking whether or not the model is identified is to choose a set of reasonable values for the parameters, say $\tilde{\pi}$, to let the LISREL program calculate $\Sigma(\tilde{\pi})$ and estimate the parameters of the model with $\Sigma(\tilde{\pi})$ as the input matrix. The estimated parameters, which are different from their corresponding elements in $\tilde{\pi}$ are usually not identified.

In the case of models with latent variables, the model is not identified if the latent variables have not been assigned measurement scales. This is a consequence of the fact that if the unit of measurement of a variable is unknown, its variance cannot be calculated without further restrictions. The nature of this kind of non-identification can easily be understood by recalling that a change in the unit of measurement of a latent variable combined with a corresponding adjustment of its regression coefficient will produce the same value of an observed variable. Formally:

$$x = \lambda \, \xi + \varepsilon = \frac{\lambda}{\alpha} \, (\alpha\xi) + \varepsilon \qquad (4.27)$$

where α is the rescaling factor.

The easiest way to fix the measurement scales of the latent variables is to set one λ-coefficient equal to 1 for each latent variable. This implies that each latent variable is measured on the scale of the corresponding observable variable with the λ-coefficient equal to 1.

We will conclude this section by mentioning that it is usually possible to fix or to constrain unidentified parameters on the basis of theoretical knowledge or ad hoc reasoning so as to render the model identified. For example, one can assume that two parameters are equal and estimate their common value. Finally, we remark that further information on identification can be found in, among others, Fisher (1966), Jöreskog (1977) and Aigner and Goldberger (1977).

4.4 Estimation of the model

As mentioned above, estimation of LISREL models consists of fitting the theoretical matrix to the sample matrix of a set of M observations on $z = (y^T, x^T)^T$ by minimizing the distance between both matrices in some metric. The exposition below will be in terms of the covariance matrices Σ and S but it has already been remarked that the matrix of moments about zero and the sample correlation matrix can also be analyzed. However, the estimates based on each of these matrices are usually not the same.

The LISREL V program (Jöreskog and Sörbom, 1981) provides three kinds of consistent estimators, i.e. the initial estimator, maximum likelihood and unweighted least squares. These estimators will be subsequentially described below.

Maximum likelihood

Maximum likelihood has been the "traditional" estimator of LISREL models in the sense that the other estimators were introduced in LISREL V for the first time. The maximum likelihood procedure is based on minimization with respect to the unknown parameters of the non-negative function:

$$F = {}^1/_2 \left[\log |\Sigma| + tr(S\Sigma^{-1}) - \log |S| -(p+q) \right] \qquad (4.28)$$

by means of a modification of the Fletcher-Powell algorithm. In (4.28) $|.|$ stands for the determinant and tr(.) for the trace of the matrix concerned. When ξ, ζ, ε, δ are multinormally distributed, and thus z, then:

$$F' = - {}^1/_2 M\left[(p+q) \log 2\pi + \log |\Sigma| + tr(S\Sigma^{-1})\right] \qquad (4.29)$$

is the log-likelihood function of the sample in the case of independent observations.

From (4.28) and (4.29) it follows that under the assumptions of normality of z and independence of the observations, minimization of F (which gives the same parameter estimates as maximization of F'), results in 'genuine' maximum-likelihood estimators. Under the usual regularity conditions, which are satisfied in the case of normality, the maximum likelihood estimator of π is asymptotically normally distributed with mean

π and covariance matrix $\frac{1}{M} \left[J(\pi) \right]^{-1}$, where $J(\pi)$ is defined in (4.26) with F' substituted for log $p(z;\pi)$. (See among others Rao, 1965). Furthermore, this estimator is consistent and asymptotically efficient.

It is obvious from (4.28) that S has to be positive definite. This condition is satisfied when there exists no exact linear relationships between any of the z variables, and if $M \geq p+q$. Furthermore, the starting values needed for the minimization algorithm, say π', should be such that $\Sigma(\pi')$, is also positive definite. The initial estimates provided by the LISREL V program usually satisfy this condition (see below).

The maximum likelihood procedure also produces an estimate of the covariance or correlation matrix of the estimators, which can be used for model judgement purposes (see section 4.6). However, it should be noted that although an estimate of the covariance or correlation matrix of the estimator is produced whatever sample matrix has been analyzed, the covariance or correlation matrix of the estimators is only valid when a sample **covariance** matrix has been analyzed.

As mentioned above, a necessary condition for the maximum likelihood procedure to give "genuine" maximum likelihood estimates is the normal distrubution of the observable variables. However, the distribution of the observables is seldomly known in practice. It also rarely happens that the theory at hand suggests a definite distribution.[1] However, when the range of the variables is in principle $(-\infty, \infty)$ and second order moments exist, the assumption of multivariate normality can be justified as a first working hypothesis on the basis of a central limit theorem or maximum entropy. The latter means that the normal distribution reflects the lack of knowledge about the distribution more completely than other distributions (see, among others, Rao, 1965).

Maximum likelihood under normality (i.e. application of maximum likelihood under the assumption of normality whereas the distribution actually devaiates from normality) may also be defended on the basis of the fact that it usually leads to a reasonable fitting function and to estimators with acceptable properties for a rather wide class of distributions. Under quite weak distributional assumptions, maximum likelihood under normality is consistent and asymptotically normal (cf. Chernoff and

---

1) For an exception see the theory of rational consumer behavior (cf. Theil, 1975, 1976).

Rubin, 1953; Dijkstra, 1981). However, in the case of deviation from normality the standard errors produced by the LISREL V computer program
should be interpreted very cautiously. The same applies to various other
judgement statics to be described below (see section 4.6).

The maximum likelihood fitting function can also be used **without**
the assumption of normality. In that case it is similar to the unweighted
least squares estimator to be described below. Under these circumstances
the resulting estimator is still consistent. However, the judgement statistics are no longer valid.

Unweighted least squares

The unweigthed least squares estimation procedure can be justified
without assumptions with respect to the distribution of the variables. The
following non-negative fitting function is minimized in the LISREL program:

$$G = \frac{1}{2} \, tr \left[(S-\Sigma)^2 \right] \tag{4.30}$$

It is minimized with respect to the unknown free and constrained parameters in an iterative procedure. The present procedure does not provide
standard errors for the estimators. Furthemore, it is not necessary for
the matrices S and Σ to be positive definite.

The discussion of the maximum likelihood and unweighted least squares
estimators is brought to a conclusion with the remark that it sometimes
happens that there are **several** local minima to which the minimization
algorithm may converge. An indication of convergence to a local minimum is
a solution of the minimization problem on the boundary or outside the
admissable parameter space, which is revealed by negative variances, correlations larger than one in absolute value, etc. It should be noted that
unacceptable estimates can be avoided by imposing inequality constraints
without the necessity for changing the computer program (see Rindskopf,
1983) However, unacceptable estimates provide important information with
respect to model identification in the case of explanatory studies.
Therefore, constraints should not be imposed at an early stage of the data
analysis (see section 4.6.3 for further details).

The occurance of several local minima is usually a consequence of a
model which is inappropriate for the data at hand or a sample size which

is too small (see, for instance, Lawley and Maxwell, 1963, for the latter case). An extensive description of model evaluation and modification of inappropriate models is given in section 4.6.

The initial estimator

The initial estimation procedure provides starting values so as to speed up the iterative procedures of unweigthed least squares and maximum likelihood. Furthermore, it may be used in its own right, especially in those situations where estimates of the parameters and other information in the output are used to improve the model under consideration (see section 4.6.2). Finally, when the model fits the data well the initial estimates are often close to the maximum likelihood or unweighted least squares estimates.

In contrast to maximum likelihood and unweighted least squares, the present procedure does not estimate the parameters simultaneously. The free and constrained parameters of each matrix mentioned in section 4.2 are estimated successively in the following order. (For a detailed overview see Folmer and Nijkamp, 1984).

–First, Λ_y and Λ_x are estimated by means of instrumental variables.

–Secondly, the matrices Θ_ε, Θ_δ, Φ, as well as the covariance matrix of the endogenous latent η variables are obtained by unweighted least squares estimators.

–Thirdly, the matrices B and Γ are estimated by means of two–stage least squares , or, if this procedure cannot be applied, by ordinary least squares (see, among others, Johnston, 1972).[1]

–Finally, the matrix ψ is obtained by means of the relationship

$$\eta = B^{-1} \Gamma \xi + B^{-1} \zeta \tag{4.31}$$

the estimated covariance matrix of the η–variables, the estimated covariance matrices B and Γ and the independence of the residuals of the ξ–variables.

1) It is well-known that when pre-determined variables and disturbances are correlated the ordinary least squares estimator is inconsistent (see, among others, Johnston, 1972).

It is obvious that because all estimates can be obtained analytically the initial estimation procedure is much faster than the iterative maximum likelihood and unweighted least squares methods.

This section on estimation is ended with the remark that when the initial estimator or the unweighted least squares estimator has been applied no estimated standard errors are produced. Moreover, when maximum likelihood has been used without the assumption of normality various judgement statistics, inter alia the standard errors, are not valid. Under these circumstances the variability of the estimators of various parameters can be investigated by means of the bootstrap or the jackknife (see chapter 8).

4.5 Estimation of the residuals

In the next chapter it will be indicated, that the estimated residuals of a LISREL model are of great importance in connection with spatio-temporal correlation. The vector of estimated residuals, say $\hat{e}_m$, for the m-th observation is defined as:

$$\hat{e}_m = y'_m - \hat{y}_m \tag{4.32}$$

where:

$\hat{y}'_m$ is the vector of observed values for the observable endogenous variables;

$\hat{y}_m$ is the vector of LISREL estimates of the observable endogenous variables.

The residuals $\hat{e}_m$ are not given by the LISREL program, but can be estimated in the following way. First the minimum variance linear estimator $\hat{\xi}$ of ξ, given x, is obtained by minimizing:

$$E(\xi - Ax)^T (\xi - Ax) = tr\Sigma_{\xi\xi} - 2\ tr(A\Sigma_{\xi x}) + tr(A^T A \Sigma_{xx}) \tag{4.33}$$

with respect to A. In (4.33) $\Sigma_{..}$ denotes the covariance matrix of the vectors mentioned in the indices. Minimization of (4.33) gives:

$$A = \Sigma_{\xi x}\ \Sigma_{xx}^{-1} \tag{4.34}$$

From the definitions and models given in section 4.2.1 it follows that:

$$A = \Phi \Lambda_x^T (\Lambda_x \Phi \Lambda_x^T + \Theta_\delta)^{-1} \tag{4.35}$$

From (4.33) we obtain:

$$\hat{\xi} = Ax \tag{4.36}$$

Next, the following standard estimators for η can be derived (see also Goldberger et al., 1971):

$$\hat{\eta} = B^{-1} \Gamma \hat{\xi} \tag{4.37}$$

Finally, the standard estimator for y is:

$$\hat{y} = \Lambda_y \hat{\eta} \tag{4.38}$$

The parameter matrices in (4.35), (4.37) and (4.38) are unknown and are to be replaced by their LISREL estimates.

So far attention has only been paid to the residuals of the structural model. However, the errors of the measurement models will also be needed in the sequel. They can be obtained as follows:

$$\hat{\delta} = x - \hat{\Lambda}_x \hat{\xi} \tag{4.39}$$

The easiest way to obtain estimates of the ε-errors is by estimating seperately a latent variables measurement model of exogenous variables only (without structural model) in which the y-variables are treated as x-variables and the η-variables as ξ-variables. The ε-errors can then be obtained via (4.39).[1]

4.6 Model judgement and model modification

4.6.1 Introduction

The purpose of model judgement is to judge how well an estimated model fits to the sample data. Various aspects of a LISREL model may be considered in this connection, such as the model as a whole, the various submodels and the individual parameters.

Two extreme forms of model judgement can be distinguished. In the

---

[1] For ease of notation both the estimated residuals and measurement errors are denoted by $\hat{e}$, if there is no risk of confusion.

first place **genuine hypothesis testing** according to the rules of statistical decisions theory (see, among others, Ferguson, 1967). Essential to this form of model judgement is the availability of a **given** model of which various aspects are tested on the sample data. The model is based on theoretical considerations or on findings of related empirical research.

The second form, denoted here as **diagnostic checking**, presents itself in analyses the purpose of which is to find a model that fits the data at hand as well as possible. Diagnostic checking is the last step in the three-stage iterative process of model fitting. The preceding steps are identification and estimation (see also section 7.4). For diagnostic checking judgement statistics are needed which reflect the change in fit of the models successively entertained. Because the data gave birth to it, the model obtained by model fitting has a data-instigated. Therefore, in such circumstances hypothesis testing is less appropriate because the accuracy of the estimator of a data-instigated model will be over-estimated to an unknown extent.

In practical research both forms of model judgement are frequently intertwined. The same data, that gave birth to the model ultimately chosen, is also used for testing purposes. Intertwining both forms, usually denoted by such fanciful expressions as "data mining", "data grubbing", "fishing" or "torturing the data", makes the greatest possible use of any and all idiosyncrasies of the data. Therefore, the goodness of model fit to the **sample** data is likely to be greater than the fit to the **population**. In chapter 8 we will return to this problem.

We will now discuss the statisic produced by the LISREL V program which can be used for model judgement. All these statistics can be used to compare the fit of the models successively estimated (i.e. for diagnostic checking purposes). Some of them, of which the distribution is known, can also be used for testing hypotheses.

The organization of this section is as follows. In section 4.6.2 an overview of all the LISREL judgement statistics is given. Diagnostic checking and the way in which a model under consideration can be improved is paid attention to in section 4.6.3. Finally hypothesis testing will be described in section 4.6.4.

4.6.2 <u>LISREL judgement statistics</u>

The statistics provided by the LISREL program are related to:

—Individual parameters;

—Separate equations of the latent variables measurement models and of the structural model;

—The latent variables measurement model for the endogenous and the exogenous variables jointly;

—The structural model;

—The model as a whole (i.e. the overall fit);

The statistics produced by the LISREL program will systematically be described below.[1)]

Individual parameters

The statistics which relate to the individual parameters are parameter estimates and, when maximum likelihood has been used, standard errors and correlations of the estimators of the individual parameters.

Separate equations

For the equation of each observed variable in each latent variables measurement model the squared multiple correlation is given. It is defined as:

$$1 - \frac{\hat{\theta}_{\varepsilon/\delta_{ii}}}{s_{ii}} \qquad (4.40)$$

where $\hat{\theta}_{\varepsilon/\delta_{ii}}$ is the estimated error variance and s_{ii} the observed variance of the corresponding i-th y/x variable.

Statistic (4.40) is a measure of the validity and reliability (see Riley, 1963, for definitions) of the observed variables as indicators of the corresponding latent variables. In other words, it shows how well the observable variable serves as a measurement instrument for the correspon-

1) In this section no attention will be paid to the distribution of the statistics. Those statistics the distribution of which is known will be taken up in section 4.6.4 again.

ding latent variable. A value of (4.40) close to one is an indication that the observable is a good instrument.

The squared multiple correlation for the i-th structural equation is defined as:

$$1 - \frac{\hat{\psi}_{ii}}{\hat{var}(\eta_i)} \tag{4.41}$$

It should be noted that the statistic (4.41) does **not** have the same interpretation as the conventional R^2 statistic. This is because η_i is a function of both exogenous and endogenous variables, the latter of which may be correlated with ζ_i. As a consequence of this correlation, (4.41) may be negative. A statistic, which does have the same interpretation as the coefficient of determination, is the coefficient of correlation, developed by Carter and Nagar (1977). This statistic is preferable to (4.41) as judgement statistic for the structural equations. However, it is not given by the LISREL V (nor by the LISREL VI) program.

The latent variables measurement models

The coefficient of determination for the latent variables measurement model (i.e. for the endogenous and exogenous latent variables jointly) shows how well the observed variables serve jointly as indicators of the endogenous and exogenous latent variables. It is defined as:

$$1 - \left| \frac{\hat{\Theta}}{S} \right| \tag{4.42}$$

where $\hat{\Theta}$ is the estimated covariance matrix of the errors of the latent variables measurement models. A value of (4.42) close to one means a satisfactory operationalization of the latent variables.

The structural model

The coefficient of determination for all structural equations jointly is defined as:

$$1 - \frac{|\hat{\psi}|}{|\hat{cov}(\eta)|} \tag{4.43}$$

where $cov(\eta)$ is the covariance matrix of the endogenous latent variables.

It should be noted that the present statistic does not always show what proportion of the variation in the endogenous variables is accounted for by the variation in the systematic part of the model. The reason is the same as the one mentioned in relation to (4.41). The coefficient of correlation for the complete system, developed by Carter and Nagar (1977), is exactly analogous to the coefficient of determination for a single equation.[1])

It should be observed that squared multiple correlations and coefficients of determination are given for all three types of estimators of the LISREL V program. Test statistics for the overall fit, however, are only given when maximum likelihood or unweighted least squares have been used.

The overall fit

For the model as a whole several statistics are provided. First, there is the χ^2-measure which is given if maximum likelihood is used. It is defired as:

$$^1/_2 \, M \left[\log \left| \hat{\Sigma} \right| + tr(S\hat{\Sigma}^{-1}) - \log |S| - (p+q) \right] \tag{4.44}$$

where $\hat{\Sigma}$ is the theoretical covariance matrix calculated on the basis of the estimated parameter vector $\hat{\pi}$. The number of degrees of freedom of the χ^2-measure is equal to:

$$^1/_2 \, (p+q) \, (p+q+1) - h \tag{4.45}$$

where h is the total number of independent parameters estimated in the hypothesized model. The interpretation of the χ^2-statistic will be given in the sections 4.6.3 and 4.6.4.

Another measure for the overall fit, when maximum likelihood is used, is the goodness of fit index (GFM) defined as:

$$GFM = 1 - \frac{tr(\hat{\Sigma}^{-1}S - I)^2}{tr(\hat{\Sigma}^{-1}S)^2} \tag{4.46}$$

This measure, adjusted for degrees of freedom (AGFM), is defined as:

$$AGFM = 1 - \frac{(p+q) \, (p+q+1)}{2h} \, (1 - GFM) \tag{4.47}$$

---

1) Carter and Nagar (1977) als describe tests for the coefficients of correlation for a single equation and for the complete system.

Measures similar to (4.46) and (4.47) are given for unweighted least squares. Then GFM is replaced by GFU defined as:

$$GFU = 1 - \frac{tr(S - \hat{\Sigma})^2}{tr(S^2)} \tag{4.48}$$

All measures (4.46) – (4.48) are expressions of the relative share of variances and covariances accounted for by the model. They usually fall between zero and one. A good fit corresponds to values close to one.

A measure of the average of the residual variances and covariances is the root mean square residual. It is given both when maximum likelihood and when unweighted least squares is used. It is defined as:

$$\left[2 \sum_{i=1}^{p+q} \sum_{j=1}^{i} (s_{ij} - \hat{\sigma}_{ij})^2 / (p + q) (p + q + 1)) \right]^{1/2} \tag{4.49}$$

A small value of this statistic in relation to the sizes of the elements in S is an indication of a good fit.

Finally, the LISREL program gives normalized residuals which are approximately standard normal variates. A normalized residual is defined as:

$$\frac{s_{ij} - \hat{\sigma}_{ij}}{\dfrac{s_{ii}s_{ij} + s^2_{ij}}{M}} \; 1/2 \tag{4.50}$$

As a rule of thumb, a normalized residual larger than 2, is an indication of specification errors. (For further details see section 4.6.3.)

The LISREL program can also give a summary of the normalized residuals taken together in the form of a so-called Q-plot. This is a plot of the normalized residuals against normal quantiles. A slope of the plotted points equal to or smaller than 1 is an indication of a moderate or a poor fit. Non-linearities in the plotted points are indications of specification errors or of deviations from normality.

4.6.3 Diagnostic checking

Model deficiency is a consequence of specification errors. The following types of specification errors can be distinguished:[1]

---

1) Detailed information on specification errors can be found in, among others, Dijkstra (1984).

a) Near non-identification;

b) Specification errors with respect to the distribution of the observable variables;[1]

c) Parameters which are incorrectly fixed (usually at zero);

d) Parameters which are incorrectly assumed to be different from zero and thus are incorrectly specified as free parameters;

e) Specification errors with respect to the form of the model, i.e. non-linearities in models which are assumed to be linear;

f) Missing variables.

Let us first pay attention to nearly non-identified parameters. This kind of problem may arise as a consequence of the fact that some parameters cannot be determined from the data. Nearly non-identified parameters usually reveal themselves in extremely large standard errors of and high correlations between the estimators of the parameters concerned. Near non-identification can usually be solved by fixing parameters or by specifying linear equality constraints between the parameters of which the estimators are highly correlated.

The other types of specification errors under consideration here, c) - f), are generally reflected in unreasonable values of one or more of the statistics mentioned in section 4.6.1: variances, squared multiple correlations or coefficients of determination which are negative; correlations which are larger than one in absolute value; covariance or correlation matrices which are not positive definite.

When one or more of these statistics have unreasonable values two problems arise:

-Which type of specification error has been made?

-When the error is of the type c) or d), the misspecified parameters have to be detected, and when the error is of the type f) the missing variables have to be counterbalanced.

Both problems are highly dependent on the nature of the investigation. The more explorative the investigation, the higher the uncertainty

---

1) This kind of specification error mainly matters in the context of genuine testing. It will be discussed in section 4.6.4 and in chapter 8.

with respect to the form of the model, the relevant variables to be included in the model and the status of the parameters.

Let us first pay attention to parameters which have incorrectly been
fixed. As mentioned in section 4.2.3, the question whether the status of a
parameter is free, fixed or constrained is in the first instance determined by theory or ad hoc knowledge. Furthermore, in case of doubt about the
status of a parameter, it is usually fixed according to the 'principle of
parsimony' (Box and Jenkins, 1976). However, incorrectly fixed parameters
usually lead to inconsistent and biased estimators for all parameters.
Therefore, when one or more judgement statistics have unreasonable values,
as mentioned above, a first step to improve the model may be to specify
'suspicious' fixed parameters as free parameters. In addition to prior
theoretical or ad hoc knowledge, the modification indices and the normalized residuals, given by the LISREL V program, may be used to detect the
suspicious parameters. The modification index, given for each fixed and
constrained parameter, is defined as:

$$\frac{M(fod)^2}{2 \; sod} \hspace{6cm} (4.51)$$

where "fod" and "sod" are the first- and second-order derivatives of the
fitting function with respect to the fixed or constrained parameter. When
maximum likelihood is used, (4.51) is equal to the expected decrease in
χ^2 (see (4.44)) if the corresponding constraint is relaxed and all estimated parameters are held fixed at their estimates (Sörbom and Jöreskog,
1981). Under these conditions the parameter with the largest modification
index in absolute value will improve the model maximally. As shown by
Dijkstra (1981), the modification indices may at best give indications
about incorrectly fixed parameters and they should only be applied to
parameters which could be relaxed from a **theoretical** point of view.

For the normalized residuals Jöreskog and Sörbom (1981) give as a
rule of thumb that an absolute value larger than 2 may be an indication of
a parameter that is incorrectly fixed. The indices i and j of such a given
normalized residual (see (4.50)) may indicate that the equations in which
the i-th and j-th observable variables are present (either directly, or
indirectly via the corresponding latent variables) contain the parameters
that are incorrectly fixed.

When the maximum likelihood fitting function has been used, the correct relaxation of a fixed or constrained parameter is reflected in a

large drop in the χ^2 value compared to the loss of degrees of freedom. Furthermore, the other relevant judgement statistics also show substantial improvements. On the other hand, changes in the χ^2 value which are close to the loss of degrees of freedom usually lead to a minor improvement of the fit. The same applies to minor changes in the other relevant statistics. When the iterative unweighted least squares procedure is used, the correct or incorrect relaxation of fixed parameters is also reflected in substantial, respectively minor improvements of the relevant statistics.

Let us now pay attention to incorrectly specified, free parameters. Such parameters have no influence on consistency, provided the model is identified. The most serious consequence of incorrectly free parameters is that the estimators are not optimal.

The way of detecting and handling incorrectly free parameters, is opposite to the way of detecting and handling incorrectly fixed parameters. Indications can be found in implausible estimates and, when maximum likelihood has been used, in the standard errors. When the model is re-estimated with the suspect parameters fixed, the relevant statistics should **not** show a substantial decrease in quality.

When there are no further indications of incorrectly fixed, constrained or free parameters and when one or more judgement statistics still have unsatisfactory values, some of the relationships in the model may be non-linear or non-additive, or essential variables may be missing. The former types of specification error may be detected by inspection of the plotted normalized residuals (see (4.50)). Many of the non-linear or non-additive relationships can be transformed into linear ones. The graph of the residuals may give hints about the kind of transformation to be used. In the case of non-linearities a logarithmic or reciprocal transformation may often be helpful (see, among others, Johnston, 1972).

When relevant variables have been omitted, the estimated coefficients may be seriously biased. Furthermore, the residual variance will have an upward bias. Therefore, substantial residual variance may be an indication of omitted relevant variables. (For detailed information on the present kind of specification error, see, among others, Theil, 1971, Dhrymes, 1978). If it is known which variables are missing but if no data is available, the use of proxy variables may be suitable (Dhrymes, 1978).

Finally, we remark here that it is possible to constrain various extreme parameter estimates by means of the specifications developed by Rindskopf (1983, 1984). The exposition given above shows that such specification should **not** be made at an early stage of an exploratory investigation because extreme parameter estimates may be helpful in identifying various kinds of specification errors. They should only be made if there is evidence of a well-specified model and if in spite of that some estimates are still extreme.

4.6.4 Hypothesis testing

When the observed variables are multinormally distributed[1], when the sample size is sufficiently large and when a covariance matrix is analyzed to investigate a given theory, model judgement may take the form of 'genuine' hypothesis testing. It is assumed here that maximum likelihood proper is used because in that case the distribution of the various test statistics is known.

Let us first pay attention to testing the overall fit of a model. In large samples this can be done by a likelihood-ratio test, which goes as follows:

Let:

$$H_0 : \Sigma = \Sigma \ (\pi) \tag{4.52}$$

and

$$H_a : \Sigma \text{ is any positive definite symmetric matrix.}$$

1) Concerning the distribution we remind the reader that normality is only of importance when "genuine" maximum likelihood estimates are wanted. When the distribution deviates from normality the tests to be discussed here are not quite valid and the results should be interpreted cautiously. Alternatively, the bootstrap or the jackknife can be used for the purpose of hypothesis testing (see chapter 8). These methods can also be used when initial estimators or unweighted least squares, which do not give standard errors and do not assume normality, are used. So, in order to avoid specification errors with respect to the distribution, multi-variate normality should be assessed (see, among others, Gnadadesikan, 1977) and when there is evidence that the observables are not normally distributed alternatives to the tests discussed in this section should be used.

In (4.52) π is the specific structure of the model under consideration. The likelihood-ratio test statistic L is:

$$L = \frac{L_0}{L_a} \qquad (4.53)$$

where

$$\log L_0 = -\tfrac{1}{2} M \left[\log \left|\hat{\Sigma}\right| + tr(S\hat{\Sigma}^{-1})\right] \qquad (4.54)$$

is the maximum of the likelihood function, given the constraints imposed by H_0. In (4.54), $\hat{\Sigma}$ stands for the estimate of Σ under H_0. The denominator in L is the maximum of the likelihood function over the parameter space for all identified models. This maximum is reached when $\hat{\Sigma} = S$. Thus:

$$\log L_a = -\tfrac{1}{2} M \left[\log \left|S\right| + (p+q)\right] \qquad (4.55)$$

So, M times F is minus 2 times the logarithm of L with F given in (4.28). Under certain regularity conditions, $-2 \log L$ is asymptotically distributed as a χ^2-variable, with $\left[\tfrac{1}{2}(p+q)(p+q+1) - h\right]$ degrees of freedom, where h is the total number of independent parameters estimated in the hypothesized model (see Rao, 1965).

A sequence of nested hypotheses can be tested sequentially by means of likelihood ratio statistics. The difference in values of $-2 \log L$ for the models under comparison is asymptotically distributed as a χ^2-variable, with degrees of freedom equal to the number of independent restrictions, which is independent of the fact whether or not the less restrictive hypothesis is true (Lehmann, 1959). So, it is possible to test whether a given model is 'worse' than a less restrictive 'bad' model. It should be noted that when testing a sequence of nested hypothese, one should start with the less restrictive hypothesis of the sequence (Malinvaud, 1970).

The maximum likelihood procedure also allows the construction of confidence intervals for individual parameters. So, the validity of the sign or specific values of each parameter can be tested. Under the prevailing conditions the standardized estimator of each parameter is asymptotically standard normally distributed.

4.7 Conclusions

In this chapter the class of LISREL models has been introduced. Its main features have been described and it has been shown that a LISREL model is a simultaneous equation model. This implies that by means of a LISREL model the multi-effective nature of economic policy can be taken into account and that indirect effects of policy can be decomposed into the constituting elements. The most important feature, however, which distinguishes LISREL models from other types of simultaneous equation models, is that the set of variables of LISREL models consists of both observable and latent variables. Both types of variables can be handled simultaneously. It has already been shown in preceding chapters that by means of latent variables effects of policy packages can be analyzed. So, LISREL models are pre-eminently suitable to measure effects of policy.

There are several other important features, which benefit the suitability of the LISREL approach to measure effects of economic policy. The first is formed by the large variety of submodels that is contained in the general framework. This variety makes it possible to capture various measurement situations. Secondly, the simple heuristic identification procedure of the LISREL V computer program is of importance because measurement models are usually so large that it may virtually be impossible to check the identifiability by examining the equations which define the elements σ_{ij} of Σ as functions of the elements of π, i.e.

$$\sigma_{ij} = f_{ij}(\pi), \quad i \leqslant j \qquad (4.56)$$

Thirdly, the LISREL V computer program provides three kinds of consistent estimators. In particular, the maximum likelihood estimator is available, which is optimal if the distribution is known to be normal. Furthermore, it provides "good" estimators for a rather wide class of distributions. When the distribution is known to deviate considerably from normality any of the three estimators of the LISREL V program can be used in a bootstrap or jackknife framework (chapter 8). Finally, insight into their stability can be obtained by comparing the sets of estimates obtained by each of the three estimators available. In the case of a correctly specified model these sets do not differ substantially.

So far, the general framework for a LISREL measurement model of effects of economic policy has been described. However, one of the purposes formulated in the preceding chapters is to develop a measurement model that can be applied to spatio-temporal data. For that purpose the general LISREL approach has to be elaborated. This will be done in the next chapter.

5.SPATIO-TEMPORAL LISREL MODELS

5.1 Introduction

In chapter 1 the advantages of the use of spatio-temporal data for impact analysis of economic policy have been pointed out. The analysis of spatio-temporal data, however, poses specific problems which will be described in this chapter. These problems stem from the fact that spatio-temporal data constists of a time series of cross-sectional observations on spatial units. The dynamic nature of this kind of data leads to the well-known problem of (temporal) autocorrelation. This problem is well-documented in the literature (see, among others, Theil, 1971, Johnston, 1972, Dhrymes, 1978). The spatial nature of this data leads to the problem of spatial correlation (see, among others, Moran, 1950, Geary, 1954, Fisher, 1971, Cliff and Ord, 1973, 1981, Hordijk, 1974, Hordijk and Nijkamp, 1977, 1978, Paelinck and Nijkamp, 1976). Thus, in the analysis of spatio-temporal data the possible presence of spatio-temporal correlation has to be considered.

The LISREL model outlined in the preceding chapter applies primarily to independent cross-sectional data. In order to analyze spatio-temporal data adequately the general LISREL model has to be modified in such a way that the specific features of spatio-temporal data can be taken into account. This modification is the purpose of the present chapter.

The organization of chapter 5 is as follows. In the sections 5.2 and 5.3 the nature and the detection of spatio-temporal correlation will be described. The specific LISREL specifications, which have to be made in order to capture the features of spatio-temporal data, will be given in section 5.4.

5.2. The nature of spatio-temporal correlation

5.2.1 Introduction

Generally speaking, spatio-temporal correlation exists if the residuals corresponding to different observations over space and/or over time are correlated. (For the sake of convenience the term residuals refers here to both the residuals of the structural model and to the measurement errors of the latent variables measurement models.) Correlated residuals are usually assumed to arise because of omitted variables.[1] It is well-known that the residuals represent the influence of all factors other than those **explicitly** included into the model. It is quite likely that in the case of spatio-temporal data the total effect of changes in the omitted variables will be distributed over space and/or over time. For example, when the residuals represent some omitted time series then it is clear that the residuals will be correlated over time because most economic time series are highly autocorrelated (see also chapter 7).

From the exposition given above it follows that spatio-temporal correlation is made up of two components: **spatial** correlation and **temporal** correlation. The former refers to the correlation of the residuals over space; the latter to the correlation over time. It should be noted that spatial correlation is usually also considered for a given period (see section 5.3 and Hordijk and Nijkamp, 1977).

Temporal correlation, usually denoted as autocorrelation, is well-known. Therefore, only a brief summary is required here. First, it is commonly assumed that temporal correlation can be captured by a first-order autoregressive process (see also chapter 7):

$$\omega_t = \rho \, \omega_{t-1} + v_t \tag{5.1}$$

where ω is the residual or error under consideration; $|\rho| < 1$ for stationarity reasons and v_t is a random variable with $E(v_t) = 0$, $E(v_t^2) = \sigma_v^2$ and $E(v_t v_s) = 0$ for $t \neq s$. It should be noted that through (5.1) there is some carry over into subsequent periods with the carry over tailing off.

The first-order autoregressive process is usually a satisfactory representation for **annual** data. For more frequently observed data other specifications are often required such as autoregressive processes of orders greater than one, moving average processes and combined autoregressive – moving average precesses (see for instance, Fuller, 1976, Nichols

---

1) For a criticism concerning the omitted variables interpretation of temporal autocorrelation, see Maddala (1977).

et al, 1975). Because in the application in chapter 9 annual data is analyzed we will work with a first-order autoregressive process throughout
this chapter.

Secondly, the consequences of the presence of temporal correlation are
dependent on the type of model under consideration. Autocorrelated residuals without lagged dependent variables do not give biased estimators but
they may be inefficient. Furthermore, the sampling variances of the estimator may be downward biased. The combination of autocorrelated residuals
and lagged dependent variables on the other hand usually gives inconsistent estimators. (For further details see, among others, Johnston, 1972,
Theil, 1971, Dhrymes, 1971). As lagged dependent variables play an important role in the LISREL measurement model of effects of economic policy,
it is of great importance to take temporal autocorrelation adequately into
account. Because lagged dependent variables only appear in the structural
model, special attention will be paid to the residuals of this model.

5.2.2 Spatial correlation

In this section the nature of spatial correlation will be discussed. In
this connection the **order of contiguity** will be needed. Therefore,
this concept will be defined first.

Following Hordijk (1974) the order of contiguity of two regions can be
described as follows. Assume an area, say A, to have been partitioned into
regions A_r, $r = 1, 2, \ldots, R$ such that:

$$\bigcup_{r=1}^{R} A_r = A$$

$$A_r \cap A_{r'} = \emptyset, \forall\ r, r', r \neq r' \tag{5.2}$$

Then any two regions of A are **first-order** contiguous if they have a
common boundary of non-zero length. A region r of A is contiguous of **k-
th order** (k>1) to a region r' of A (r' $\neq$ r) if region r is first-order
contiguous to one of the regions of A, which is contiguous of order k-1 to
r' and is not already contiguous of an order less than k. It should be
noted that a region is defined as **non-contiguous** with itself. (Examples of various orders of contiguity can be found in Appendix 9.III).

Let us now turn to the nature of spatial correlation. Two forms can be distinguished:
-Spatial auto-correlation;
-Spatial cross-correlation.

In the case of **spatial autocorrelation**, a phenomenon in a given region, say region r, is influenced by the **same** phenomenon in other regions from multiple and different directions in the current or in previous periods. Furthermore, there may be a reverse influence: the phenomenon in other regions may be influenced by the phenomenon in region r in the current or in previous periods. When two **different** phenomena are involved we will speak of **spatial cross-correlation.**[1]) It may be helpful to illustrate the difference between both kinds of spatial correlation by means of an example. Consider the investments in a given region r. In the case of spatial autocorrelation the investments in region r are influenced by or they themselves influence investments in one or more other regions of the spatial system. In the case of spatial cross-correlation the investments in region r are influenced by or they themselves influence e.g. sales in other regions.

It is worthwhile pointing out the differences between spatial and temporal correlation here. In the case of temporal correlation the relationship of influence is **uni-directional** in the sense that a phenomenon at time t is influenced by the same or another phenomenon in a previous period. A reverse relationship is not possible. Spatial correlation on the other hand allows mutual relationships: the phenomenon under study may both influence the same or another phenomenon in other regions and itself be influenced by the same or another phenomenon in other regions. The second difference is that in the case of spatial correlation a phenomenon in a given region in a given period may be influenced by the same or another phenomenon in **various** regions. In the case of temporal correlation only **one** relationship of influence is possible, given the period.

In the remainder of this section the nature of spatial correlation will be considered further. It should be noted that **one** single equation of a system of equations is under consideration. This means that the depen-

---

1) Spatial crosscorrelation is usually also called spatial autocorrelation.

dent variable of another equation than the one under consideration is an explanatory variable for that equation.

First, the notion of a "spatially lagged variable" will be used here in a way similar to the notion of a "temporally lagged variable". That is, a k-th order spatially lagged variable indicates the spatial correlation for a variable in regions which are k-th order contiguous.

Secondly, when spatial correlation is considered in connection with LISREL models (and other types of econometric models as well) two non-exclusive cases should be distinguished.

-Spatial correlation caused by variables **included** in the model. This kind of correlation will be denoted as "omitted spatial correlation". When omitted spatial correlation is not accounted for, relevant variables, e.g. regional input-output linkages, are excluded from the relations concerned. This is a type of specification error as described by Theil (1957). Depending on the correlations between the included and excluded variables and the population coefficients of the excluded variable the estimators of the population coefficients of the included variables will be biased. Furthermore, the estimator of the residual variance will be biased upwards.

-Spatial correlation caused by variables represented by the residuals, which will be denoted as "residual spatial correlation" here. Residual spatial correlation may be the consequence of the presence of non-linear relationships between the dependent and independent variables or it may be caused by the fact that the omitted variables are spatially correlated. In both cases the estimators are inconsistent and asymtotically biased when spatially lagged dependent variables are present (see, for instance, Whittle, 1954). In models without spatially lagged variables residual spatial correlation leads to inefficient estimators of the coefficients, to downwards biased estimators of the variances of the estimators of the coefficients and to inflated values of the R^2 when the standard LISREL estimators are applied.

The upshot of the present and the preceding section is that spatio-temporal correlation is a serious econometric problem. Its existence should be carefully investigated and remedial action should be taken when necessary. Since we assume that spatial correlation due to non-linear relationships between the dependent and explanatory variables has been taken into account along the lines described in the preceding chapter, attention will only be paid to the other kinds of spatial correlation here.

5.2.3 The structure of the spatio-temporal LISREL model

In this section we will formulate the spatio-temporal LISREL model which in subsequent chapters will be used to measure effects of economic policy. Suppose that a sample of observations on R spatial units over T periods is available. It is assumed that the coefficients of the time-dependent variables are the same for all R regions over all periods and that the residuals and measurement errors of the equations capture differences over time and over regions. This assumption may be reasonable in many circumstances, but it may also be rather restrictive. The reason to make it here is to keep the required number of observations as small as possible, because one of the problems one usually has to face in policy analysis is the scarcity of data (see also chapter 1). (For an overview of standard linear models with coefficients that vary over individuals (i.e. non-spatial cross-sectional units) and over time see Judge et al, 1980). It should be noted that for the time-invariant variables in the structural model the assumption of constant coefficients is not made.

The spatio-temporal LISREL model with constant coefficients reads as:

$$
\begin{aligned}
B \, \eta_{r,t} &= \Gamma^{(1)} \xi_{r,t} + \Gamma_t^{(2)} \tilde{\xi}_r + u_{r,t} & \text{(a)} & \\
y_{r,t} &= \Lambda_y \, \eta_{r,t} + \varepsilon_{r,t} & \text{(b)} & \quad r = 1, 2, \ldots, R; \\
x_{r,t} &= \Lambda_x \, \xi_{r,t} + \delta_{r,t} & \text{(c)} & \quad t = 1, 2, \ldots, T \quad (5.3) \\
\tilde{x}_r &= \Lambda_{\tilde{x}} \, \tilde{\xi}_r + \tilde{\delta}_r & \text{(d)} &
\end{aligned}
$$

with:

$\xi_{r,t}$: a vector of explanatory latent variables which may be current or lagged endogenous variables;

$\tilde{\xi}_r$: a vector of explanatory variables which are assumed to be constant over time;

$\tilde{x}_r$: a vector of indicators corresponding to $\tilde{\xi}_r$;

$u_{r,t}$: a vector of residuals.

All other variables and matrices are defined as in chapter 4.

Because of the specific nature of the observations, the residuals and measurement errors are likely to be spatio-temporally correlated. In this section a temporal correlation model will be formulated. Spatial correlation will be dealt with in subsequent sections.

As mentioned above, temporal correlation of the residuals is most serious because of the possible presence of lagged dependent variables. The residuals $u_{r,t}$, are assumed to be composed of two mutually uncorrelated parts:

-A vector of regional components μ_r, which do not vary over time. This component is assumed to capture differences over regions.

-A vector of autocorrelated components $\omega_{r,t}$, which follow a first-order autoregressive scheme.

Formally:

$$u_{r,t} = \mu_r + \omega_{r,t} \tag{5.4}$$

where:

$$\omega_{r,t} = D \, \omega_{r,t-1} + \zeta_{r,t} \tag{5.5}$$

with:

$$D = \text{diag} \, (d_1, \, d_2, \, \ldots, \, d_m), \; |d_i| < 1, \; i=1,2,\ldots,m. \tag{5.6}$$

and the ζ-terms uncorrelated in different periods.

For the errors no decomposition assumption is made. It is simply assumed that the errors of the latent variables measurement equations are generated by first-order autoregressive processes, which leads to the usual structures of the covariance matrices (see section 5.4.2).

At the end of this section the following remarks are in order. First, by means of (5.4) and (5.5) temporal autocorrelation has been taken into account. In addition to temporal autocorrelation spatial correlation has to be taken into account in order to obtain residuals which are uncorrelated both within and between periods. The identification of spatio-temporal correlation is the purpose of section 5.3. Secondly, as mentioned above, the residuals and errors are assumed to capture differences over time and over regions. Consequently, the residuals and errors may have different variances over time and regions. This is the problem of heteroscedasticity, which has been extensively described in econometric textbooks such as Theil (1971) and Judge et. al. (1980). Various tests for heteroscedasticity have been developed. (For an overview see Judge et. al., 1980). Most of these tests can be applied in a straight forward way to the residuals and errors estimated according to (4.32) - (4.38).

When there is evidence of heteroscedasticity for the residuals or errors of a given equation it is most easily accounted for by identifying an appropriate heteroscedastic error model, by transforming the data according to the error model and by applying one of the LISREL-estimators. If one has strong a priori notions about the form of heteroscedasticity the model should be chosen accordingly. Otherwise it has to be identified on the basis of the data at hand. (An overview of various models and their identification procedures can be found in Judge et. al., 1980).

It should be noted that the transformed data is added to the original data set and is used in only that equation of which the residual or error is heteroscedastic. The reason for this is that the use of transformed data in equations other than that of which the residual or error is heteroscedastic could lead to heteroscedasticity of residuals or errors which were originally homoscedastic.

5.3 Detection of spatio-temporal correlation

In this section some measures and detection procedures of spatio-temporal correlation will be considered. As in section 5.2, we concentrate on spatial correlation.

5.3.1 Measures of spatial correlation

The measures of spatial correlation to be discussed here are for ordinal and interval data because this type of data is most frequently used in policy analysis.[1]

In the literature there exists three types of measures of spatial autocorrelation for ordinal and interval data, which are closely related: the Moran coefficient (Moran, 1950), the Geary coefficient (Geary, 1954) and the Cliff and Ord coefficient (Cliff an Ord, 1969). As shown by Hordijk (1974), the Geary coefficient is inferior to the Moran coefficient and the

---

1) Measures for nominal data can be found in Cliff and Ord (1981).

Cliff and Ord coefficient represents a weighted Moran coeffient, which is rather time consuming to construct. Therefore, the Moran coefficient is usually preferred as a measure to detect spatial correlation. Various variants of the Moran coefficient have been developed (see Hordijk and Nijkamp, 1977). For our purpose the variant which applies to autocorrelation of contiguity order s of time lag ℓ is most appropriate. It is defined as:

$$M_\ell^s (y,y) = \frac{\sum\limits_{r=1}^{R} (y_{r,t} - \bar{y}_t) (L^s y_{r,t-\ell} - \bar{y}_{t-\ell})}{\{\sum\limits_r (y_{r,t} - \bar{y}_t)^2\}^{1/2} \{\sum\limits_r (y_{r,t-\ell} - \bar{y}_{t-\ell})^2\}^{1/2}} \qquad (5.7)$$

$$s=1,2,\ldots,S$$
$$\ell=0,1,2,\ldots,T$$

where:

$y_{r,t}$ is the variable under consideration in region r at time t;

L^s is the spatial lag operator satisfying the condition that:

$$L^s y_{r,t} = \sum_{i\in A_{s,r}} w_{r,i}^s y_{i,t} \qquad (5.8)$$

where:

$A_{s,r}$ is the set of all regions of contiguity order s with respect to region r;

$w_{r,i}^s$ is a contiguity weight between regions r and i such that:

$$\sum_{i\in A_{s,r}} w_{r,i}^s = 1, \; \forall \, r,s \qquad (5.9)$$

Furthermore:

$$\bar{y}_t = \frac{1}{R} \sum_{r=1}^{R} y_{r,t} \qquad (5.10)$$

The Moran coefficient of spatial cross-correlation for two variables y and x of contiguity order s and of time lag ℓ is defined as:

$$M_\ell^s (x,y) = \frac{\sum\limits_{r=1}^{R} (y_{r,t} - \bar{y}_t) (L^s x_{r,t-\ell} - \bar{x}_{t-\ell})}{\{\sum\limits_r (y_{r,t} - \bar{y}_t)^2\}^{1/2} \{\sum\limits_r (x_{r,t-\ell} - \bar{x}_{t-\ell})^2\}^{1/2}} \qquad (5.11)$$

$$s=1,2,\ldots,S$$
$$\ell=0,1,2,\ldots,T$$

Positive correlation implies $M_\ell^s (.,.) > 0$ and negative correlation $M_\ell^s (.,.) < 0$, where $M_\ell^s (.,.)$ refers to both $M_\ell^s(y,y)$ and $M_\ell^s(y,x)$. Absence of spatial correlation implies $M_\ell^s (.,.) = 0$. It should be noted that, although $M_\ell^s (.,.)$ is referred to as a coefficient of spatial correlation, it is not restricted to the interval $[-1, 1]$. In general, however, the upper bound for $|M_\ell^s(.,.)|$ will be less than one (see Cliff and Ord, 1981).

It is clear that for each variable, a Moran coefficient of spatial autocorrelation can be calculated for each time lag and for each contiguity order. Similarly, for each pair of different variables a Moran coefficient of spatial cross-correlation can be calculated. Thus a matrix of spatial auto- and cross-correlation coefficients can be constructed (see Martin and Oeppen, 1975, and Hordijk and Nijkamp, 1977). It will be shown below that in the present situation, where spatially correlated residuals and errors have to be remedied, only part of this matrix is needed, viz. that part in which the **endogenous** observable variables are involved. This matrix will be denoted as the matrix C. As an example of the matrix C consider a model with one dependent variable y and two explanatory variables, x_1 and x_2. Furthermore, two orders of contiguity and one time lag are assumed, i.e. s=1,2 and ℓ=0,1. Then C reads as:

$$C = \begin{bmatrix} M_0^1 (y,y) & M_0^2 (y,y) & M_0^1 (y,x_1) & M_0^2 (y, x_1) & M_0^1 (y,x_2) & M_0^2 (y,x_2) \\ M_1^1 (y,y) & M_1^2 (y,y) & M_1^1 (y,x_1) & M_1^2 (y,x_1) & (M_1^1 (y,x_2) & M_1^2 (y,x_2) \end{bmatrix} \qquad (5.12)$$

In the detection procedure of omitted spatial auto- and cross-correlation a check on the presence of spatially autocorrelated residuals is of crucial importance. For this the moments of $M_\ell^s (\hat{e}, \hat{e})$, where $\hat{e}$ denotes the estimated LISREL residual or error of a given single equation (see section 4.5), are needed. Cliff and Ord (1973, 1981) have derived the first and second order moments of $M_\ell^s (\hat{e}, \hat{e})$ for the standard regression model estimated by means of ordinary least squares. Under rather limiting conditions, in particular the absence of spatially lagged dependent variables, these authors have shown that $M_\ell^s (\hat{e}, \hat{e})$ is asymptotically normally distributed. Furthermore, they have outlined a randomization procedure for use with small samples or in situations where the assumption of normality does not hold. However, when spatially **lagged** variables are present the tests by Cliff and Ord may lead to serious under-estimation of significance. Because spatially lagged variables play essential roles in the detection procedure and in the remedy for omitted spatial correlation (see below) we will not develop a testing procedure for the LISREL approach similar to the one developed by Cliff and Ord. Instead we will resort to the bootstrap. By means of this technique the distribution of $M_\ell^s(\hat{e},\hat{e})$ will be approximated and used to construct a confidence interval for $M_\ell^s(e,e)$, where e denotes the true residual or error of the equation under consideration. On the basis of the confidence interval a decision about the presence of omitted spatial correlation will be made. This problem will be taken up again in chapter 8.

5.3.2 Detection of omitted spatial correlation

As mentioned above, omitted spatial correlation is caused by variables explicitly included in the model, i.e. by the dependent variable (spatial autocorrelation) or by the explanatory variables (spatial cross-correlation). Although an alternative exists to detecting spatial autocorrelation, which will be briefly described below, the procedure to be developed here applies simultaneously to both kinds of spatial correlation. The procedure consists of the following steps:

-Estimate the model without specifications for spatial correlation but with specifications for possible temporal autocorrelation (using either of the methods to be described in section 5.4) and calculate the residuals by means of (4.32) - (4.38).[1])

-Check the residuals for spatial autocorrelation.

-If the hypothesis of spatially correlated residuals is rejected, omitted spatial correlation need **not** be considered further.

---

1) The notion "residuals" refers here to both te residuals of the structural model and the measurement errors.

-If the hypothesis concerned is not rejected the matrix C is calculated for all the variables in those equations for which the residuals may be spatially autocorrelated.

-Spatial correlation indicated by the element of largest absolute value in the matrix C, denoted as $\max\left|C_{ij}\right|$, is taken into account using the method which will be described in section 5.4.

-If the coefficient of the variable representing spatial correlation, indicated in the previous step, is significantly different from zero this variable is included into the model.

-Otherwise, spatial correlation indicated by the element with the next largest absolute value in the matrix C is considered.

-This searching process continues as long as a coefficient of a variable representing spatial correlation, which is significantly different from zero, is found and as long as the number of relevant observable variables in the model, which may be spatially correlated, is not exhausted.

-The residuals of the model extended with a variable representing spatial correlation are calculated, tested for spatial autocorrelation, and so on.

The procedure described above is summarized in Figure 5.1. In this figure "s.a.c." and "s.c.c." denote spatial autocorrelation and spatial correlation, respectively. Furthermore, the matrix $\tilde{C}$ has as (i, j)-th element $\max\left|C_{ij}\right|$ and zero's elsewhere. The number of x and y variables in the matrix C is put equal to n.

The procedure described here can be made more rapid by simultaneously considering several equations for which there is evidence of omitted spatial correlation. To each of these equations a spatial correlation variable is added at each run.

If the procedure stops when the number of relevant variables is exhausted and the residuals are still spatially autocorrelated, there must be spatial auto- or cross-correlation in the variables represented by the residual or error term (i.e. residual spatial correlation). The way to deal with this is described in section 5.4.1.

It should be marked that the detection procedure outlined above is rather "mechanical" of nature. Therefore, a variable should only be inclu-

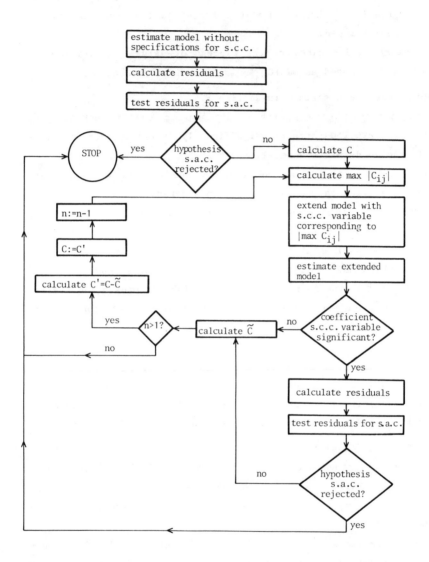

FIGURE 5.1   Schematic representation of the procedure to detect spatial
            correlation.[1])

1) It should be noted that hypothesis testing should not be understood in
   the sense of genuine testing because of the data-instigated nature of
   the model.

ded if this can be justified from a theoretical point of view. On the other hand spatial correlation is a serious problem which should be adequately accounted for, even if this requires the application of a "mechanical" procedure.

This section continues with a brief description of a direct test of spatial autocorrelation. This test can be used in situations where a priori hypotheses of spatially correlated variables are given.

Cliff and Ord (1973, 1983) have derived the moments of $M_\ell^s(y,y)$ under the null hypothesis of no spatial autocorrelation. In this connection, they distinguish two situations:

-The observations are random independent drawings from one (or separate identical) normal population(s): situation N.

-The observations are random independent drawings from one (or separate identical) population(s) with unknown distribution function(s): situation R. In this situation the observed value of $M_\ell^s(y,y)$ is considered relative to the set of all possible values which $M_\ell^s(y,y)$ could take if the y_r were repeatedly randomly permuted around the regional system.

In both the situations N and R:

$$E\ (M_\ell^s(y,y)) = -\frac{1}{R} \tag{5.13}$$

In situation N:

$$E\ ((M_\ell^s(y,y))^2) = \frac{R^2\ S_1 - R\ S_2 + 3\ S_o^2}{S_o^2\ (R^2 - 1)} \tag{5.14}$$

and in situation R:

$$E\ ((M_\ell^s(y,y))^2) = \frac{R\left[(R^2-3R+3)S_1-RS_2+3S_o^2\right] - b\left[(R^2-R)S_1-2RS_2+6S_o^2\right]}{(R - 1)^3\ S_o^2} \tag{5.15}$$

where:

$$S_o = \sum_{\substack{i=1 \\ (i \neq j)}}^{R} \sum_{j=1}^{R} w_{ij} \tag{5.16}$$

$$S_1 = \frac{1}{2} \sum_{\substack{i=1 \\ (i \neq j)}}^{R} \sum_{j=1}^{R} (w_{ij} + w_{ji}) \tag{5.17)[1]}$$

$$S_2 = \sum_{i=1}^{R} (\sum_{j=1}^{R} w_{ij} + \sum_{j=1}^{R} w_{ji}) \tag{5.18}$$

$$b = \frac{3(3\ R^2 - 7)}{5(R^2 - 1)} \tag{5.19)[2]}$$

In (5.16) – (5.18) w_{ij} denotes the contiguity weights defined in (5.9).

Cliff and Ord (1973, 1981) have also shown that $M_\ell^s(y,y)$ is asymptotically normally distributed under the hypothesis of no spatial autocorrelation in both the situations N and R.

After this extensive discussion of the detection of spatial correlation we will turn in brief to the detection of temporal correlation in the next section.

5.3.3 Detection of temporal autocorrelation

Because temporal autocorrelation is a topic extensively described in econometric textbooks, only a few short remarks are necessary here. Durbin and Watson (1950, 1951) developed the following statistic for testing the presence of first-order autocorrelation:

$$d = \frac{\sum_{t=2}^{T} (\hat{e}_t - \hat{e}_{t-1})^2}{\sum_{t=1}^{T} \hat{e}_t^2} \tag{5.20}$$

with $\hat{e}_t$ the estimated residual or error of a given structural or measurement equation.

---

1) It is assumed here that the investigator may choose weights such that $w_{ij} \neq w_{ji}$.

2) It should be noted that for $n \to \infty$ $b \to 1.8$

Tables for testing purposes can be found in most econometric textbooks. It is well-known that the test is inconclusive for a given interval. An overview of approximate methods for the inconclusive interval can be found in Judge et al (1980).

In the present situation of a time series of cross section observations the Durbin-Watson test can be based on the sum of (5.20) over the R regions, i.e. on:

$$\tilde{d} = \sum_{r=1}^{R} d_r \qquad\qquad (5.21)$$

When (5.21) is used the number of observations equals $R(T-1)$.

In the presence of lagged dependent variables the test for temporal autocorrelation based on the statistics (5.20) or (5.21) is likely to have reduced power and is biased toward 2 (see Nerlove and Wallis, 1966, and Durbin, 1970). Alternatives have been developed by Durbin (1970). For our purpose the variant which regresses $\hat{e}_t$ on $\hat{e}_{t-1}$ and X, where X is the set of explanatory variables including the relevant lagged y-variables, is appropriate. When spatial correlation has been accounted for, the $R(T-1)$ observations can be pooled in a model with constant coefficients. The test for temporal autocorrelation consists of testing the significance of the coefficient of $\hat{e}_{t-1}$ in the regression model using OLS.

We want to end this section with the remark that because of the serious consequences of neglecting temporal autocorrelation it may be preferable to err on the cautious side and to assume the presence of temporal auto-correlation (see, for instance, Johnston, 1972).

5.4.   Specification of spatio-temporal LISREL models

In this section the LISREL specifications, which have to be made in order to take spatio-temporal correlation into account, will be described. In section 5.4.1 spatial correlation will be dealt with; in section 5.4.2 temporal correlation.

5.4.1 LISREL specifications for spatial correlation

5.4.1.1 Introduction

When the procedure described in Figure 5.1 in the preceding section leads to the rejection of spatially independent variables spatial correlation has to be corrected. This is the subject of the present section. Furthermore, it will be shown that LISREL models are well suited to cope with a specific problem generally encountered in spatio-temporal models of the non-LISREL kind. This problem can be made clear by considering the following general single equation spatio-temporal model of the non-LISREL type:

$$y_{r,t} = \sum_{\ell=1}^{T} \alpha_{\ell} \, y_{r,t-\ell} + \sum_{s=1}^{S} \sum_{\ell=0}^{L} \beta^{s}_{\ell} (L^{s} y_{r,t-\ell}) + \sum_{j=1}^{J} \sum_{\ell=0}^{T_j} \gamma_{j,\ell} \, x_{r,j,t-\ell}$$

$$+ \sum_{j=1}^{\tilde{J}} \sum_{p=1}^{P_j} \sum_{\ell=0}^{\tilde{T}_j} \delta^{p}_{j,\ell} \, (L^{p} \, x_{r,j,t-\ell}) + \zeta_{r,t} \qquad (5.22)$$

where

$y_{r,t}$ is the endogenous variable in region r at time t;

$x_{r,j,t}$ is the j-th exogenous variable in region r at time t;

α, β, γ, δ are unknown parameters;

$\zeta_{r,t}$ represents a disturbance term.

The subscript ℓ refers to temporal lags and the superscripts s and p to spatial lags.

It is obvious that several explanatory variables in (5.22) are likely to be highly correlated. As mentioned in chapter 4, one of the main consequences of this is that the variances of the estimators of the coefficients tend to increase so that variables may incorrectly be dropped from the equation. It will be shown below how this problem of multicollinearity can be mitigated by using the LISREL approach.

5.4.1.2 LISREL specifications for omitted spatial correlation

Suppose there is evidence that the j-th exogenous observable variable x_j is spatially correlated with y_i for several temporal and spatial lags.

This kind of correlation can be dealt with by defining a new exogenous latent variable, say $\xi_{n',r,t}$, of which $L^p x_{r,t-\ell}$ are the indicators for the various combinations of p and ℓ concerned.

If spatial correlation only holds for the residuals of the structural model the new latent variable is included into the structural equation of the endogenous latent variable of which y_i is an observable indicator. If spatial correlation also holds for the exogenous latent variables measurement model it must also be included into the measurement equation concerned. This can be done by making explicitly use of the fact that an observable can be an indicator of more than one latent variable. As an example consider the following measurement model:

$$
\begin{bmatrix} x_{r,1} \\ x_{r,2} \end{bmatrix} = \begin{bmatrix} 1 \\ \lambda_1 \end{bmatrix} \begin{bmatrix} \xi_{r,1} \end{bmatrix} + \begin{bmatrix} \delta_{r,1} \\ \delta_{r,2} \end{bmatrix} \tag{5.23}
$$

Furthermore, let $x_{r'}$ and $x_{r''}$ be spatially lagged variables of $x_{r,1}$ responsible for the spatial correlation. Then spatial correlation in the first equation can be accounted for as follows:

$$
\begin{bmatrix} x_{r,1} \\ x_{r,2} \\ x_{r'} \\ x_{r''} \end{bmatrix} = \begin{bmatrix} 1 & \lambda_2 \\ \lambda_1 & 0 \\ 0 & 1 \\ 0 & \lambda_3 \end{bmatrix} \begin{bmatrix} \xi_{r,1} \\ \xi_{\tilde{r}} \end{bmatrix} + \begin{bmatrix} \delta_{r,1} \\ \delta_{r,2} \\ \delta_{r'} \\ \delta_{r''} \end{bmatrix} \tag{5.24}
$$

From this exposition it follows that instead of using the observable x-variable spatially lagged for various orders in the structural model, as in equation (5.21), one latent variable, which represents the variable under consideration in spatial units of several orders of contiguity in several periods, is used. It is obvious that this may lead to a considerable reduction in multicollinearity.

The following remarks are in order. First, when, on the basis of prior information or data analysis, the sequence $\{L^p x_{r,t-\ell}, p=1,2,\ldots,P; \ell = 0, 1, 2,\ldots, L\}$ is assumed to exhibit spatial or temporal transient features in its structure, more than one latent exogenous variable may be used (see Folmer and Van der Knaap, 1981, for the case of temporal transients).

Secondly, if x_j and x_h are indicators of the same latent variable and if both are spatially correlated with y_i, both the sequences $\{L^P x_{h,r,t-\ell}\}$ and $\{L^{P'} x_{j,r,t-\ell'}\}$ can be used as indicators of $\xi_{n',r,t}$.

An analogous approach can be used, if there is evidence of spatial auto- or cross-correlation among endogenous observable variables. In the case of a structural equation, a new endogenous latent variable, say $\eta_{m',r,t}$, is defined. Because it is not the intention to explain $\eta_{m',r,t}$ in terms of the other variables in the model, it is a **quasi**-endogenous variable, which is set equal to its residual. Spatial correlation in the measurement model of the endogenous latent variables can be handled in the same way as in the measurement model of the exogenous latent variables.

The procedure described above can be applied to all equations for which spatial correlation holds. A problem that may arise when R and T are small, is that the ratio of the number of observations with respect to the number of observables becomes equal to or smaller than one and, consequently, the sample covariance matrix S becomes singular. If this is a problem, as in the case of the maximum likelihood estimator, several indicators of a single latent variable representing spatial correlation could be combined to only one indicator, which is an externally defined function (e.g. the average) of the relevant variables. This procedure can be applied to both endogenous and exogenous spatially correlated observables.

5.4.1.3 Tranformations for residual spatial correlation

The present kind of spatial correlation can be accounted for by two methods developed by Hordijk (1974): the iterative method and Durbin's method. These methods, will briefly be described here in slightly modified forms. It should be observed that the models to be presented below refer to each period and the transformations have to be applied for each period. Moreover, in the case of estimation the observations may be pooled over time, if temporal correlation has been taken into account (see section 5.4.2). We will first consider the iterative procedure.

Assume that there is evidence of residual spatial correlation for the i-th element of the vector of errors or residuals (see section 4.5) of contiguity orders s, s + h , ..., $\tilde{k}$ of time lag ℓ. For ease of notation, the orders of contiguity are appropriately re-ordered and written as $1, 2, \ldots, k'$, $k' \leqslant K$, where K is the maximum order of contiguity. For the sake of convenience the indices i and ℓ are omitted in the notation.

The following notation is introduced:

(r'_{kr}) i.e. $(1_{kr}), \ldots, (R_{kr})$, is the subscript denoting the regions contiguous of order k to region r;

D_k ($R \times (R-1)$), $k = 1, 2, \ldots k'$ is the matrix with elements

$$d_{r',r}(k) \quad = \begin{cases} 1 \text{ if the regions } r' \text{ and } r \text{ are contiguous of order } k; \\ 0 \text{ if they are not.} \end{cases}$$
$(r' \neq r)$

e_r is the true residual or error for the r-th region of which $\hat{e}_r$ is an estimate.[1])

The residuals e_r ($r = 1, 2, \ldots, R$) are assumed to follow a generalized stationary Markov scheme:

$$e_r = \sum_{k=1}^{k'} \sum_{r'=1}^{R} \rho_k e_{r'_{kr}} + v_r, \qquad r = 1, 2, \ldots R \quad (5.25)$$
$$(r \neq r')$$

with:

$E(v_r) = 0$, $E(v_r^2) = \sigma_v^2$, $r = 1, 2, \ldots, R$; $E(v_r\, v_{r'}) = 0$ for $r \neq r'$.

In matrix notation (5.25) reads as:

$$\overset{\approx}{e} = D* \rho + v \qquad (5.26)$$

with:

$$D* = \left[D_1 \tilde{e} \; \vdots \; D_2 \tilde{e} \; \vdots \ldots \vdots \; D_k \tilde{e} \right] \qquad (5.27)$$

$\overset{\approx}{e}$ and $\tilde{e}$ R-and $(R-1)$-vectors, respectively;

ρ a k'-vector.

From the estimated residuals the vector ρ can be estimated as:

$$\hat{\rho} = (\hat{D}*^T \hat{D}*)^{-1} \hat{D}*^T \hat{e} \qquad (5.28)$$

where $\hat{e}$ is the R-vector of estimated residuals and $\hat{D}*$ is $D*$ with the true residuals replaced by their estimates.

In order to facilitate notation, all the observable explanatory variables (both endogenous and exogenous), which are directly or indirectly (via latent variables) related to y_i, are denoted here as x-variables. The

---

1) The term residual denotes both errors and residuals in the remainder of this section.

following transformations are applied to the observations y_r and the observed explanatory variables $x_{r,j}$:

$$y^*_r = y_r - \sum_{k=1}^{k'} \sum_{\substack{r'=1 \\ (r' \neq r)}}^{R} \hat{\rho}_k y_{r'}{}_{kr} , \; j \qquad\qquad r = 1, 2, \ldots, R \qquad (5.29)$$

$$x^*_{r,j} = x_{r,j} - \sum_{k=1}^{k'} \sum_{\substack{r'=1 \\ (r' \neq r)}}^{R} \hat{\rho}_k x_{r'}{}_{kr} , \; j \qquad\qquad r = 1, 2, \ldots, R \qquad (5.30)$$

where j ranges over the set E of all explanatory variables of y_i.

Transformations like (5.29) and (5.30) reduce spatial correlation in the i-th residual. Because we are dealing with a model consisting of a system of equations the use of transformed data with regard to equations other than those corresponding to the i-th residual should be avoided. The reason for this is that the transformed data could lead to spatial correlation in equations which were originally not contaminated. Therefore, the variables y^*_r and $x^*_{r,j}$, j ε E, are added to the data set in addition to the original variables.

The next step in the iterative procedure is to re-estimate the model on the basis of the extended data set. The new i-th residual is calculated and checked for spatial autocorrelation. In the case the residual is still spatially correlated the procedure described in (5.25) – (5.30) is repeated. This process goes on as long as there is evidence that the i-th residual is spatially correlated.

The procedure described here has to be applied to all elements of the vector of residuals for which there is evidence of spatial correlation.

Let us now turn to Durbin's method. The same notational conventions as in the iterative method are in order here. In particular, both the endogeneous and exogeneous explanatory observable variables are denoted as x-variables. Furthermore, for the residuals model (5.25) is again assumed. The equation under consideration is specified in observables only and for the r-th region it is written as:

$$y_r = \sum_{j=1}^{J} \alpha_j x_{r,j} + \epsilon_r \qquad (5.31)$$

Repeated application of (5.25) and (5.31) gives:

$$y_r - \rho_1 \sum_{\substack{r'=1 \\ r' \neq r}}^{R} y_{r'}{}_{1r} - \ldots - \rho_{k'} \sum_{\substack{r'=1 \\ r' \neq r}}^{R} y_{r'}{}_{k'r} = \sum_{j=1}^{J} \alpha_j x_{r,j} + \rho_1 (\sum_{j=1}^{J} \alpha_j x_{1_{1r},j}$$

$$+ \ldots + \sum_{j=1}^{J} \alpha_j x_{r-1_{1r},j} + \sum_{j=1}^{J} \alpha_j x_{r+1_{1r},j} + \ldots + \sum_{j=1}^{J} \alpha_j x_{R_{1r},j}) + \ldots$$

$$+ \rho_{k'} (\sum_{j=1}^{J} \alpha_j x_{1_{k'r},j} + \ldots + \sum_{j=1}^{J} \alpha_j x_{r-1_{k'r},j} + \sum_{j=1}^{J} \alpha_j x_{r+1_{k'r},j} + \ldots$$

$$+ \sum_{j=1}^{J} \alpha_j x_{R_{k'r},j} + v_r), \qquad\qquad r = 1, 2, \ldots R \quad (5.32)$$

In matrix notation (5.32) reads as:

$$y = - \left[D_1 y' \vdots D_2 y' \vdots \ldots \vdots D_{k'} y' \right] \rho + X\alpha + \left[D_1 X' \alpha \vdots D_2 X' \alpha \vdots \ldots D_{k'} X' \alpha \right] \rho + v$$

$$\qquad\qquad (5.33)$$

where:

y and v are R-dimensional vectors;

y' is an (R-1)- dimensional vector;

X and X' (R×J) and ((R-1)×J) matrices, respectively;

α is a J-vector;

Least squares regression applied to (5.33) yields inter alia an estimate of ρ. Then the following transformations are applied:

$$y^* = y - \hat{\rho}_1 D_1 y' - \hat{\rho}_2 D_2 y' - \ldots - \hat{\rho}_{k'} D_{k'} y' \qquad (5.34)$$

and

$$X^* = X - \hat{\rho}_1 D_1 X' - \hat{\rho}_2 D_2 X' - \ldots - \hat{\rho}_{k'} D_{k'} X' \qquad (5.35)$$

Next the original data set is extended with the starred variables and the model is re-estimated (see the description of iterative procedure).

In contrast to the iterative procedure the present method operates from the assumption that by means of the transformations (5.34) and (5.35) residual correlation has adequately been accounted for so that there is no need to repeat the whole process.

Several remarks are in order here. First, it is difficult to express a preference for either of the methods described here. The iterative procedure has the advantage that it continues as long as there is evidence of residual spatial correlation. However, this may lead to convergence problems (see Hordijk, 1974). Durbin's method on the other hand, may not lead to a satisfactory remedy of residual spatial correlation (see Hordijk, 1974). Therefore, the best way to proceed is probably to use the iterative procedure and to resort to Durbin's method only when the former does not converge. Secondly, the procedures described here clearly lead to a data-instigated model. Finally, this section is ended by mentioning two other approaches to spatial auto- and cross-correlation which are worthwhile examining in the framework of LISREL models. First, Hordijk and Nijkamp (1978) describe the use of Markov schemes for spatio-temporal models. Secondly, Streitberg (1979) showed for the standard linear model without latent variables that, when information on a particular dependence structure of the spatial units is available, the covariance structure of the endogenous variables can be decomposed.

5.4.2 LISREL specifications for temporal autocorrelation

In this section we will pay attention to the problem of temporal autocorrelation. The structural model is considered first (see also Jöreskog, 1977b). Let us once again consider model (5.3). Using Kronecker products, equation (5.3a) may be combined for $t=1,2,\ldots,T$ into one single equation:

$$(I \otimes B) \, \eta_r = (I \otimes \Gamma^{(1)}) \, \xi_r + \tilde{\Gamma}^{(2)} \, \tilde{\xi}_r + u_r, \quad r = 1, 2, \ldots, R \qquad (5.36)$$

where:

$$\eta_r = (\eta_{r,1}^T, \eta_{r,2}^T, \ldots, \eta_{r,T}^T)^T;$$

$$\xi_r = (\xi_{r,1}^T, \xi_{r,2}^T, \ldots, \xi_{r,T}^T)^T; \qquad (5.37)$$

$$u_r = (u_{r,1}^T, u_{r,2}^T, \ldots, u_{r,T}^T)^T;$$

$$\tilde{\Gamma} = ((\Gamma_1^{(2)})^T, (\Gamma_2^{(2)})^T, \ldots, (\Gamma_T^{(2)})^T)^T$$

I is the T x T identity matrix;
$\otimes$ denotes a Kronecker product.

For simplicity of notation, the index r will be dropped. Thus, equation (5.36) reads as:

$$(I \boxtimes B)\eta = (I \boxtimes \Gamma^{(1)}) \xi + \tilde{\Gamma}^{(2)} \tilde{\xi} + u \qquad (5.38)$$

Without the index r equation (5.5) reads as:

$$\omega_t = D \, \omega_{t-1} + \zeta_t \qquad (5.39)$$

Models (5.38), (5.39) and (5.4) can now be combined as follows:

$$
\begin{bmatrix} I \boxtimes B & -(I \boxtimes \tilde{I}) \\ 0 & A \end{bmatrix}
\begin{bmatrix} \eta \\ \varepsilon \end{bmatrix}
=
\begin{bmatrix} I \boxtimes \Gamma^{(1)} & \tilde{\Gamma}^{(2)} \\ 0 & 0 \end{bmatrix}
\begin{bmatrix} \xi \\ \tilde{\xi} \end{bmatrix}
+
\begin{bmatrix} \iota \boxtimes \tilde{I} & 0 \\ 0 & I \boxtimes I \end{bmatrix}
\begin{bmatrix} \mu \\ \zeta \end{bmatrix}
$$

where: $\qquad\qquad (5.40)$

$\mu = (\mu_1, \mu_2, \ldots, \mu_m)^T$;

$\zeta = (\zeta_1^T, \zeta_2^T, \ldots, \zeta_T^T)^T$ with ζ_t^T a m-dimensional vector, t = 1, 2, ..., T;

$\omega = (\omega_1^T, \omega_2^T, \ldots, \omega_T^T)^T$ with ω_t^T a m-dimensional vector, t=1, 2, ..., T;

ι is a column vector with T elements equal to one;

$\tilde{I}$ is the m x m identity matrix;

A is a block matrix of order mT x mT of the following form:

$$
A =
\begin{bmatrix}
\tilde{I} & 0 & 0 & \cdots & 0 & 0 \\
-D & \tilde{I} & 0 & \cdots & 0 & 0 \\
0 & -D & \tilde{I} & \cdots & 0 & 0 \\
\cdot & \cdot & \cdot & \cdot & \cdot & \cdot \\
\cdot & \cdot & \cdot & \cdot & \cdot & \cdot \\
\cdot & \cdot & \cdot & \cdot & \cdot & \cdot \\
0 & 0 & 0 & \cdots & -D & \tilde{I}
\end{bmatrix}
\qquad (5.41)
$$

The latent variables measurement model for the vector $(\eta^T \, \omega^T)^T$ is specified as follows:

$$y = \begin{bmatrix} I \boxtimes \Lambda_y & I \boxtimes \bar{\Lambda}_y \end{bmatrix} \begin{bmatrix} \eta \\ \omega \end{bmatrix} + \varepsilon \qquad (5.42)$$

where:

$y = (y_1^T, y_2^T, \ldots, y_T^T)^T$

$\varepsilon = (\varepsilon_1^T, \varepsilon_2^T, \ldots, \varepsilon_T^T)^T$;

$\bar{\Lambda}_y$ is similar in structure to Λ_y with unknown coefficients $\bar{\lambda}$.

The measurement model for the ξ variables reads as:

$$x = \begin{bmatrix} I & \Lambda_x \end{bmatrix} \xi + \delta \qquad (5.43)$$

where:

$$x = (x_1^T, x_2^T, \ldots, x_T^T)^T;$$

$$\delta = (\delta_1^T, \delta_2^T, \ldots, \delta_T^T)T$$

Finally, the usual measurement model for the $\tilde{\xi}$ variables applies.

As temporal correlation for the residuals of the structural model has been taken into account by means of (5.40) no particular specifications for the covariance matrix Ψ of the vector $(\mu^T \ \zeta^T)^T$ are required. The temporal correlation for the exogenous and endogenous observable variables can be directly expressed in the matrices Θ_ε and Θ_δ by specifying the covariance matrices of subsequent vectors of errors as free submatrices of Θ_ε and Θ_δ. It should be observed that a similar procedure could be applied with regard to temporal correlation of the residuals. That is to say, that the following structural model could be specified:

$$(I \otimes B)\eta = (I \otimes \Gamma^{(1)}) \ \xi + \Gamma^{(2)} \ \tilde{\xi} + (I \otimes I) \ \zeta \qquad (5.44)$$

and that temporal correlation of the residuals should be expressed in the matrix Ψ by specifying free covariance matrices for subsequent vectors of residuals. Moreover, this procedure allows for more general autoregressive schemes than the first-order scheme.

The following remarks are in order here. First, with regard to both procedures the covariance or correlation matrix to be analyzed has to be positive definite when the maximum likelihood estimation procedure is used. This means that the number of regions has to be larger than p+q (the sum of the number of observable variables) for t=1,2,...,T. Secondly, both procedures may be hampered by identification problems. In particular, with regard to the former identification problems are likely to arise in the case of latent variables which are identical to their single observable indicators.

If identification problems with either procedure cannot satisfactorily be handled by imposing plausible constraints on the parameter matrices, such as constraining the covariance matrices for subsequent vectors of errors or residuals to be equal for the various periods or by constraining the $\bar{\lambda}$-coefficients in (5.42) to be equal to one, one could ultimately resort to transforming the observations for which temporal autocorrelation holds. For instance, in the case of endogenous observables the transformed observations are given by

$$y^*_{i,r,t} = y_{i,r,t} - \hat{\rho}_{i,r}\, y_{i,r,t-1}, \qquad \begin{array}{l} t=2,3,\ldots,\ T \\ r=1,2,\ldots,\ R \end{array} \qquad (5.45)$$

with

$$\hat{\rho}_{i,r} = \frac{\sum\limits_{t=2}^{T} \hat{e}_{i,r,t}\, \hat{e}_{i,r,t-1}}{\sum\limits_{t=2}^{T} \hat{e}^2_{i,r,t}}$$

where $\hat{e}_{i,r,t}$ is the residual or error obtained via (4.32) - (4.38) from the LISREL model without specifications for temporal correlation.

As in section 5.4.1.3 the original data set is extended with the transformed observations and they are analyzed in those equations for which temporal autocorrelation holds.

Another way to handle persistent identification problems is a **covariance analytical** approach, which is well-known method of correcting statistically for the effects of uncontrolled variables (see among others, Johnston, 1972), i.e. in the present case for time-specific features which lead to temporal autocorrelation. The uncontrolled variables are generally represented by dummy variables. In the case of model (5.3), this means that dummy variables $a_{r,t}$ are defined as:

$$a_{r,t} = \begin{cases} 1 & \text{for period } t \\ 0 & \text{for period } s, \ s \neq t \end{cases} \qquad r=1,2,\ldots,R; \ t=2,3,\ldots,T \qquad (5.46)$$

In the measurement models of the latent variables the dummy variables are identical to their corresponding latent variables. It should be noted that dummy variables can be used to correct for time-specific effects in both the structural and the measurement models.

The use of dummy variables has been criticized by, among others, Maddala (1971). His objections are the following. First, the dummy variable technique eliminates a major portion of the variation among both the explained and explanatory variables, if the between time-period variation is large. Secondly, in some cases there is a substantial loss in the number of degrees of freedom. Thirdly, it is usually difficult to give meaningful interpretations to the dummy variables.

A possible way to overcome these drawbacks in the LISREL framework is to use 'real' information instead of dummy variables (Folmer, 1981). In this case, an observable variable or several observable variables which are possibly combined to a latent variable may be used to represent information on the various periods under consideration (see also chapter 9).

It should be observed that the present variant of the covariance analytical approach also allows to take autocorrelation in the measurement models into account by adding time-specific explanatory variables to the equations of the measurement models (see Appendix 9.VII for an example).

5.5 Conclusions

In this chapter the analysis of spatio-temporal data in the LISREL framework has been considered. The nature, detection and LISREL specifications of spatial auto- and crosscorrelation have been described extensively. Furthermore, the detection of temporal autocorrelation has been touched upon and various methods to deal with this kind of correlation have been discussed.

The most important characteristic of spatio-temporal LISREL-models, compared with the general LISREL model presented in the preceding chapter, is that they make it possible to take spatial spill-overs and the dynamic nature of regional systems into account.

In the next chapter the various characteristics of LISREL models described in this and the preceding chapter, will be used in the design of a LISREL measurement model of the effects of regional economic policy.

6 THE SPATIO-TEMPORAL LISREL IMPACT MODEL.

6.1 Introduction

In chapter 3 several methodological requirements for adequate measurement of effects of economic policy have been formulated. Furthermore, in the chapters 4 and 5 the main characteristics of LISREL models in general and of spatio-temporal LISREL models have been described. The purpose of this chapter is to combine the various aspects outlined in the chapters 3-5 into a spatio-temporal LISREL measurement model of effects of regional economic policy.

The present chapter consists of three sections. In section 6.2 the various specifications of the measurement model will be extensively described. Point estimators of effects based on the parameter matrices of a LISREL model will be derived in section 6.3. Finally, in section 6.4 attention will be paid to interval estimators.

We will end this introduction by summarizing the reasons, mentioned throughout the preceding chapters, for using latent variables in the framework of an impact model of effects of economic policy. These reasons are:

-First, economic policy often takes the form of policy packages, in which various instruments are combined. A policy package is viewed here as a latent variable of which the instruments are observable indicators. From the discussion in chapter 4 it should be clear that single instruments can also be handled in the LISREL framework by defining an identity relationship between the single instrument and the corresponding package. In addition to the policy variables several of the non-policy variables appearing in a measurement model are also latent variables, such as economic expectation, socio-cultural environment, etc.

-Secondly, as described in chapter 5, the use of latent variables has important advantages in the framework of spatio-temporal models. In particular, they can be used to remedy omitted spatial correlation.

6.2   The structure of a spatio-temporal LISREL measurement model

In this section the requirements for adequate impact analysis of economic policy, which have been formulated in chapter 3, will be elaborated
first (section 6.2.1). On the basis of the resulting guidelines the formal
LISREL impact model will be specified in section 6.2.2.

6.2.1 Basic requirements of a measurement model

We start this subsection by recalling from chapter 2 that an instrument
of regional economic policy may be intended to operate on several policy
objectives and that one objective may be striven after by several instruments. Furthermore, an instrument may have effects on policy objectives
and on additional impact variables. Finally, an objective may be influenced indirectly via a set of intermediate variables. As a consequence of
these characteristics of economic policy, the following types of variables
have to be specified as **endogenous** variables in the measurement model:
-The policy objectives
-The ultimate additional impact variables.
-The intermediate impact variables in a causal chain between an instrument
and an ultimate policy objective or additional impact variable. [1]) It
should be observed that the instruments should be specified as explanatory
variables in the equations of all the directly influenced impact variables.

It may often be useful to incorporate the policy packages also into the
model as **endogenous** variables. This follows from the fact that economic policy comes into being as a reaction to the developments of the economic system. When the policy packages are endogenous it is possible to
estimate the sensitivity and the vigilance of policy to changes in the
economic system.

Another methodological requirement, mentioned in section 3.6, concerns

1) It should be noted that the additional impact variables may be difficult to detect when no adequate theory is available. In such a case
   intuition and ad hoc knowledge play important roles.

the disentanglement of policy effects from **autonomous developments**. In order to meet this requirement both the policy packages and the variables causing the autonomous developments have to be included into the model as explanatory variables of the endogenous variables which they affect. As mentioned in the preceding chapters, omission of important explanatory variables is a kind of specification error which may give seriously biased estimators of the coefficients and biased variance estimators. One of the problems one has to face in this connection is the operationalization of the notion of autonomous developments. In this study this concept will be understood as developments induced by non-policy variables. Usually economic theory provides clues to the selection of explanatory non-policy variables to be incorporated into a specific equation (for further details and an example see chapter 9).

It is worthwhile paying attention here to a special category of explanatory variables which will frequently be used in the measurement model to be presented below, viz. **lagged variables**. The situations in which these kinds of variables are required will briefly be described here.

-Lagged predetermined variables may be necessary when predetermined variables are effective over several periods or when their effects occur after some periods of time (delayed response). For example, investment expenditures in a given period are usually (partly) based on information about demand in previous periods.

-Lagged dependent variables may be necessary for several reasons. First, they may arise when an explicit form is assumed for the coefficients of the lagged exogenous variables, such as in the Koyck distributed lag scheme (Koyck, 1954; see also Dhrymes, 1971, Johnston, 1972). Secondly, lagged dependent variables may be needed when, for reasons of inertia, ignorance or costs of change, regional systems move only part of the way to the optimal level of a given dependent variable. The model describing this kind of behaviour is the so-called partial adjustment model. (For further details see, among others, Johnston, 1972, Griliches, 1967.) A third model form which is related to the partial adjustment model and which requires lagged dependent variables, is the adaptive expectations model. In this kind of model it is assumed that the actual value of the dependent variable depends on the expected level of an exogenous var-

126

iable. Operationalization of the adaptive expectations model may lead to lagged dependent variables. (For further details see, among others, Johnston, 1972.)

The last remark to be made here before the formal presentation of the LISREL measurement model concerns the status of the explanatory variables. Usually the interest of the present kind of analyses is primarily in measuring effects given the values of the exogenous variables. In such cases the fixed-x option applies. However, this limitation is not necessary. Therefore, the measurement model presented here will be in terms of stochastic exogenous variables.

6.2.2 The formal LISREL impact model

Suppose we have data on R regions over T periods. For the r-th region the following vectors of variables are defined:[1]

$n^a_{r,t}$ as a vector of jointly dependent endogenous impact variables (i.e. goal variables, intermediate and additional impact variables);

$n^p_{r,t}$ as a vector of endogenous latent policy variables;

$\xi^a_{r,s}$ as a vector of lagged latent impact variables at time s, s < t;

$\xi^p_{r,s}$ as a vector of lagged latent policy variables at time s, s < t;

$\xi^o_{r,s}$ as a vector of exogenous latent variables, other than the elements of $\xi^a_{r,s}$ and $\xi^p_{r,s}$, at time s, s $\leq$ t;

ξ^c_r as a vector of time-invariant background variables;

1) As mentioned before, an observable variable can also be represented as a latent variable. In that case the corresponding λ-coefficient is equal to 1 and the mesurement error to zero. (See also section 4.2). This means that a vector which contains both latent and observable variables may be called a vector of latent variables.

The following remarks are in order here. First, concerning the observable variables a division similar to the one of the latent variables is made. That is, the vector $y^a_{r,t}$ corresponds to $\eta^a_{r,t}$, the vector $x^p_{r,s}$ to $\xi^p_{r,s}$ and so on. Secondly, it should be noted that it is assumed that spatial correlation has been taken into account in the way described above. That is, variables representing omitted spatial correlation are assumed to have been added to the original set of variables. The same applies to variables which result from transformations for residual spatial correlation.

With the notions formulated above the structural impact model for the periods $\max \{m, u, v\}$, $\max \{m, u, v\} + 1$, $\ldots$, t reads as:

$$
\left[B^a : B^p \right]
\begin{bmatrix} \eta^a_{r,t} \\ \eta^p_{r,t} \end{bmatrix}
= \sum_{s=t-m}^{t-1} \Gamma^a_s \xi^a_{r,s} + \sum_{s=t-u}^{t-1} \Gamma^p_s \xi^p_{r,s} + \sum_{s=t-v}^{t} \Gamma^o_s \xi^o_{r,s} +
$$

$$
+ \Gamma^c_t \xi^c_r + \zeta_{r,t} \qquad\qquad r = 1,2,\ldots,R; \qquad (6.1)
$$

where:

B^a represents the effects of $\eta^a_{r,t}$ on each other and on $\eta^p_{r,t}$;

B^p represents the effects of $\eta^p_{r,t}$ on each other and on $\eta^a_{r,t}$;

Γ^a_s, Γ^p_s, Γ^o_s represent the effects, respectively, of $\xi^a_{r,s}$, $\xi^p_{r,s}$, $\xi^o_{r,s}$ on $\eta^a_{r,t}$ and $\eta^p_{r,t}$;

Γ^c_t represents the effects of ξ^c_r on $\eta^a_{r,t}$ and $\eta^p_{r,t}$.

Model (6.1) belongs to the class of models formulated in (5.3.a). The latent variables measurement models are similar to (5.3.b)-(5.3.d) and are omitted here.

For the sake of simplicity of notation model (6.1) is rewritten as:

$$
B \, \eta_{r,t} = \Gamma^a \, \tilde{\xi}^a_{r,t} + \Gamma^p \, \tilde{\xi}^p_{r,t} + \Gamma^o \, \tilde{\xi}^o_{r,t} + \Gamma^c_t \, \tilde{\xi}^c_r + \zeta_{r,t} \qquad r= 1,2,\ldots,R; \quad (6.2)
$$

where:

$$
B = \left[B^a : B^p \right]
$$

$$\Gamma^a = [\Gamma^a_{t-1} \vdots \Gamma^a_{t-2} \vdots \cdots \vdots \Gamma^a_{t-m}]$$

$$\Gamma^p = [\Gamma^p_{t-1} \vdots \Gamma^p_{t-2} \vdots \cdots \vdots \Gamma^p_{t-u}]$$

$$\Gamma^o = [\Gamma^o_t \vdots \Gamma^o_{t-1} \vdots \Gamma^o_{t-v}]$$

$$\eta_{r,t} = [(\eta^a_{r,t})^T, (\eta^p_{r,t})^T]^T$$

$$\tilde{\xi}^a_{r,t} = [(\xi^a_{r,t-1})^T, (\xi^a_{r,t-2})^T, \ldots, (\xi^a_{r,t-m})^T]^T$$

$$\tilde{\xi}^p_{r,t} = [(\xi^p_{r,t-1})^T, (\xi^p_{r,t-2})^T, \ldots, (\xi^p_{r,t-u})^T]^T$$

$$\tilde{\xi}^o_{r,t} = [(\xi^o_{r,t})^T, (\xi^o_{r,t-1})^T, \ldots, (\xi^o_{r,t-v})^T]^T$$

Similar modifications are assumed to apply to the observable variables. As mentioned above, model (6.1), and thus model (6.2), belongs to the class of LISREL models given by (5.3.a). Therefore, when the latent variables appearing in (6.2) have been operationalized, the structural model (6.2) and its corresponding latent variables measurement models can be estimated by the methods described in chapter 5.

6.3   Point estimators of effects of economic policy

6.3.1 Introduction

In this section, point estimators of the effects of policy packages and of individual instruments on the impact variables are derived from the estimated structural and latent variables measurement models. (In order to facilitate notation the presentation will be in terms of population parameter matrices. In practice these matrices have to be replaced by their estimated counterparts).

For rather simple models the impacts can usually easily be derived by means of a so called **path diagram.**[1] Such a diagram is a graphic representation of the system of equations under consideration. A hypothetical example is given in Figure 6.1.

---

1) A path diagram is also a useful device to give a comprehensive overview of the model equations and specifications.

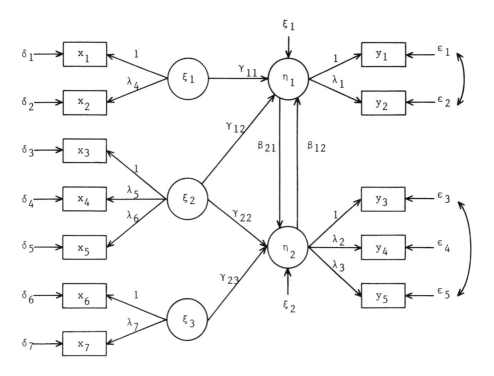

FIGURE 6.1. Path diagram of a hypothetical LISREL model.

The parameter matrices of the example read as:

$$\Lambda_y = \begin{bmatrix} 1 & 0 \\ \lambda_1 & 0 \\ 0 & 1 \\ 0 & \lambda_2 \\ 0 & \lambda_3 \end{bmatrix}, \quad 0_\varepsilon = \begin{bmatrix} \theta_{11} & & & & \\ \theta_{21} & \theta_{22} & & & \\ 0 & 0 & \theta_{33} & & \\ 0 & 0 & 0 & \theta_{44} & \\ 0 & 0 & \theta_{53} & 0 & \theta_{55} \end{bmatrix}, \quad \Lambda_x = \begin{bmatrix} 1 & 0 & 0 \\ \lambda_4 & 0 & 0 \\ 0 & 1 & 0 \\ 0 & \lambda_5 & 0 \\ 0 & \lambda_6 & 0 \\ 0 & 0 & 1 \\ 0 & 0 & \lambda_7 \end{bmatrix}$$

$$B = \begin{bmatrix} 1 & -\beta_{12} \\ -\beta_{21} & 1 \end{bmatrix} \quad \Gamma = \begin{bmatrix} \gamma_{11} & \gamma_{12} & 0 \\ 0 & \gamma_{22} & \gamma_{23} \end{bmatrix} \quad \phi = \begin{bmatrix} \phi_{11} & 0 & 0 \\ 0 & \phi_{22} & 0 \\ 0 & 0 & \phi_{33} \end{bmatrix}$$

$$\Psi = \text{diag} (\Psi_{ii}), \quad \theta_\delta = \text{diag} (\theta_{\delta ii})$$

where diag (.) means a matrix with free elements on the main diagonal and zero's elsewhere.

In Figure 6.1 observed variables are enclosed in rectangles, latent variables in circles and measurement errors and disturbances are not enclosed. A one-way arrow indicates a postulated direct causal relationships and a two-way arrow indicates correlation without any causal interpretation.

According to Duncan (1975), the **partial** effect of a given variable on another variable along a given causal chain is equal to the product of the estimated coefficients which appear in that particular causal chain between both variables. In the present example the effect of ξ_1 on y_5 equals $\gamma_{11} \cdot \beta_{21} \cdot \lambda_3$. The **total** effect of a given variable on another given variable is obtained by summing the partial effects along **all** causal chains between both variables. In the example the total effect of ξ_2 on η_2 equals $\gamma_{22} + \gamma_{12} \cdot \beta_{21}$.

The use of path diagrams is often very illustrative and point estimates of the effects can be easily derived. However, it is usually difficult to depict complex systems with many variables by such diagrams. Such systems are more appropriately represented by means of the parameter matrices. The formal derivation of the effects from the parameter matrices will be dealt with below. In this regard the following remarks are in order.

First, although our interest is primarily in the effects of policy packages on the impact variables, the presentation below will be of a more general kind. We will describe the mutual effects of the latent endogenous variables on each other as well as the effects of the exogenous latent variables on the impact variables. From the former the effects of the current policy packages on the current impact variables and vice versa can be derived. The latter allows for the derivation of effects of the lagged latent policy packages on current impact variables as well as of lagged profile elements on the current policy packages.

Secondly, it may be of interest to obtain the effects of η and ξ-varia-

bles on the observable indicators of the latent impact variables. Therefore, attention will also be paid to the derivation of this kind of effects.

Thirdly, the derivation of the **sum** of the effects of latent policy
packages applied in a given period, say t–s, over a set of periods: t–s,
t–s+1,..., t, will be discussed. This is important because the impact
patterns of policy packages over time may be quite different. For instance, some policy packages may have substantial, lasting effects not until
several periods have elapsed, whereas other packages may be immediately
slightly effective for a short period only. Adequate impact analysis, in
particular comparison of effects, requires that the total effects of policy packages over various periods can be obtained.

Finally, the derivation of effects of the endogenous observables on
each other and of the exogenous observables on the endogenous observables
will be discussed. Two situations will be distinguished. First, the case
where the causal latent variable is identical to its **single** indicator.
It is obvious that in that case the derivation of the impacts of η on y
(section 6.3.3) or of ξ on y applies (section 6.3.5). Secondly, there is
the situation with **several** indicators for a given latent variable. In
that case, the effect of a given instrument will be obtained by isolating
the instruments concerned from the policy package. Effects over a set of
periods will also be considered for both situations distinguished.

Finally, it is remarked here that for ease of notation the subscript r
will be dropped in the following sections.

6.3.2 Effects of latent endogenous variables on each other

For the current period:

–The **direct** causal effects of the η_t variables on each other can be
found in the matric $\tilde{B}$, defined in (4.3);

–The **direct** effects of the η_t variables on each other by paths of
length k, k $\geq$ 2, are given by $\tilde{B}^k$. For example, in Figure 6.1 it is
seen that the effect of η_1 on η_2 by the path of length 3 is equal to

$\beta_{21}^2 \cdot \beta_{12}$ which is the (1,1)-th element of $\tilde{\beta}^3$;

The **total** effects of the η_t variables on each other are formed by the sum of the effects by all possible paths, i.e., by

$$\sum_{k=1}^{\infty} \tilde{B}^k = (I - \tilde{B})^{-1} - I = B^{-1} - I \qquad (6.3)$$

where I is the unitary matrix.

It should be noted that (6.3) is only valid if the infinite series converges. This is the case for all recursive models and for non-recursive models if and only if all eigenvalues of

$$B = (I - \tilde{B})$$

are within the unit circle (see, among others, Fisher, 1970).

This sections ends with the remark that, although there are never direct effects of an η variable on itself, there is a total effect of each η on itself. However, this can only occur in non-recursive models in which there is a causal relationship going from one η, passing over some other η's and returning to the original η.

6.3.3 Effects of latent endogenous variables on observable endogenous variables

For the current period:

–The **direct** causal effects of the η_t variables on the observable variables y_t are given by Λ_y.

–The **indirect** effects of η_t on y_t in the current period arise via η-variables which are mutually connected by paths of length $1,2,\ldots$ Because the total effects of the η_t variables on each other are given by (see (6.3)):

$$(B^{-1} - I)$$

the present indirect effects can be found in:

$$\Lambda_y (B^{-1} - I) \qquad (6.4)$$

From (6.3) and (6.4) it follows that the **total** effects of η_t on y_t in the current period are given by:

$$\Lambda_y (B^{-1} - I) + \Lambda_y = \Lambda_y B^{-1} \qquad (6.5)$$

6.3.4 Effects of exogenous latent variables on endogenous latent variables

In chapter 4 the matrix Γ was defined as the matrix of **direct** effects of the ξ variables on the η variables. So, the direct effects of, e.g. ξ^p_{t-u} on η^a_t in the current period are given by:

$$\Gamma^p_{t-u} \tag{6.6 -}$$

The **total** effects of the exogenous variables on the endogenous variables are in general given by the matrix of the reduced form (see, for instance, Duncan, 1975), i.e. by:

$$B^{-1} \Gamma \tag{6.7}$$

From (6.7) the effects of the several subvectors of $\tilde{\xi}^p_t$ can be derived. For instance, the effects of ξ^p_{t-u} on η_t in the current period are given by:

$$B^{-1} \Gamma^p_{t-u} \tag{6.8}$$

-The **indirect** effects of the ξ variables on the η variables can be derived by subtracting the direct effect from (6.7). This gives:

$$B^{-1} \Gamma - \Gamma \tag{6.9}$$

6.3.5 Effects of exogenous latent variables on observable endogenous variables

Because the direct effects of ξ on η are given by Γ and of η on y by Λ_y the indirect effects of ξ on y with only one intermediate η variable can be found in:

$$\Lambda_y \Gamma \tag{6.10}$$

Graff and Schmidt (1982) derived that the **total** effects of ξ on y are given by:

$$\Lambda_y B^{-1} \Gamma \tag{6.11}$$

With the aid of (6.10) and (6.11), the effects of several subvectors of exogenous variables on y_t in the current period can be calculated. For example, the effects of ξ^p_{t-u} on y_t are given by $\Lambda_y B^{-1} \Gamma^p_{t-u}$.

Finally, it is obvious that indirect effects of ξ-variables on y-variables can be obtained by subtracting (6.10) from (6.11). This gives:

$$\Lambda_y \, (B^{-1} - I)\Gamma \tag{6.12}$$

6.3.6 The sum of effects of policy packages over several periods

In the introduction to this section it was argued that adequate comparison of policy packages requires that the sum of the effects over several periods be obtained. This is the subject of the present section. For the derivation to be presented below it is assumed that the effects of policy packages on observable y variables are wanted. Effects on the η-variables can be obtained in a similar way by means of section 6.3.4 and will not be discussed here.

Suppose that the packages were applied in a given period, say t^*, $t^* < t$. Their effects may be realized in the periods t^*, $t^* + 1$, ..., t and consist of the following components:

−First, the **total** effects on y_{t^*}, which, according to (6.5) are given by $\Lambda_y \, B^{-1}$.

−Secondly, the **direct** effects on y_{t^*+1}, y_{t^*+2}, ..., y_t **without** the intervention of latent impact variables. According to (6.11) they are given by $\Lambda_y \, B^{-1} \, \Gamma^p_{t^*+1}$, $\Lambda_y \, B^{-1} \Gamma^p_{t^*+2}$, ..., $\Lambda_y \, B^{-1} \, \Gamma^p_t$, respectively.

−Thirdly, the **indirect** effects by way of latent impact variables. According to (6.11), the effects of the latent impact variables on y_{t^*+1}, y_{t^*+2}, ..., y_t are given by $\Lambda_y \, B^{-1} \, \Gamma^a_{t^*+1}$, $\Lambda_y \, B^{-1} \, \Gamma^a_{t^*+2}$, ..., $\Lambda_y \, B^{-1} \, \Gamma^a_t$. This means that the indirect effects of the policy packages on y_{t^*+1}, y_{t^*+2}, ..., y_t by way of latent impact variables are given by $\Lambda_y \, B^{-1} \, \Gamma^a_{t^*+1} \, Q$, $\Lambda_y \, B^{-1} \, \Gamma^a_{t^*+2} \, Q$, ..., $\Lambda_y \, B^{-1} \, \Gamma^a_t \, Q$ where Q is the block of the matrix $B^{-1} - I$ which represents the total effects of the policy packages on the latent impact variables (see (6.3)).

By summing the various effects described above the total effect of a policy package can be obtained.

6.3.7 Effects of endogenous and exogenous observable variables on endogenous observable variables

It may be of great interest to know what the effect is of an individual, observable instrument on a latent or an observable impact variable, and vice versa. In general, the present kinds of effects cannot be obtained in a straightforward way from the parameter matrices of the LISREL model, because the effects of the indicators on their corresponding latent variables, which are needed in this connection, are not given by the parameter matrices of the LISREL model.[1] The simplest procedure to obtain these effects is probably by adding an additional equation to the structural model in which the instrument concerned is separated from the original policy package and specified as identical to an additional latent variable. As an example, consider a policy package n_2 made up by three instruments y_3, y_4 and y_5. If the effect of, say y_5, on the impact variable n_1 with observable indicators y_1 and y_2 is wanted, the following measurement model is specified:

$$
\begin{bmatrix} y_1 \\ y_2 \\ y_3 \\ y_4 \\ y_5 \end{bmatrix}
=
\begin{bmatrix} 1 & 0 & 0 \\ \lambda_1 & 0 & 0 \\ 0 & 1 & 0 \\ 0 & \lambda_2 & 0 \\ 0 & 0 & 1 \end{bmatrix}
\begin{bmatrix} n_1 \\ n_2 \\ n_3 \end{bmatrix}
+
\begin{bmatrix} \varepsilon_1 \\ \varepsilon_2 \\ \varepsilon_3 \\ \varepsilon_4 \\ 0 \end{bmatrix}
\qquad (6.13)
$$

The structural model reads as:

$$
n_1 = \beta_{12} \, n_2 + \beta_{13} \, n_3 + \zeta_1 \qquad (6.14)
$$

The effect of y_5 on y_2 is given $\beta_{13} \cdot \lambda_1$.

In this section 6.3 attention has been paid to point estimators of effects. Usually, one also wants a measure of the variability, in particu-

---

[1] As mentioned above, the present kind of effects can be obtained in a straightforward way when the causal observable is identical to the corresponding latent variable.

lar of the statistical significance, of a point estimator. Such a measure is, inter alia, provided by a confidence interval. Therefore, this subject is dealt with in the next section.

6.4. Confidence intervals

6.4.1 Introduction

In this section attention will be paid to the construction of confidence intervals. We will first deal with direct effects and next with indirect effects which arise along causal chains of length ≥ 2.

Before starting on this purpose the discussion on genuine hypothesis testing and assessment of model fit in section 4.6 is recalled. Because interval estimation and genuine hypothesis testing are closely related the remarks made in section 4.6 also apply here. That is, a confidence interval is of level $(1-\alpha)$ only if a given model is available. In the case of a data-instigated model the accuracy of the estimator will usually be overestimated.

6.4.2 Direct effects

As described in, inter alia, the sections 2.5 and 4.2, a direct effect is given by one single element of one of the matrices $\tilde{B}$, Γ, Λ_y, Λ_x. Under the conditions mentioned in section 4.6.4, a standardized estimator of each single parameter is asymptotically standard normally distributed. When the assumptions of 4.6.4 do not apply because the distribution of η, ξ, ε and δ deviates from normality or when a correlation matrix has been analyzed, confidence intervals can be obtained by means of the bootstrap or the jackknife (see chapter 8).

6.4.3 Indirect effects

Concerning interval estimators of indirect effects two approaches can be distinguished: a crude, simple method and a more efficient one.

Let us first turn to the crude and simple method. Its main feature is that it does not take into account dependencies between the individual parameters, which appear in a given causal chain. It goes as follows. Let "b" denote the indirect effect of a policy package or an instrument of policy on a given impact variable along a given causal chain. Furthermore, let u_i and l_i denote the upper and lower limits of a confidence interval of level $(1-\alpha_i)$ for the **individual** parameters involved in the chain. Then, assuming the model is correct

$$P\left[b \in (\prod_{i=1}^{k} l_i, \prod_{i=1}^{k} u_i) \geqslant 1 - \sum_{i=1}^{k} \alpha_i\right] \tag{6.16}$$

where "P" denotes probability.

If the total effect, say b', of a policy instrument, which arises along m causal chains with lower and upper limit l'_j and u'_j of a $(1-\alpha'_j)$ confidence interval, then, assuming the model is correct

$$P\left[b' \in (\sum_{i=1}^{m} l'_j, \sum_{i=1}^{m} u'_j) \geqslant 1 - \sum_{i=1}^{m} \alpha'_j\right] \tag{6.17}$$

It is obvious that the present method is simple to apply. However, the intervals obtained are unduly large. Therefore, we will now turn to the second method, which is usually more efficient.

The second method takes the dependencies between the estimators of the individual parameters explicitly into account. It goes as follows. Under the assumptions made in LISREL, the estimator $\hat{\pi}$ of the vector of all the independent, free, and constrained parameters, π, has an asymptotic normal distribution in the sense that $\sqrt{n}(\hat{\pi}-\pi)$ converges in distribution to a normal distribution with expectation π and variance-covariance matrix $\Sigma(\pi)$. Notation:

$$L\left[\sqrt{n}(\hat{\pi}-\pi)\right] \rightarrow N(0, \Sigma(\pi)) \tag{6.18}$$

where n is the sample size.

Suppose f is a function defined on an open subset of a s-dimensional space taking values in an r-dimensional space, i.e.

$$f(\pi) = (f_1(\pi), \ldots, f_r(\pi))^T \tag{6.19}$$

It is assumed that f has the following expansion as $w \rightarrow \pi$:

$$f(w) = f(\pi) + (\frac{\partial f}{\partial \pi})^T (w-\pi) + 0(\|w-\pi\|) \tag{6.20}$$

where $(\frac{\partial f}{\partial \pi})$ denotes the s x r matrix whose (i, j)th entry is the partial derivative of f_i with respect to the j-th element of w evaluated at $w = \pi$ and $0(\|w-\pi\|)$ means that the norm of the vector $w-\pi$ converges to zero.

Under the assumptions (6.18) an (6.20) the asymptotic distribution of $f(\hat{\pi})$ is given by:

$$L\left[\sqrt{n}(f(\hat{\pi}) - f(\pi))\right] \rightarrow N(0, (\frac{\partial f}{\partial \pi})^T \Sigma(\pi) (\frac{\partial f}{\partial \pi})) \tag{6.21}$$

A proof of this theorem can be found in Bishop et.al. (1975).

The equation (6.21) is estimated by substituting $\hat{\pi}$ for π in the matrix $(\frac{\partial f}{\partial \pi})$ and by using the LISREL estimate for $\Sigma(\pi)$. It should be observed that in the present case the function f is the product of the parameters in a given causal chain.

As mentioned above, the total effect of an instrument of policy may involve the sum of the effects along several causal chains. Confidence intervals for such total effects can be obtained by means of the multiple comparison test, first suggested by Scheffé and described by, among others, Dhrymes (1978) for the general linear model. Under the assumptions made in LISREL the estimator of a subvector $\pi*$ of say k elements is normally distributed with expectation $\pi*$ and variance-covariance matrix $\Sigma(\pi*)$.

Let there be a test of the hypothesis:

$$H_0 : \pi* = \bar{\pi}* \tag{6.22}$$

as against the alternative

$$H_1 : \pi* = \bar{\pi}* \tag{6.23}$$

Then the probability is $1-\alpha$ that simultaneously, for all vectors g in the Euclidian k-space, the intervals:

$$(g^T\hat{\pi}* - \sqrt{(k \, F_\alpha \, \hat{Var}(g^T \hat{\pi}*))}, \; g^T \hat{\pi}* + \sqrt{(k \, F_\alpha \, \hat{Var}(g^T \hat{\pi}*))}) \tag{6.24}$$

will contain the true parameter point, where F_α is a number such that

$$P\{F_{k, \, 1/2(p+q) \, (p+q+1) - h} \leq F_\alpha\} = 1-\alpha \tag{6.29}$$

where:

$F_k,\ ^1/_2(p+q)\ (p+q+1)\ -\ h$ is a central F-distributed variable with k and

$^1/_2\ (p+q)\ (p+q+1)\ -\ h$ degrees of freedom;

h is the number of independent parameters in π (see section 4.3).

A proof of this theorem can be found in Dhrymes (1978).

6.5 Conclusions and summary of the main features of a spatio-temporal LISREL measurement model

In this chapter the various methodological requirements for adequate measurement of effects of regional economic policy and the characteristics of spatio-temporal LISREL models have been combined in the design of a measurement model. The structure of the model has been described and attention has been paid to point and interval estimators of effects of policy packages and of individual policy instruments.

Before leaving the LISREL measurement model, its main features, which have been described in this and preceding chapters, will be summarized.

- The LISREL approach can be used to measure effects of economic policy of both the control type and of the influencing type under various conditions. It can be applied to cross-sectional and to spatio-temporal data.[1] In the former case spatial and in the latter case spatio-temporal correlation has to be taken into account. The detection of and the specifications for both types of correlation have been dealt with. An important characteristic of LISREL meausurement models is that they, like other general simultaneous equations models, may give detailed information about the effects of policy and non-policy variables on various impact variables. Direct, indirect, and, in the case of spatio-temporal data, effects of orders higher than one, can be estimated.

- A specific feature of the LISREL approach is that it allows of handling of both latent and observable variables simultaneously. Advantages of simultaneously including both types of variables in a model are a closer

1) The LISREL approach can also be applied to micro data. Both cross-sectional and panel data can be analyzed.

correspondence between theory building and empirical data analysis, and the mitigation of the multi-collinearity problem. Concerning multi-collinearity, latent variables may play an important role in spatio-temporal models because they can be used to take omitted spatial correlation into account. In the context of impact analysis latent variables are of great importance because they can be used to model policy packages.

The spatio-temporal LISREL approach belongs to the class of simultaneous equation models, which are aimed at giving a relatively detailed description of a set of regional economic systems. Such a description usually requires observations on a relatively large number of variables. In practice, however, it happens that observations on some of the relevant variables are missing. If the missing information is not accounted for one runs the risk of making specification errors (see section 6.2.1). The LISREL approach does not allow for missing information and under these circumstances its use should be avoided. In such situations the two-stage time-series approach, which will be discussed in the next chapter, can be used.

Considering the advantages and disadvantages described above, one may conclude that the LISREL approach can succesfully be used to measure effects of economic policy in a variety of situations, provided relatively detailed information is available.

7. TWO-STAGE TIME SERIES ANALYSIS[1])

7.1 Introduction

The conclusion of the preceding chapter was that the LISREL approach can not be used to measure effects of policy, when essential information needed for the description of a set of regional systems is missing. If this is the case application of the LISREL approach (and many other approaches as well) would lead to biased estimators of the effects of the included policy and non-policy variables if the missing variables are correlated with the included explanatory variables. Furthermore, the residual variance would be biased upwards (see, among others, Theil, 1957, and Dhrymes, 1978). (Missing information in the data matrix is usually called "specification error". Although it was defined in a more general sense above, it will be used in this particular sense in this chapter).

In the preceding chapters it was also mentioned that missing information frequently occurs in economic research. Therefore, there is a need for a measurement method which can be used when information on important explanatory variables is missing and which does not suffer from specification error. In section 3.4.3 two-stage time series analysis was touched upon in this connection. At that place it was also mentioned that a prerequisite for the application of two-stage time series analysis is the availability of a univariate time series of the impact variable for the pre-intervention period and a multivariate time series of the impact variable and the instruments of policy for the policy-on period. This condition is often met in practice. So, the applicability of this measurement approach is quite large. In this chapter measurement by means of two-stage time series analysis will be described in detail.

Before starting on this purpose, the following remarks are in order. First the present method is of the **single** equation type. This implies that the multi-dimensional nature of the regional profile is not explicitly taken into account. However, by applying the method to several impact variables separately, an insight into the effects on several elements

1) This chapter is partly based on Fischer and Folmer (1983).

of the regional profile can be gained. The total effect along a causal chain can be obtained by applying two-stage time series analysis to successive links of the causal chain and by multiplying the coefficients on the links. Furthermore, confidence intervals can be obtained by means of the methods described in section 6.4.3. Secondly, two-stage time series analysis is essentially a single region method, i.e., the impact variable in only **one** region is observed over time. It should be marked, however, that this method may also be used to estimate spatial spill-over effects (see section 7.5). When intraregional effects are under consideration we will speak of the **intraregional measurement** model and when spatial spill-over effects are estimated the measurement model will be called the **interregional** model. Thirdly, the present measurement method does not allow of the simultaneous use of observable and latent variables. However, by first applying dynamic factor analysis (see Geweke, 1977) to the time series of the instruments and next analyzing the multivariate time series of the impact variable and the estimated factors[1]), latent variables can be introduced in the present measurement approach.[2])

The organization of this chapter is as follows. In section 7.2 some important definitions for time series modelling will be presented. Section 7.3 is devoted to theoretical and methodological aspects of the intra-regional measurement model. Section 7.4 deals with the process of fitting the measurement model. This process consists of the stages of model identification, estimation of the identified model and diagnostic checking of the estimated model.[3]) Finally, in section 7.5 attention is paid to the spill-over model.

1) In factor analysis latent variables are usually called "factors".

2) Dynamic factors analysis wil not be dealt with in this study because it has been described extensively in Geweke (1977). Furthermore, in the application in chapter 9 only one instrument of policy will be considered so that there is no reason to apply factor analysis at that place.

3) When a model is a priori given the stage of model identification is redundant.

7.2   Some definitions for time series modelling

A time series is a sequence of observations generated sequentially in time.   In this chapter we are concerned with **discrete** time series, i.e. with time series where observations are taken only at separated time points t_j ($j=1,\ldots,T$).[1])

The elements of a discrete time series are usually denoted by z (t_j) for $j=1,2,\ldots,T$. If the intervals are equally spaced (which is usually the case in economic research) then $t_{j+1}-t_j=c$, $j=1,2,\ldots,T$. The observations are then made at $t_1+ c,\ldots,t_1+Tc$. If t_1 is adopted as the origin and c as the unit of time, z_t is regarded as the observation at time t, $t=1,2,\ldots$, T. In the sequel of this chapter the intervals are assumed to be equally spaced.

The basic idea of statistical time series analysis is to consider the set of observations as a realization of the underlying stochastic process or, in other words, as a realization of jointly distributed random variables z_t ($t=1,\ldots,T$).[2]) Therefore, the set of observational values $\{z_t$, $t=1,\ldots,T\}$ can be thought of as being drawn from a probability function $P(z_1,\ldots,z_T)$. (It should be observed that a sequence say, $\ldots,x_{t-1}$, x_t, $x_{t+1},\ldots$ is denoted here as $\{x_t\}$).

A stochastic process can be described by means of the moments of the process, especially the mean function (μ), the variance function (σ^2) and the autocovariance function (γ). These functions are defined as:

$$\mu(t) = E(z_t) = \mu_t \qquad\qquad\qquad t=1,\ldots,T \quad (7.1)$$

$$\sigma^2(t) = \text{var}(z_t) = \sigma^2_t \qquad\qquad t=1,\ldots,T \quad (7.2)$$

and

---

[1]) It should be noted that the term "discrete" is used for time series of this type, even when the measured variable itself is continuous.

[2]) From the context it is clear whether a random variable or a realization is meant. Therefore, no distinction in notation is made here.

$$\gamma(t,s) = cov(z_t, z_j) = E(z_t - \mu(t))(z_s - \mu(s)) \qquad\qquad t,s=1,..,T \quad (7.3)$$

where $\sigma^2(t)$ is a special case of $\gamma(t,s)$, i.e. when $t=s$.

In the sequel of this chapter only strictly **stationary** stochastic processes are considered. A stochastic process is said to be strictly stationary if the joint distribution is invariant with respect to a displacement in time, i.e. if:

$$P(z_{t_1}, z_{t_2}, \ldots, z_{t_m}) = P(z_{t_1+k}, z_{t_2+k}, \ldots, z_{t_m+k}) \qquad k=\pm1, \pm2,.. \quad (7.4)$$

where t is any point in time.[1]

Stationarity has a number of general implications. For instance, the expected values (7.1) and variances (7.2) are constant and no more dependent on time, i.e.

$$E(z_t) = E(z_{t+k}) = \mu \qquad\qquad (7.5)$$

and

$$var\ (z_t) = var(z_{t+k}) = \sigma^2 \qquad\qquad (7.6)$$

Stationarity implies furthermore that the covariance between z_t and z_s ($s=t+k$) depends only on the number k of time periods separating them:

$$cov(z_t, z_{t+k}) = E((z_t-\mu)(z_{t+k}-\mu)) = \gamma_k \qquad\qquad (7.7)$$

γ_k is called the **autocovariance** at lag k. In particular $\gamma_0 = \sigma_z^2 = \sigma^2$ is the variance of z_t for all t.

It is remarked here that a convenient way of gaining the autocovariances γ_k is by means of the autocovariance generating function, defined as:

$$\gamma(B) = \sum_{k=-\infty}^{\infty} \gamma_k B^k \qquad\qquad (7.8)$$

where B is a backshift operator such that

$$B^s z_t = z_{t-s} \qquad\qquad (7.9)$$

The variance of the process, γ_0, is the coefficient of B^0 and the autocovariance at lag k, γ_k, is the coefficient of B^k and B^{-k}.

[1] In the sequel the term "stochastic process" will frequently be referred to as "process" simply.

Evidently, the size of γ_k is dependent on the measurement scale of z_t. Comparability is achieved by transforming the autocovariances γ_k into so-called **autocorrelations** ρ_k at lag k which are defined as:

$$\rho_k = \frac{\gamma_k}{\gamma_0} \qquad (7.10)$$

ρ_k as function of lag k is termed the autocorrelation function $\{\rho_k, k=0,1, 2,\ldots\}$ of the process. The matrix of autocorrelations has several characteristics, above all the property of positive definiteness. Another related important notion, which will be needed in the sequel is the **partial autocorrelation function** $\{\phi_{kk}, k=1,2,\ldots\}$ defined as:

$$\phi_{kk} = \frac{|P*|}{|P|} \qquad (7.11)$$

where $|P_k|$ is the determinant of the $(k \times k)$-autocorrelation matrix P_k

$$P_k = \begin{bmatrix} 1 & \rho_1 & \rho_2 & \cdots & \rho_{k-1} \\ \rho_1 & 1 & \rho_1 & & \rho_{k-2} \\ \rho_2 & \rho_1 & 1 & & \rho_{k-3} \\ \cdot & \cdot & \cdot & & \cdot \\ \cdot & \cdot & \cdot & & \cdot \\ \cdot & \cdot & \cdot & & \cdot \\ \rho_{k-1} & \rho_{k-2} & \rho_{k-3} & \cdots & 1 \end{bmatrix} \qquad (7.12)$$

P_k^* is obtained from P_k by replacing the last column by $(\rho_1,\rho_2,\ldots,\rho_k)$.

The autocorrelations of a time series are estimated by means of a sample analog to (7.7). Given T observations $z_1,\ldots,z_T$ the autocovariances can be estimated by:

$$c_k = \frac{1}{T} \sum_{t=1}^{T-k} (z_t - \bar{z})(z_{t+k} - \bar{z}) = \hat{\gamma}_k \qquad k=0,1,2,\ldots,K \qquad (7.13)$$

where $\bar{z}$ denotes the sample mean:

$$\bar{z} = \frac{1}{T} \sum_{t=1}^{T} z_t = \hat{\mu} \tag{7.14}$$

Using (7.13) the estimates of the autocorrelations are computed as:

$$r_k = \frac{c_k}{c_0} = \hat{\rho}_k \tag{7.15}$$

Adequate estimates of γ_k require in general that N should be larger than 50 and k not greater than T/4 (cf. Box and Jenkins, 1976). The estimates of the partial autocorrelations, denoted by $\hat{\phi}_{kk}$, can be obtained from the sample analog of (7.11) by replacing ρ_i by r_i.

Up to now, only univariate time series have been considered. Multivariate time series $\{y_t,\ x_{1t}, x_{2t}, \ldots, x_{gt}\}$ can be used to describe the relationship in time between a dependent variable y and one or more independent x-variables. In the case of a stationary multivariate time series the definitions of the mean, the variance and the autocorrelations apply to each univariate element of the multivariate series. Further details, in particular the crosscorrelation function, will be discussed in section 7.4.1.2.2.

7.3 The intraregional measurement model

7.3.1 Introduction

This section is devoted to some theoretical and methodological aspects of the intraregional measurement model. The discussion starts from the assumption that policy interventions will lead to changes in the autonomous time pattern of an impact variable if the interventions have had any effects. If policy has had no effect, the autonomous pattern will be continued.

Let x denote the vector of policy variables under consideration and v the vector of the other relevant explanatory variables of the impact variable y. As mentioned above, the measurement problem consists of determining the effects of the policy instruments without specification errors, when data on important explanatory variables is missing. In order to describe the present measurement method, it is convenient to refer first to the situation where observations for all relevant variables are available. Then:

$$y_t = F(\alpha, \alpha', v, x, t) + u_t \qquad (7.16)$$

where $F(\alpha, \alpha', v, x, t)$ is an adequate function in v and x as well as in α, a set of unknown parameters referring to v, and α', a set of unknown parameters referring to x, and t. $F(...)$ is called a **transfer** model. The term u_t is the disturbance term.

Let us now turn to the basic idea to avoid specification errors when data on one or more v-variables is missing. Let $\{y_t^{(1)}\}$ denote the time series of the affected variable y prior to the first policy intervention, say at time t=T'. Then $y_t^{(1)}$ can be modelled as:

$$y_t^{(1)} = n_t, \ t < T' \qquad (7.17)$$

where n_t represents a function of the aggregate of v-variables and stochastic variation of the impact variable. For $t > T'$ the series of the impact variable, say, $\{y_t^{(2)}\}$, is affected by policy instruments in addition to the v-variables represented implicitly in the n_t-model. Under the conditions that:

- In both the pre-intervention and the intervention periods the same relationships hold between the impact variable and the v-variables;
- The policy instruments are independent of the v-variables;
- A linear additive model structure applies;

the series $\{y_t^{(2)}\}$ can be modelled as:

$$y_t^{(2)} = n_t + f(\alpha', x, t) \quad \text{for } t > T' \qquad (7.18)$$

where $f(\alpha', x, t)$ is a reduced transfer or intervention model. Model (7.18) is called the n_t-intervention model.

Referring to the n_t-intervention model (7.18) two questions arise immediately:

- How should the n_t-model be specified?

- What kind of intervention model should be used?

Answers to both questions will be given in subsequent sections. In section 7.3.2 the family of **multiplicative seasonal autoregressive integrated moving average models** (abbreviated as SARIMA-models), forming the most general and flexible specification of the n_t-model, is described. Section 7.3.3 is devoted to a discussion of a general class of intervention models.

7.3.2 The general class of SARIMA models

The time pattern of socio-economic phenomena is often characterized by seasonal characteristics. Therefore, we consider a seasonal time series $\{y_t^{(1)}\}$ with period s.[1]) When a phenomenon is characterized by seasonal characteristics, two kinds of relationships should be taken into account: correlations between successive observations **within** seasonal periods and dependencies **between** different seasons. This fact motivates the use of a candidate out of the general class of multiplicative seasonal autoregressive integrated moving average models, as developed by Box and Jenkins (1976), to model n_t. Such a multiplicative seasonal model can be formulated in the following form:

$$\phi_{p_1}(B) \, \Phi_{p_2}(B^s) \, (1-B)^d \, (1-B^s)^D \, n_{r,m} = \theta_{q_1}(B) \, \Theta_{q_2}(B^s) \, a_{r,m} \qquad (7.19)$$

The following remarks are in order with respects to (7.19). First, r and m are time indices, for example, corresponding to year r and month m.

Secondly, B denotes the backshift operator and $(1-B)^d$ and $(1-B^s)^D$ are the regular and seasonal differencing operators, respectively. The differing operators serve to remove non-stationary characteristics of the non-stationary process such as shifts in level, trends and seasonal variation, so as to achieve stationarity. Sometimes differencing is not sufficient

---

1) For instance, in the case of monthly unemployment data for the building sector, s is usually equal to 12 with peaks during the winter seasons.

to obtain a stationary series. In such situations it may be helpful to use some appropriate transformation (for instance, a logarithmic transformation) of the series and to consider the transformed values differenced by $(1-B)^d$ or $(1-B)^D$. Stationarity implies that the roots of the characteristic equations:

$$\phi_{p_1} (B) (1-B)^d = 0$$

and

$$\Phi_{p_2} (B^s) (1-B^s)^D = 0$$

lie outside the unit circle in the complex plane (Box and Jenkins, 1976). Thirdly, the process described by (7.19) is said to be of order $(p_1, d, q_1) \cdot (p_2, D, q_2)_s$, where p_1 is the non-seasonal and p_2 the seasonal autoregressive average order; q_1 the non-seasonal and q_2 the seasonal moving average order. Furthermore, the parameters D and d denote the degrees of seasonal and regular differencing. The nonseasonal autoregressive polynomial $\phi_{q_1} (B)$ and the nonseasonal moving average polynomial $\theta_{q_1} (B)$ are defined as:

$$\phi_{p_1} (B) = 1 - \sum_{i=1}^{p_1} \phi_i B^i \tag{7.20}$$

and

$$\theta_{q_1} (B) = 1 - \sum_{i=1}^{q_1} \theta_i B^i \tag{7.21}$$

The corresponding seasonal polynomials are:

$$\Phi_{p_2} (B^s) = 1 - \sum_{i=1}^{p_2} \Phi_i B^{si} \tag{7.22}$$

$$\Theta_{q_2} (B^s) = 1 - \sum_{i=1}^{q_2} \Theta_i B^{si} \tag{7.23}$$

Finally, $\{a_{r,m}\}$ in (7.19) is a sequence of independently normally distributed random variables with mean zero and variance σ_a^2. It is usually called **white noise** . If $\{a_{r,m}\}$ has a non-zero mean, a constant term has to be added to the right-hand side of (7.19).

Because of the multiplicative nature of the model, $n_{r,m}$ may be thought of as being generated by a seasonal ARIMA model, called the **between-periods** component:

$$\Phi_{P_2}(B^s) \ (1-B^s)^D \ n_{r,m} = \Theta_{q_2}(B^s) \ \tilde{a}_{r,m} \qquad (7.24)$$

where it is supposed that the $\tilde{a}_{r,m}$ are serially correlated rather than independent. Therefore the $\tilde{a}_{r,m}$ are described by a non-seasonal ARIMA-model termed the **within-periods**-component of (7.19):

$$\phi_{P_1}(B) \ (1-B)^d \ \tilde{a}_{r,m} = \theta_{q_1}(B) \ a_{r,m} \qquad (7.25)$$

It is evident that this general family of SARIMA-models includes non-seasonal ARIMA models (s=0, D=0) as well as non-seasonal ARMA-models (s=0, D=0, d=0) as special cases.

In the sequel the double indices r,m in (7.19) and (7.24) - (7.25) will be assumed to be appropriately mapped on the set of positive integers and therefore only a single index, t, will be used.

7.3.3 A general class of intervention models

When an adequate n_t-model (7.19) has been obtained, the intervention model $f(\alpha',x,t)$ must be specified. Box and Tiao (1975) suggest the following type of model:

$$f(\alpha',x,t) = f(\delta,\varepsilon,x,t) = \sum_{h=1}^{H} f_{ht} = \sum_{h=1}^{H} \frac{\varepsilon_h(B)}{\delta_h(B)} \ x_{ht} \qquad (7.26)$$

where H denotes the number of policy variables and f_{ht} represents the dynamic transfer of x_{ht}, the policy variable h measured at time t. The set α' of unknown parameters in (7.18) is disaggregated into two subsets $\varepsilon = \{\varepsilon_{h0}, \varepsilon_{h1}, \dots, \varepsilon_{hm_h}, h=1,\dots,H\}$ and $\delta = \{\delta_{h1}, \dots, \delta_{hr_h}, h=1,\dots,H\}$.

The polynomials $\varepsilon_h(B)$ and $\delta_h(B)$ are defined as:

$$\varepsilon_h(B) = \varepsilon_{h0} - \varepsilon_{h1} B - \dots - \varepsilon_{hm_h} B^{m_h} \qquad (7.27)$$

$$\delta_h(B) = 1 - \delta_{h1} B - \ldots - \delta_{hr_h} B^{r_h} \tag{7.28}$$

where m_h and r_h denote the degrees of $\varepsilon_h(B)$ and $\delta_h(B)$, respectively. In practice, it is hard for m_h and r_h to exceed 2.

It should be noted that the various policy instruments must be mutually distinguishable in time and/or in intensity in order to create sufficient variation of the impact variable. Otherwise the polynomials $\varepsilon_h(B)$ and $\delta_h(B)$ are not discernable for different values of h.

It is assumed that the roots of $\varepsilon_h(B)=0$ lie outside of and the roots of $\delta_h(B)=0$ on or outside of the unit circle in the complex plane. This assumption implies that a finite incremental change in an exogenous variable results in a finite incremental change in the endogeneous variable.

According to (7.26), equation (7.18) can be specified as:

$$y_t^{(2)} = n_t + \sum_{h=1}^{H} \frac{\varepsilon_h(B)}{\delta_h(B)} x_{ht} \tag{7.29}$$

Attention should be paid to the following remarks. First, the policy variables x_{ht} (h=1,...,H) in (7.26) an (7.29) can be variables measured at interval, ratio or binary levels. In the case of binary variables a distinction between step variables, denoted by $s_{ht}^{(\tilde{T})}$, and (im)pulse variables, denoted by $p_{ht}^{(\tilde{T})}$, has to be made. It should be observed that $\tilde{T}$ denotes the moment of intervention. The variable x_{ht} is a step variable if it represents a **permanent** change from a given level to a new level (see, among others, Bennett, 1979). Formally:

$$s_{ht}^{(\tilde{T})} = \begin{cases} 0 & t < \tilde{T} \\ 1 & t \geq \tilde{T} \end{cases} \tag{7.30}$$

The variable x_{ht} is a pulse variable if it represents a **temporal** change from a given level, followed by the return to the original level.

$$p_{ht}^{(\tilde{T})} = \begin{cases} 0 & t = \tilde{T} \\ 1 & t \neq \tilde{T} \end{cases} \tag{7.31}$$

An incidental temporal tax increase is an example of a pulse variable whereas the relocation of a government activity is an example of a step

variable. The second remark refers to the situation that during the intervention period new variables, which are different from the policy variables under study and the non-policy variables modelled in the pre-intervention period, have affected the impact variable. Such variables must
also be included into the n_t-intervention model so as to avoid the risk of
specification error. Similar remarks apply to structural changes in the
relationship between the non-policy variables and the impact variable
during the intervention period. The new or changed variables can be handled in the same way as the policy variables, i.e. they are included into
the reduced intervention model $f(\alpha',x,t)$ as additional explanatory non-
policy variables.

7.4. Fitting the intra-regional measurement model

As mentioned in chapter 4 and in the introductory section 7.1, model
fitting consists of a three-stage iterative process of model **identification, estimation** of the identified model and diagnostic **checking** of
the estimated model (see also Box and Tiao, 1975; Box and Jenkins, 1976;
Droth and Fischer, 1981). In this section these stages will be described
briefly and applied to the measurement model presented in section 7.3.

7.4.1 The stage of model identification

Model identification means the operation of tentatively choosing an
appropriate model, in the present context an adequate n_t-model as well as
an adequate intervention model, from the classes of possible models by
means of inspecting the data at hand,[1] by using a priori information and
by a priori reasoning about the process generating the time series. These
various methods should be regarded as complementary.

1) As mentioned in chapter 4 a priori inspection of the data in order to
   find an appropriate model may lead to a data-instigated model. The
   discussion of this problem will be continued in chapter 8.

Below the n_t-model will be considered first. In particular the auto-correlation and the partial autocorrelation functions are basic tools for identifying the n_t-model because they reveal several characteristics of the underlying process. Furthermore, plots of the raw data may often give valuable hints.

7.4.1.1   The pre-intervention model

7.4.1.1.1 The period

The first parameter to be identified in (7.19)-(7.23) is the period s. Inspection of the raw data, in particular of their plots, usually gives valuable hints for determining s. Furthermore, the estimated autocorrela-tions r_k and the partial autocorrelations $\hat{\phi}_{kk}$ can provide useful informa-tion. In the case s=s', the autocorrelations $\rho_{s'}$, $\rho_{2s'}$,... and the partial autocorrelattions $\phi_{s's'}$, $\phi_{2s'2s'}$,... will turn up to be significant at a given level.

If the periodic effects dilute themselves among several autocorrela-tions they may not clearly be revealed by the estimated autocorrelation function. Then more sensitive methods, such as for example the Schuster periodogram, (Box and Jenkins, 1976) may be used.

The autocorrelation and the partial autocorrelation functions, as well as the mean and the variance of a series can be calculated e.g. by means of the computer program by Pack (1974).

7.4.1.1.2 Degrees of differencing

The second step of the identification process involves the choice of values for the parameters d en D. Anderson (1976) proposes to investigate the behavior of the variances of successively differenced series as a criterion for deciding upon the values of d and D. Differencing will in the first instance remove deterministic trends as well as stochastic var-iation, thus reducing the variance of the series. Overdifferencing, how-ever, will at least lead to a rapid enlargement of the stochastic variat-ion, thus increasing the variance of the series again. So, the optimal values of d and D can be found by:

$$\min_{d,D} \text{var}\left[(1 - B)^d (1 - B^s)^D y_t^{(1)}\right] \tag{7.32}$$

When the adequate values of d and D have been obtained, the autocorrelation function for the differenced series dies out rather quickly.

7.4.1.1.3 Model order

The third step in the identification process of the n_t-model comprises the determination of the values of the parameters p_1, p_2 and q_1, q_2. This problem can be approached via autocorrelation and partial autocorrelation analysis, where the autocorrelation and the partial autocorrelation functions are derived and compared with the theoretical patterns for different orders of the models.

The autocovariance generating function is an important tool for deriving the autocovariances of the process. Box and Jenkins (1976) have shown that the autocovariance generating function $\Gamma(B)$ of the multiplicative process described by a model of type (7.19) is equal to the **product** of the autocovariance generating functions $\gamma(B^s)$ and $\tilde{\gamma}(B)$ of the between-periods-model (7.24) and the within-periods-model (7.25):

$$\Gamma(B) = \gamma(B^s) \, \tilde{\gamma}(B) \tag{7.33}$$

Because SARIMA $(p_1,d,q_1) \cdot (p_2,D,q_2)_s$-models imply a structure determined by the multiplication of the (p_1,d,q_1)- and $(p_2,D,q_2)_s$-polynomials, the structure of $(p_1,d,q_1) \cdot (p_2,D,q_2)_s$-models can be deduced from the behaviour of the (p_1,d,q_1)- and $(p_2,D,q_2)_s$-models **separately** , by taking the rules of polynomial multiplication into account. So, the degrees p_1,q_1 and p_2,q_2 of the polynomials (7.20), (7.21) and (7.22), (7.23) respectively can be derived **separately**, but in the same way, from the estimated autocorrelation and partial autocorrelation functions of the appropriately differenced series. For this reason we will deal with just an ARIMA process in the remainder of this section which may refer to both the between-period and the within-period component. Furthermore, p and q without indices will be used below. However, one has to keep in mind that compared with (7.25) the determination of the degrees of the polynomials in (7.24) usually requires relatively long autocorrelation and partial autocorrelation functions.

The characteristic behaviour of autocorrelations and partial autocorrelations associated with special types of ARIMA processes can provide
valuable hints for the choice of the degree of the moving average polynomial as well as for the autoregressive polynomial. A detailed discussion
of these topics, especially referring to the admissible regions of moving
average and autoregressive parameters for several values of p and q, p + q
≤ 2, can be found in Box and Jenkins (1976) and in Nelson (1973).[1] A
summary of this discussion will be given below. In this respect it is
important to notice that non-stationary features are assumed to have been
taken into account.

- The autocorrelation and the partial autocorrelation functions for an
ARMA (p,q)-process of the appropriately differenced series tail off
with mixtures of exponentials or damped sinoids from the first lag.
- The autocorrelation function of a **pure autoregressive** process (i.e.
ARMA (p,o) process) decays to zero and its partial autocorrelation function cuts off (i.e. $\phi_{kk} = 0$, k>p).
- The characteristics of a **pure moving average** (i.e. ARMA (o,q) process) are quite opposite. Its autocorrelation function cuts off for k>q
and its partial autocorrelation function tails off.
- For the sake of completeness, the characteristics of a white noise process are also mentioned, viz. neither ρ_k nor ϕ_{kk} is different from zero,
except for randomness.

The specific theoretical properties mentioned above can be used as
aids to determine the order of the model. However the **estimated** autocorrelation and partial autocorrelation functions usually do not correspond exactly to the underlying true autocorrelation, respectively partial
autocorrelation functions because of sampling errors. Instead, the estimated functions only roughly follow the behavior of the corresponding
theoretical functions. However, they can serve as keys for the identification of the several parameters.

From the discussion of the characteristics of the autocorrelation and
foltial autocorrelation functions of ARMA models of various orders it
follows that significance checks of the estimated autocorrelations and

---

1) As mentioned above, it is hard for p + q to exceed 2 in practice.

partial autocorrelations being zero beyond some given lag usually have to be performed. A simple significance check for a process, for which the autocorrelations are assumed to be zero for lags k greater than some limit q, has been derived by Box and Jenkins (1976) from Bartlett's (1946) approximation for the variance r_k of a stationary normal process. The variance of the estimated autocorrelations under the hypothesis that the process is a moving average process of order q is given by:

$$\text{var } (r_k) \approx (\frac{1}{T_1} (1 + 2 \sum_{j=1}^{q} r_j^2)), \quad k>q \tag{7.34}$$

where T_1 is the number of observations in $\{y_t^{(1)}\}$. For large T_1, r_k is approximately normally distributed.

The variance needed to perform a significance check for the estimated partial autocorrelations under the hypothesis that the process is autoregressive of order p is given by (cf. Quenouille, 1947):

$$\text{var } (\hat{\phi}_{kk}) \approx (\frac{1}{\tilde{n}}), \quad k>p \tag{7.35}$$

where $\tilde{n}$ is the number of unrestricted observations in $\{y_t^{(1)}\}$. For fairly large $\tilde{n}$, $\hat{\phi}_{kk}$ is approximately normally distributed. Significance checks of the autocorrelations and partial autocorrelations as well as their plots are useful aids to indicate the appropriate model order.

7.4.1.2 The intervention model

The final step in the identification process regards the model, which describes the relationship between the impact variable and the policy variables. In principle, there are many possible response patterns to a policy variable. Theory, a priori knowledge or inspection of the raw data $\{y_t^{(2)}\}$ or of its plot may be of great help to select a tentative model.

The discussion of intervention models is made up by two parts. First, attention is paid to single step and pulse variables describing interventions which take place only once (section 7.4.1.2.1). Next, repeated pulse interventions are discussed (section 7.4.1.2.2). In this respect the following remark is in order. It is obvious that step interventions are usually single interventions. If this is not the case, as in the situation of the relocation of a governmental organization in **stages**, the interventions can be modelled as separate, single interventions or as one single comprehensive intervention. The choice is dependent on the kind of effect one is interested in. For instance, when direct employment effects of the relocation are wanted it would be appropriate to consider separate interventions so as to obtain the effects for each stage. If the effect on e.g. the location profile is wanted it would be more appropriate to consider the relocation as one intervention.

7.4.1.2.1 Single interventions

Box and Tiao (1975) have described some simple models which can be applied in a large variety of situations. These models will be summarized below. Before going into detail, it is remarked that a distinction is made here between responses to step and pulse variables.[1] The former will be considered first. It is assumed that the step intervention takes place in period $\tilde{T}$.

- The simplest pattern of response to a step input is an **abrupt** and **constant** change of size ε_{h0} in the impact variable: Formally:

$$f_{ht} = \varepsilon_{h0} \, s_{ht}^{(\tilde{T})} \tag{7.36}$$

It should be observed that this type of response is of a permanent nature in the case of a step input.

- A **gradual** change in the affected variable can be represented by a first-order intervention model of the form:

$$f_{ht} = \frac{\varepsilon_{h0}}{1 - \delta_{h1} B} \, s_{ht}^{(\tilde{T})} \tag{7.37}$$

where the change is determined by $\varepsilon_{h0}/(1-\delta_{h1})$. The parameter δ_{h1} is constrained to the interval $-1 < \delta_{h1} < 1$. When $\delta_{h1} = 1$, the first-order intervention model becomes:

$$f_{ht} = \frac{\varepsilon_{h0}}{1 - B} \, s_{ht}^{(\tilde{T})} \tag{7.38}$$

---

1) Because $(1-B) \, s_{ht}^{(\tilde{T})} = p_{ht}^{(\tilde{T})}$, it is possible to represent responses to both types of variables within one model framework. For the sake of clearness, however, both types of variables are treated separately here.

158

In many cases a step intervention would not be expected to lead to an immediate response as assumed in (7.36) - (7.38), but rather to a delayed response, i.e. to an unknown change in the impact variable with a delay of m_h periods. Then (7.36) - (7.38) have to be modified by replacing ε_{h0} by the term $\varepsilon_{hm_h} B^{hm_h}$ where the delay parameter m_h is a positive integer.

As we will now turn to pulse interventions, a distinction is made between single and repeated interventions. The former is considered first. The intervention is again assumed to take place in period $\tilde{T}$.

- A response consisting of an initial **increase** of size ε_{h1} in the period following the intervention and a rate of **decay** of the increase of size δ_{h1} is given by the model:

$$f_{ht} = \frac{\varepsilon_{h1} B}{1 - \delta_{h1} B} \; p_{ht}^{(\tilde{T})} \tag{7.39}$$

- When the intervention also has a **lasting** effect of size ε_{h2}, model (7.39) could be extended as follows:

$$f_{ht} = \{ \frac{\varepsilon_{h1} B}{1 - \delta_{h1} B} + \frac{\varepsilon_{h2} B^2}{1 - B} \} \; p_{ht}^{(\tilde{T})} \tag{7.40}$$

- When the intervention leads to an initial effect of ε_{hm_h} on the impact variable, which is changed incrementally by δ_{h1} in the period (m_h, m_h^*) with a lasting effect of $\tilde{\varepsilon}_{m_h}^*$, the following compound model arisis:

$$f_{ht} = (\varepsilon_{hm_h} B^{m_h} + \frac{\varepsilon'_{hm_h^*} B^{m_h^*}}{1 - \delta_{h1} B} + \frac{\tilde{\varepsilon}_{hm_h^*} B^{m_h^*}}{1 - B}) \; p_{ht}^{(\tilde{T})} \tag{7.41}$$

where the delay parameters m_h and m_h^* are positive integers with $m_h < m_h^*$.

7.4.1.2.2 <u>Repeated pulse interventions</u>

Economic policy frequently takes the form of a sequence of interventions. For example, the extra employment programs in the Netherlands,
which will be discussed in detail in chapter 10, consisted of yearly
spendings on infrastructural projects during the period 1972 - 1976. This
kind of policy can formally be viewed as a sequence of pulse variables. In
the sequel only policy variables measured at ratio or interval level,
which are by far the most important, are considered.

The type of model to analyse effects of the present kind of policy is
of the same type as model (7.26). However, it is convenient to include the
dead time (b), i.e. the time that expires before the system responds to
the intervention, explicitly into the notation. This gives in terms of
model (7.26):

$$\sum_{h=1}^{H} f_{ht} = \sum_{h=1}^{H} \frac{\varepsilon_h(B)}{\delta_h(B)} x_{ht-b_h} \tag{7.42}$$

For ease of exposition only one policy variable is now considered. In
terms of model (7.29) this gives:

$$y_t^{(2)} = n_t + \frac{\varepsilon(B)}{\delta(B)} x_{t-b} \tag{7.43}$$

or

$$y_t^{(2)} = \lambda(B) x_{t-b} + n_t \tag{7.44}$$

with

$$\lambda(B) = \lambda_0 + \lambda_1 B + \lambda_2 B^2 + \dots \tag{7.45}$$

From (7.43) and (7.44) it follows that

$$\lambda(B) = \frac{\varepsilon(B)}{\delta(B)} \tag{7.46}$$

The weights λ_0, λ_1, λ_2,... in (7.45) are called the **impulse response**
weights. As will be shown below, these weights play an important role in
the identification process of the present type of intervention model.

With regard to identification, the **cross-correlation function** may be used te obtain crude values of b, r, and m in (7.43), if theory does not point to a specific pattern of impact. This function is defined as:

$$\{\rho_{xy}(k) = \frac{\gamma_{xy}(k)}{\sigma_x \sigma_y} = \frac{E\left[(x_t - \mu_x)(y_{t+k} - \mu_y)\right]}{\sigma_x \sigma_y} \quad , \quad k = 0, \pm 1, \pm 2, \pm \ldots\} \quad (7.47)$$

In contrast to the aurocorrelation function, the cross-correlation function is not symmetric about k=0, i.e. $\rho_{xy}(k)$ is generally not equal to $\rho_{xy}(-k)$. However, $\rho_{xy}(k) = \rho_{yx}(-k)$.
An appropriate estimator of $\rho_{xy}(k)$ is:

$$c_{xy}(k) = \begin{cases} \frac{1}{n} \sum_{t=1}^{n-k} (x_t - \bar{x})(y_{t+k} - \bar{y}) & k = 0,1,2, \\ \frac{1}{n} \sum_{t=1}^{n+k} (y_t - \bar{y})(x_{t-k} - \bar{x}) & k = 0,-1,-2,.. \end{cases} \quad (7.48)$$

where $n = T_2 - \max\{d_1, d_2\}$, where d_1 and d_2 are the degrees of differencing of $\{y_t\}$ and $\{x_t\}$ to obtain stationary series and T_2 is the number of observations on the impact variable for $T \geq T'$. Estimators $r_{xy}(k)$ of cross correlations can be obtained by dividing $c_{xy}(k)$ by $(\hat{\sigma}_y \cdot \hat{\sigma}_x)$.

The identification process is facilitated by pre-whitening the input appropriately differenced, i.e. by fitting a model of type (7.19) to the policy variable which transforms the correlated series of observations on the policy variable $\{x_t\}$ to an uncorrelated white noise series, say $\{w_t\}$. The same transformation is applied to $\{y_t\}$ which gives the transformed series $\{f_t\}$.[1] From the pre-whitened policy variable and the transformed impact series the estimated impulse response weights are obtained as

---

1) It is obvious that $\{f_t\}$ is usually not a white noise series because of the applied transformation

$$\lambda_k = \frac{r_{wf}(k)\hat{\sigma}_f}{\hat{\sigma}_w} \qquad (7.49)$$

The impulse response weights are used to obtain crude values of b, r and m in model (7.44). For this model the weights have the following pattern (cf. Box and Jenkins, 1976):

(i)   b weights $\lambda_0, \lambda_1, \ldots, \lambda_{b-1}$ have zero values;

(ii) a further s-r+1 weights λ_b, $\lambda_{b+1}, \ldots, \lambda_{b+s-r}$ follow no fixed pattern; if s<r no such values occur;

(iii) weights λ_j, j ⩾ b+s-r+1, follow the pattern dictated by an r-th order difference equation:

$$\delta(B)\,\lambda_j = 0, \quad j>b+s \qquad (7.50)$$

Equation (7.50) has r starting values $\lambda_{b+s}, \ldots, \lambda_{b+s-r+1}$.

From this scheme it is clear that (approximate) standard errors of crosscorrelation estimators are needed to check whether certain values of $\rho_{xy}(k)$ could be effectively zero. Bartlett (1955) has derived the covariance between two cross-correlation estimators $r_{xy}(k)$ and $r_{xy}(k+1)$ on the assumption of normality. The variance of $r_{xy}(k)$ and of some related particular cases, which have been derived from Bartlett's formula, can be found in Box and Jenkins (1976). Of particular interest is the case that two processes are not correlated and that one is white noise, because, as mentioned above, pre-whitening facilitates identification. Under these conditions:

$$\mathrm{var}\left[r_{fw}(k)\right] \simeq (n - k)^{-1} \qquad (7.51)$$

where $\{w_t\}$ is white noise, $\{f_t\}$ is the transformed series $\{y_t\}$ and n is defined as in (7.48).

Before ending this section the following remark is in order. In the preceding discussion of intervention models it has been assumed implicitly that responses to policy variables take place **after** the actual interventions. As pointed out in chapter 2, however, policy interventions may also be anticipated by the agents in the economic system. Information on such anticipations usually has to be derived from external sources. Evidence on anticipations should be taken into account when the present measurement method is applied by an appropriate displacement in time in the intervention models described in the sections 7.4.1.2.1 and 7.4.1.2.2.

With this overview of the identification of repeated pulse inverventions models the discussion of the indentification stage is finished. In the next section the subsequent stage of the model fitting process, viz. estimation, is taken up.

7.4.2 The stage of estimating the model parameters

Whereas the stage of identification is concerned with defining the structure of a model, the stage of estimation is devoted to the determination of the magnitudes and signs of the model parameters. Let us first pay attention to the n_t-model. For the time period, prior to the first policy intervention, model (7.17) is valid, i.e.

$$y_t^{(1)} = n_t, \qquad t < T' \qquad (7.17)$$

Model (7.17) is estimated by minimizing with respect to the unknown parameter vectors:

$$\sum_{t=-Q}^{T_1} [a_t | y_t^{(1)}, \phi, \Phi, \theta, \Theta]^2 \qquad (7.52)$$

where

$[a_t | y^{(1)}, \phi, \Phi, \theta, \Theta]$ is the expected value of a_t conditional on the observations $\{y_t^{(1)}\}$ and the parameter vectors ϕ, Φ, θ, Θ;

Q is some positive integer.

(For further details see Box and Jenkins, 1976.)

Under the assumptions with respect to $\{a_t\}$ made in (7.21), the least squares estimator (7.52) is approximately normally distibuted. Furthermore, the estimation results closely approximate maximum likelihood estimates (Box and Tiao, 1975). For the estimation procedure there exist computer programs like Pack's (1974) program, which also calculates the variance-covariance matrix of the estimator.

Let us denote the estimated version of model (7.17) by

$$n_t = \hat{\Lambda} a_t, \qquad t < T' \qquad (7.53)$$

where Λ is defined as:

$$\Lambda = \frac{\theta_{q_1}(B) \; \Theta_{q_2}(B^s)}{\phi_{p_1}(B) \; \Phi_{p_2}(B^s) \; (1-B)^d \; (1-B^s)^D} \qquad\qquad (7.54)$$

If it can be assumed that the relationship between the impact variable and the variables determining n_t can still be represented by (7.53) for $t \geqslant T'$, the effect of the policy interventions can be estimated without specification error by imposing $\hat{n}_t$ instead of n_t on (7.18).[1]) This leads to:

$$y_t'^{(2)} = \hat{\Lambda} \, a_t + f(\alpha', x, t), \qquad\qquad t \geqslant T' \qquad\qquad (7.55)$$

Pre-multiplication of (7.55) by $\hat{\Lambda}^{-1}$ gives a series

$$\{\tilde{y}_t^{(2)}, \; \tilde{x}_{1t}, \; \tilde{x}_{2t}, \ldots, \tilde{x}_{ht}\}, \qquad\qquad t \geqslant T', \qquad\qquad (7.56)$$

which can be modeled as:

$$\tilde{y}_t^{(2)} = a_t + f(\alpha', \tilde{x}, t), \qquad\qquad t \geqslant T' \qquad\qquad (7.57)$$

Model (7.57) is a standard model, which can be estimated by a standard least squares routine.

As mentioned above, the least squares estimator (7.52) is asymptotically normally distributed under the assumption that $\{a_t\}$ is white noise. The same applies to the least squares estimators of model (7.57). If only a small number of observations is available, or in the case of serious deviations of normality the parameters in model (7.57) can be estimated by means of the bootstrap. Bootstrap estimation of the two-stage time series measurement model will be discussed in the next chapter.

---

[1]) It should be noted that estimation errors in the estimated n_t model (7.53) are ignored. Some insight in the consequences of this ignorance could be obtained by repeating the transformation with the point estimates replaced by their lower and upper limits of the confidence interval.

164

7.4.3 The stage of diagnostic checking

The final stage of the model fitting process involves checking the adequacy of the identified and estimated n_t- intervention model for the data at hand and, moreover, discovering if and in what respect the chosen model is inadequate. A distinction has to be made between checking of individual parameters and of the overall fit of the model. The latter will be discussed first.

Diagnostic checking strategies of the **overall** fit usually rely on properties of the estimated residuals $\{\hat{a}_t\}$ of the n_t-and of the combined n_t-intervention models. The residuals belong to the standard output of the computer programs mentioned above. For a correctly identified and estimated model the estimated residuals $\{\hat{a}_t\}$ should be close to white noise.

Various tests and checks are available for investigating these properties.[1] In this chapter only checks of the distribution of the estimated residuals will be presented.

The so-called **cumulative sum** check tries to detect model inadequacy by examining the autocorrelation function $\{r_k(\hat{a})\}$ of the estimated residuals. When the cumulative sum check is applied to the n_t-model, the statistic to be used, say κ_1, is defined as:

$$\kappa_1 = (T_1 - d - sD) \sum_{k=1}^{K} r_k^2(\hat{a}) \tag{7.58}$$

where K should be taken sufficiently large. (Usually larger than 20.) If the functional form of the n_t-model is adequate, κ_1 is approximately chi-square distributed with $K-(p_1 + p_2 + q_1 + q_2)$ degrees of freedom.

The check based on the autocorrelation function of the estimated residuals is also instrumental in checking the adequacy of the n_t-intervention model. In this case, however, (7.58) has to be changed. First, T_1 must be replaced by T_2. Secondly, because it was postulated in (7.57) that $\{a_t\}$ is white noise, d and sD are equal to zero. This gives the following statistic κ_2:

---

1) In the sequel of this section we will only speak of "checks". However, the various remarks also apply to "tests".

$$\kappa_2 = T_2 \sum_{k=1}^{K} r_k^2 (\hat{a})$$

where κ_2 is approximately chi-square distributed with K degrees of freedom, if the n_t-intervention model is adequate.

For checking the adequacy of the intervention model **solely** a test similar to the cumulative sum check can be obtained by means of the cross-correlation $r_{\hat{a}w}(k)$ between the estimated residuals and the pre-whitened policy variable w_t. The relevant statistic, κ_3, is defined as:

$$\kappa_3 = b \sum_{k=0}^{K} r_{\hat{a}w}^2 (k) \tag{7.60}$$

with

$$b = T_2 - \max(r_1, \ldots, r_h, m_1 \ldots, m_h, \ h=1, \ldots, H) - \max(d^*, D^*) \tag{7.61}$$

where r_h and m_h denote the degrees of the polynomials (7.27) and (7.28) and d^* and D^* denote the degrees of regular, respectively, seasonal differencing of the multivariate series $\{y_t, x_t, \ldots, x_{ht}\}$ necessary to obtain stationarity. Again K has to be chosen sufficiently large. κ_3 is approximately distibuted as a chi-square variate with $K-(r_1+\ldots+r_h+m_1+\ldots+m_h)$ degrees of freedom.

The checks described above are usually performed sequentially. The n_t-model is checked by means of κ_1 before it is used to transform the multivariate intervention series. At the next stage model (7.57) is checked by means of κ_2. If this leads to a rejection of the n_t-intervention model, the n_t-model and/or the intervention model may be inappropriately specified. However, if the κ_3-cross-correlation check does not indicate inadequacy of the transfer model, the inadequacy of the complete model is caused by the fitted n_t-model, either by an inappropriate functional form with respect to the pre-intervention series (which has been checked by means of κ_1 at a previous stage), or by the fact that the fitted n_t-model is not valid for $t \geqslant T'$. In the latter case of model rejection one finds oneself in a stalemate. Under such circumstances the present measurement approach is not applicable.

When the n_t-intervention model is rejected, the **over-fitting** approach may be used to re-identify and re-specify more adequate n_t- or intervention model candidates. The general idea of the over-fitting approach is to compare sequentially the improvement of a model fit by enlarging the order of the model. The over-fitting procedure is briefly summarized here. The n_t-model is discussed first.

The estimated residuals form an important tool in the over-fitting approach of the rejected n_t-model. First, a SARIMA model for the estimated residuals of the rejected model is identified, estimated and checked. Next, the model for the residuals is combined with the rejected n_t-model. An example may be helpful to clarify this procedure. Suppose the (inadequate) original model is

$$\phi_{p_1} (B) (1-B)^d z_t = a_t'$$

(7.62)

and for the residuals we find

$$a_t' = \theta_{q_1} (B) d_t$$

(7.63)

with $\{d_t\}$ white noise. Substitution of (7.63) in (7.62) gives:

$$\phi_{p_1} (B) (1-B)^d z_t = \theta_{q_1} (B) d_t$$

(7.64)

Model (7.64) is estimated and checked. If necessary this procedure is repeated. (For further details, see, among others, Bennett, 1979; Box and Jenkins, 1976.)

A relationship between policy and impact variables, which has been wrongly fitted, can be restored as follows. Let $\tilde{\lambda}_0$, $\tilde{\lambda}_1$, $\tilde{\lambda}_2$, ... denote the incorrect impulse response weights and λ_0, λ_1, λ_2, ... the correct ones. Furthermore, let:

$$v_t = f_t - \tilde{\lambda} (B) w_t$$

(7.65)

where $\tilde{\lambda} (B)$ is a polynomial in the backshift operator B with the incorrect response weights as coefficents and f_t and w_t defined in section 7.4.1.2.2. Then the correct response weights can be obtained as:

$$\lambda_k = \tilde{\lambda}_k + \frac{r_{wv} (k) \hat{\sigma}_v}{\hat{\sigma}_w} , \qquad k = 0, 1, 2, ...$$

(7.66)

By means of the weights (7.66) the fitting process is repeated until a correct model has been found.

When a model with an acceptable fit has been obtained, a check on the significance of the **individual** parameters should be performed. In this regard the theory that the various parameters in the n_t and n_t-intervention model have Student's t-distribution can be used.

This section ends with the following remarks. First, in chapter 8 further attention will be paid to diagnostic checking and testing. Secondly, in the preceding sections of this chapter we have been concerned with a measurement method of effects of economic policy in a single region. In addition to intra-regional effects economic policy in a given region usually also has interregional effects. Measurement of the latter will be dealt with in the next section.

7.5 The interregional model

Let r denote the region where policy interventions have taken place. Furthermore, let p denote the region, in which effects of the intervention in region r, are to be estimated. As in section 7.3, the vector x denotes the policy variables and y the impact variable.

It is assumed that observations on the explanatory non-policy variables are missing but that a pre-intervention series $\{y_{p,t}^{(1)}\}$ for the impact variable in region p, prior to the first policy intervention at time t=T', is available. Under the conditions mentioned in section 7.3.1, the series $\{y_{p,t}^{(2)}\}$ for t≥T' can be modelled as:

$$y_{p,t} = n_{p,t} + f(\beta, x_r, t) \tag{7.67}$$

where $n_{p,t}$ is the model for the pre-intervention series and $f(\beta, x_r, t)$ is the reduced transfer model of the policy variables in region r.

The class of multipicative seasonal SARIMA models considered in section 7.3.2, can be used to specify the n_t-model and the class of models, dealt with in section 7.3.3, can be chosen to specify the intervention model $f(\beta, x_r, t)$. Furthermore, the fitting process of model identification, estimation and diagnostic checking (section 7.4) applies here as well.

This section ends with the remark that in the case of policy interventions in **several** regions, model (7.67) can be extended with the instruments in the regions concerned.

7.6 Conclusions

Two-stage time series analysis is a measurement method which does not require explicit information about the explanatory non-policy variables. The latter can indirectly be taken into account by means of a model of the pre-intervention time series of the impact variable, provided the same relationships hold between the non-policy variables and the impact variable in both the pre-intervention and the intervention periods. Because of this characteristic two-stage time series analysis may be used to measure effects of economic policy without specification error when information on systematic non-policy variables is missing.

In this chapter, the structure of a general class of two-stage time series measurement models and the process of model fitting, consisting of model identification, estimation and diagnostic checking, have been described. Attention has been paid to intraregional and interregional measurement models.

This section ends with the conclusion that the two-stage time series measurement approach may yield good estimates of effects of policy if information about essential explanatory variables is missing. However, it provides no detailed insight into the working of an instrument with respect to, **inter alia**, the composition of effects (direct, indirect, n-th order effects). Furthermore, it relies heavily on the assumption that the **same** relationships between the impact and the non-policy variables in both the pre-intervention and the intervention period holds. If this assumption does not hold 'effects' on the impact variable, which have **actually** been caused by changes in the omitted non-policy variables, are easily attributed to policy variables which happen to covary with the omitted non-policy variables. However, when information about the changes in the non-policy variables is available, it can be taken into account by adding the relevant variables to the transfer model. Furthermore, the multiple group time-series design, proposed by Campbell (1963, 1966), may provide a way out for this problem.

8. THE BOOTSTRAP, THE JACKKNIFE AND MODEL SELECTION

8.1 Introduction

It has been pointed out in several places above that the LISREL and two-stage time series approaches rely heavily on the assumption of normality in as far as model testing is concerned. For data sets, which do not satisfy this assumption, the results of tests are less reliable or invalid.

In the recent past an upsurge of interest in statistical techniques, providing freedom from the constraints of traditional parametric theory can be observed. They take full advantage of the facilities of high-speed computers and constitute a computer-based distribution-free statistical methodology which is founded on resampling procedures. The jackknife (Quenouille, 1949) and the bootstrap (Efron, 1979) are probably the best known members of the class of resampling procedures. Some other well-known resampling procedures are cross-validation (Stone, 1974; Geiser, 1975), half-sampling (Kish and Frankel, 1974) and random subsampling (Hartigan, 1969).

The key feature of resampling procedures is the evaluation of a statistic of interest at reweighted versions of the empirical distribution. For this purpose, "fake" data sets are generated from the original data. The actual variability of a statistic is assessed from its variability over the "fake" data (see Diaconis and Efron, 1983). The individual resampling methods mainly differ from one another in the way in which the "fake" data sets are generated. Another important feature of the bootstrap, the jackknife and especially cross-validation is that they may be used to gain an insight into the consequences of model fitting, in particular of data-mining. This problem was touched upon above, in partcular in section 4.6.

In this chapter attention is paid to distribution-free testing procedures and to model selection. Section 8.2 describes the general idea and the main characteristics of the bootstrap in the context of univariate situations (section 8.2.1) and of the two-stage time series method and the LISREL approach (section 8.2.2). In section 8.3 the jackknife is dealt with in connection with the LISREL approach. Finally, in section 8.4 model selection is discussed.

8.2 The general idea and main characteristics of the bootstrap

The key idea of the bootstrap in both univariate and multivariate situations is to resample the original measurements and to construct bootstrap samples to which the estimator of interest is applied. Nonparametric measures of variability, confidence intervals and estimates of bias may then be computed which can be applied to describe the appropriate finite sample behavior of the statistic of interest.

Before going into detail it should be mentioned that subsection 8.2.1 is based on Efron (1979, 1982), Bickel and Freedman (1981), and Freedman (1981) and Folmer and Fischer (1985).

This section ends with the remark that only **functional** statistics are considered here. Such statistics depend on the sample observations through the empirical probability distribution.

8.2.1 Univariate situations

The only univariate statistis, to which the bootstrap will be applied in the cases studies of the chapter 9 and 10, is the Moran coefficient of spatial autocorrelation. However, the exposition is facilitated by first describing the bootstrap in general terms and,subsequently, by turning to the Moran coefficient.

Before going into detail the following notation is introduced. A "conventional" estimator or estimate of a parameter θ based on the empirical distribution is denoted as $\hat{\theta}$. A bootstrap estimator or estimate is written as $\hat{\theta}^*$.

Consider an independent and identically distributed (IID) sample x_1, x_2, ..., x_n of size n, which is drawn from an unknown population distribution F on some space S. On the basis of the observed values of the sample the parameter of interest, say

$$\theta = \theta \ (F) \tag{8.1}$$

is estimated by an appropriate standard estimator, such as least squares, as:

$$\hat{\theta} = \hat{\theta} \ (\hat{F}) \tag{8.2}$$

In (8.2) $\hat{F}$ denotes the empirical probability distribution putting probability mass $1/n$ on each x_i (i=1, ...,n). The standard deviation of $\hat{\theta}$ is

$$\sigma(F,n,\hat{\theta}) = \sigma(F) \tag{8.3}$$

The bootstrap estimates of $\theta(F)$ and $\sigma(F,n,\hat{\theta})$ are obtained as follows:

STEP 1: Draw a **bootstrap sample** $x_1^*,...,x_n^*$ of size n from $\hat{F}$ with sampling probabilities $1/n$ for each x_i (i=1,...,n) (i.e. an IID random sample drawn with replacement from $x_1,...,x_n$).

STEP 2: The standard estimator (8.2) is applied to the bootstrap sample:
$$\hat{\theta}^* = \hat{\theta} \ (x_1^*,...,x_n^*) \tag{8.4}$$

STEP 3: STEP 1 and 2 are independently repeated a finite, but large number of times, say B times, which leads to **bootstrap replications** $\hat{\theta}_1^*,..., \hat{\theta}_B^*$.

STEP 4: Calculate the **bootstrap estimator** for θ as:
$$\hat{\theta}.^* = \frac{1}{B} \sum_{b=1}^{B} \hat{\theta}_b^* \tag{8.5}$$

STEP 5: Compute the bootstrap estimator of the standard deviation of $\hat{\theta}.^*$ as:
$$\hat{\sigma}^*(\hat{F}^*,n,\hat{\theta}.^*) = \left(\frac{1}{B-1} \sum_{b=1}^{B} (\hat{\theta}_b^* - \hat{\theta}.^*)^2\right)^{1/2} \tag{8.6}$$

where $\hat{F}^*$ is the empirical proability distribution of the bootstrap sample.

Several remarks are in order here. First, let b denote the bias of an estimator $\hat{\theta}$:

$$b = E_F \; \hat{\theta}(F) - \theta(F) \qquad (8.7)$$

The bootstrap estimator of b is given by:

$$\hat{b}^* = \frac{1}{B} \sum_{b=1}^{B} \hat{\theta}_b^* - \hat{\theta} = \hat{\theta}_\cdot^* - \hat{\theta} \qquad (8.8)$$

Secondly, the bootstrap can also be carried out in a parametric framework ('parametric bootstraping'). Furthermore, 'smoothed bootstrapping' arises when the resampling in STEP 1 is not done from the empirical distribution $\hat{F}$ which assigns probabilities 1/n at each data point $x_1, \ldots, x_n$ but from the convolution of $\hat{F}$ with a parametric distribution. (For further details see Efron, 1982.)

So far attention has been focussed on the bootstrap point estimator, its variance estimator and the bootstrap estimator of bias. Now attention will be paid to bootstrap procedures for setting a confidence interval for θ and estimating significance levels.

Singh (1981) as well as Bickel and Freedman (1981) give asymptotic theory for various situations. In particular, they show that the asymptotic distribution of the bootstrap pivot

$$\hat{u}^* = \frac{\sqrt{n} \; (\hat{\mu}^* - \hat{\mu})}{\hat{s}^*} \qquad (8.9)$$

where:
$\hat{\mu}$ is the sample average and

$$\hat{s}^{*2} = \frac{1}{n} \sum_{i=1}^{n} (x_i^* - \hat{\mu}^*)^2 \qquad (8.10)$$

is the standard normal. It should be noted that in (8.9) μ is replaced by $\hat{\mu}$, the sample average. Moreover, $\hat{\mu}^*$ and $\hat{s}^*$ are based on one bootstrap replication. The bootstrap distribution of $\sqrt{n}\ (\hat{\mu}^* - \hat{\mu})$ could be used to approximate the sampling distribution of $\sqrt{n}\ (\hat{\mu} - \mu)$ since the behaviour of $\hat{u}^*$ mimics that of $\hat{u}$, the conventional pivotal quantity. Finally, Singh (1981) shows that in the non-lattice case the bootstrap approximation of the distribution of the standardized sample mean is asymptotically more accurate than approximation by the limiting normal distribution.

Although the asymptotic theory for the bootstrap is interesting, the small sample theory is definitively of greater practical interest. For the small sample situation Efron (1982) suggests the **percentile method** for assigning approximate confidence intervals to any real-valued parameter θ based on the bootstrap distribution of $\hat{\theta}^* = \theta(\hat{F}^*)$. This method goes as follows.

Let:

$$\hat{c}^*(\lambda) = P\{\hat{\theta}^* \leq \lambda\} \tag{8.11}$$

be the **cumulative distribution function of** $\hat{\theta}^*$. In the framework of the nonparametric bootstrap based on Monte Carlo sampling as outlined above, $\hat{c}^*(\lambda)$ is simply obtained as:

$$\hat{c}^*(\lambda) = \#\ \{\hat{\theta}_b^* \leq \lambda\}\ B^{-1} \tag{8.12}$$

where $\#$ denotes "the number of times". So, in (8.12) $\hat{c}^*(\lambda)$ simply gives the fraction of $\hat{\theta}_b^*$'s smaller than λ.

For a given level α, $0 < \alpha < 0.5$, the following definitions apply:

$$\hat{\theta}_1^*(\alpha) = \hat{c}^{*-1}(\alpha) \tag{8.13}$$

and

$$\theta_u^*(\alpha) = \hat{c}^{*-1}(1 - \alpha) \tag{8.14}$$

where $\hat{c}*^{-1}(\alpha)$ is the inverse of $\hat{c}*(\alpha)$.[1]

The essential feature of the percentile method is to take

$$[\hat{\theta}_l^*(\alpha),\ \hat{\theta}_u^*(\alpha)] \tag{8.15}$$

as a $(1-2\alpha)$ central confidence interval for θ.

It should be noted that usually a large number of bootstrap replications is needed to get reasonable accuracy in the tails of the distribution.

Now a variant of the percentile method will be described which should be applied if:

$$P\{\hat{\theta}* < \hat{\theta}\} \neq 0.5 \tag{8.16}$$

The variant, called the **bias-corrected percentile** method can be briefly characterized as follows. Define:

$$z_o = \Phi^{-1}(\hat{c}*(\hat{\theta})) \tag{8.17}$$

where Φ is the cumulative distribution function for a standard normal variate. Then the bias-corrected approximate $(1-2\alpha)$ central confidence interval for θ is defined as:

$$[\hat{c}*^{-1}(\Phi(2 z_o - z_\alpha)),\ \hat{c}*^{-1}(\Phi(2 z_o + z_\alpha))] \tag{8.18}$$

where z_α is the upper α point for the standard normal, i.e.:

$$\Phi(z_\alpha) = 1 - \alpha \tag{8.19}$$

It is worthwhile mentioning that if $P\{\hat{\theta}* \leq \hat{\theta}\} = 0.5$ then $z_o = o$ and the uncorrected percentile method applies.

The percentile method is justified from a Bayesian point of view and there is evidence that it works well in many situations. Furthermore, it is shown to coincide with the standard theory for the median. (For further

[1] In other words, $\hat{c}*^{-1}(\alpha)$ gives the values of λ such that $P(\hat{\theta}* \leq \lambda) = \alpha$.

details, see Efron, 1982.)

As mentioned above, the bootstrap will be applied in chapter 9 to estimate the Moran coefficient of spatial autocorrelation and its variability. Application of the bootstrap to the Moran coefficient involves some specific requirements. In particular, the spatial structure of the data should be preserved. This could be done by drawing bootstrap samples consisting of R multivariate tuples $(x_r, x_{j_{kr}}, j = 1, 2, ..., n_r)$ where $x_{j_{kr}}$ are neighboring values of order of contiguity k. Next, the Moran coeficient is calculated as indicated in (5.7). The steps 3-5 are the same again as in the general bootstrap algorithm.

In Folmer and Fischer (1985) the bootstrap has been applied to estimate the Moran coefficient of spatial autocorrelation of Geary's Irish data (cf. Geary, 1954). The Moran coefficient of this data has also been estimated by "conventional methods" by Geary (1954) and later by Cliff and Ord (1973). Comparisons of the various results leads to the conclusion that the bootstrap performs quite well. (For further details see Folmer and Fischer, 1985.)

8.2.2 Multivariate situations

The key idea of the bootstraps in multivariate situations is similar to that in univariate situations. In this section the bootstrap will be applied to the LISREL and two-stage time series measurement approaches. First the bootstrap algorithm for the latter will be outlined.

Consider again the pre-intervention model (7.21), written in a slightly different form:

$$\phi_{p_1}(B)\, \Phi_{p_2}(B^S)\, (1-B)^d\, (1-B^S)^D\, y_t = \theta_{q_1}(B)\, \Theta_{q_2}(B^S)\, a_t \qquad (8.20)$$

With respect to model (8.20) the assumption is made that $...a_{t-1}, a_t, a_{t+1},...$ is a sequence of independently, identically distributed random variables having mean zero and variance σ_a^2. It should be observed that in chapter 7 the additional assumption was made that the residuals a_t are normally distributed. This additional assumption is dropped here. As in the preceding section, the form of the distribution is assumed to be unknown.

It is also assumed that for the particular data set at hand an appropriate candidate out of the class of SARIMA-models (8.20) has been identified according to the lines described in section 7.4.1.; that this model has been preliminarily estimated by means of the least squares estimator mentioned in section 7.4.2 and that it has been checked and possibly modified in the ways as described in section 7.4.3. It should be noted that if an a priori given model is avaible only estimation by means of the squares estimator is required before proceeding to the bootstrap procedure.

Before turning to the bootstrap algorithm it is remarked that in the literature two ways of generating the bootstrap data with respect to linear models are distinguished. First, Freedman and Peeters (1984) suggest to generate this data by resampling from the estimated residuals. Secondly, Efron and Gong (1983) argue to generate the bootstrap data by drawing independently with replacements rows from the data matrix:

$$[y|X] \qquad (8.21)^{1)}$$

where:

y is the T x 1 vector of observations on the dependent variable;

X is the T x K matrix of predetermined explanatory variables.

In the framework of model (8.20) the latter procedure is to be preferred, inter alia because the number of estimated residuals is usually substantially smaller than the number of data points. This is because of regular and seasonal differencing and because of the estimation of the parameters (see Box and Jenkins, 1976, for details). Moreover, the latter procedure is to be preferred in the context of model selection. Therefore, resampling from the data points will be assumed in the sequel.

For ease of notation the set of independent parameters to be estimated is denoted as π and the least squares estimator of π as $\hat{\pi}$.

---

[1]) This way of arranging the data is different from the data input required by the computer program by Pack (1974). It is only introduced here to facilitate the description of the bootstrap data generation procedure. It should be observed that one representation can easily be transformed to the other.

The bootstrap procedure with respect to a SARIMA model goes as follows. Given a data set of T observations on the basis of which π has been identified, estimated, checked and possibly modified according to the lines described in chapter 7.

STEP 1: Construct bootstrap data sets

$$[y_b^* | X_b^*] \qquad (8.22)$$

by drawing independently with replacement rows from $[y|X]$, i.e.

$$P([y_{bi}^* | x_{bi}^{*T}] = [y_t | x_t^T]) = \frac{1}{T}, \qquad i, t = 1,2,\ldots,T \qquad (8.23)$$

STEP 2: The standard estimator for SARIMA models described in chapter 7 is applied to the bootstrap dataset $[y_b^* | X_b^*]$

STEP 3: Steps 1 and 2 are independently repeated a finite, but large number of times, say B times, which leads to the bootstrap replications $\hat{\pi}_1^*, \hat{\pi}_2^*, \ldots, \hat{\pi}_B^*$

STEP 4: Calculate the bootstrap estimator for π as

$$\hat{\pi}_\cdot^* = \frac{1}{B} \sum_{b=1}^{B} \hat{\pi}_b^* \qquad (8.24)$$

and the covariance matrix of $\hat{\pi}_\cdot^*$ as:

$$\hat{C}^* = \frac{1}{B} \sum_{b=1}^{B} (\hat{\pi}_b^* - \hat{\pi}_\cdot^*)(\hat{\pi}_b^* - \hat{\pi}_\cdot^*)^T \qquad (8.25)$$

In the case of the transformed n_t-intervention model (7.56) the bootstrap algorithm is similar to the algorithm with respect to the pre-intervention model (8.20). The main difference is that each problem requires its own specific estimator.

Let us now turn to the spatio-temporal LISREL model. It should be recalled that we have R regions observed over T periods, which gives a total of RT observations. As above, it is assumed that an appropriate model for the data at hand has been identified; in particular, that spatial and temporal correlation have been accounted for along the lines described in chapter 5.

In the present case the bootstrap algorithm is rather similar to that with respect to SARIMA models. However, the data matrix is now made up by two submatrices instead of a vector and a matrix. It reads as follows:

$$[Y|X] \qquad\qquad (8.26)$$

where:

Y is a RTX p matrix of observations on the endogenous variables;

X is a RTX q matrix of observations on the predetermined variables.

The bootstrap data are constructed by drawing independently with replacement rows from (8.26) with probability $(RT)^{-1}$.

Concerning the estimators to be used in the bootstrap algorithm, both the initial estimator, the unweighted least squares and maximum likelihood estimators can be used in principle[1]. The latter two iterative estimators, however, are rather time consuming. Therefore, the initial estimator is usually to be preferred, in particular when the number of replications is large.

Let us now turn to the problem of setting confidence intervals for the parameters in the two classes of models considered above. As an introduction, it is remarked that Freedman (1981) gives some asymptotic theory for single equation models. The case of fixed explanatory variables and homoscedastic errors as well as the case of random explanatory variables and heteroscedastic errors are considered. The main result is that in both situations the bootstrap approximation to the distribution of the least squares estimator is valid.

Although the asymptotic theory for the bootstrap is interesting, the small sample theory is definitely of greater practical interest. In this situation the easiest way to obtain confidence intervals is probably by means of an analog of the percentile method in the univariate case, i.e. by estimating quantiles from the histogram (see also Kieviet, 1984). To be more specific, consider the hypothesis:

[1] The maxiumum likelihood estimator is to be used without the distributional assumption.

$$g^T \pi = a \qquad (8.27)$$

where g is a vector containing known elements and a is a known scalar. The p-th quantile of $g^T \hat{\pi}*$, to be denoted as $Q_p(g^T\hat{\pi}*)$, is defined as:

$$P(g^T \hat{\pi}* \le Q_p(g^T \hat{\pi}*)) = p \qquad (8.28)$$

$Q_p(g^T \hat{\Pi}*)$ can be estimated as (cf. Mood, Graybill and Boes, 1974):

$$\hat{q}_p*(g^T \hat{\pi}*) = g^T \hat{\pi}*_{b'} + (g^T \hat{\pi}*_{b'+1} - g^T \hat{\pi}*_{b'})[(B+1)p - b'] \qquad (8.29)$$

where:

$\{g^T \hat{\pi}*_{b'}, b' = 1,2,\ldots, B\}$ are order statistics corresponding to

$\{g^T \hat{\pi}*_{b}, b = 1,2,\ldots, B\}$ i.e. the values $g^T \hat{\pi}*_{b'}$ are arranged in order of increasing magnitudes;

b' is such that

$$\frac{b'}{B+1} \le p \le \frac{b'+1}{B+1} \qquad (8.30)$$

An $(1-2\alpha)$ confidence interval for $g^T \pi$ with equal tail probabilities is given by:

$$[\hat{q}_\alpha* (g^T \hat{\pi}*), \hat{q}_{1-\alpha}* (g^T \hat{\pi}*)] \qquad (8.31)$$

The statistic

$$P (g^T \hat{\pi}* \le a) = \frac{b'}{B+1} \qquad (8.32)$$

is an estimator of the cumulative distribution function of $g^T \hat{\pi}*$ in a, where

[1]) For ease of exposition the vector π is assumed to be h-dimensional for both the LISREL and the two-stage time series approach.

$$g^T \hat{\pi}^*_{b'} \leq a < g^T \hat{\pi}^*_{b'+1} \tag{8.33}$$

It should be observed that k hypothesis

$$R \pi = r \tag{8.34}$$

where R is a k x h matrix of full row rank with known elements and r is a k-vector of known elements could be tested by means of the statistic

$$\frac{1}{k} (R \hat{\pi}^* - r) [R \hat{C}^* R^T]^{-1} (R \hat{\pi}^* - r) \tag{8.35}$$

and the F-distribution.

This section ends with the remark that the bootstrap theory with respect to linear models is still in its developing stage. In particular, setting confidence intervals in small sample non-parametric situations is rather speculative. Furthermore, it should be pointed out that the application of an appropriate estimator for the data at hand is likely to be highly important. Kiviet (1984) has shown that the small sample bias of the ordinary least squares estimator in autoregressive models disrupts bootstrap inferences even more seriously than it hampers the classical standard approach. Finally, we remark that in Folmer (1985) the bootstrap applied along the lines described above has been found by Monte Carlo simulation to perform well with respect to SARIMA models. With regard to LISREL models no information about the performance of the bootstrap is yet available.

8.3. The jackknife

The jackknife is, just as the bootstrap, an estimator which is exercised on "pseudeo data" constructed from the original observations. As shown by Efron (1982) the bootstrap is in fact a generalization of the jackknife.

There is some evidence that the jackknife performs less well than the bootstrap (cf. Efron, 1982). This applies in particular to interval estimators in small sample situations. From a computational point of view, however, the jackknife is far more efficient than the bootstrap. Therefore, it may be applied in those situations where the estimator is a computational spend-thrift, as in the case of the iterative LISREL estimator. Therefore, attention is briefly paid here to the jackknife with respect to the LISREL approach.

The jackknife algorithm goes as follows (see also Mosteller and Tukey, 1977). Assume the availability of G groups of observations, each group containing H elements. For example, the number of groups may be equal to the total number of observations so that each group contains only 1 element or in the case of R regions observed over T periods G may be equal to T and H to R. Let $\hat{\pi}$ be the estimate of the vector of unknown independent parameters based on all G groups of observations and $\hat{\pi}_{(g)}$, $g = 1,2,\ldots, G$, the estimate of π based on G-1 groups, with the g-th group deleted. It should be observed that either of the LISREL estimators can be applied to obtain the estimates $\hat{\pi}$ and $\hat{\pi}_{(g)}$. A **pseudo value** $\hat{\pi}_g$ is defined as:

$$\hat{\pi}_g = G \hat{\pi} - (G-1) \hat{\pi}_{(g)} \tag{8.36}$$

The jackknife estimate $\hat{\pi}'_{.}$ of π is defined as:

$$\hat{\pi}'_{.} = \frac{1}{G} \sum_{g=1}^{G} \hat{\pi}_g \tag{8.37}$$

The jackknife estimate of the covariance matrix D' of $\hat{\pi}$ is defined as:

$$\hat{D}' = \frac{1}{G(G-1)} \sum_{g=1}^{G} [\hat{\pi}_g - \hat{\pi}'_{.}][\hat{\pi}'_g - \hat{\pi}'_{.}]^T \tag{8.38}$$

The following remarks are in order here. First, in a wide variety of situations the pseudo values may be treated as independent and identically distributed random variables (cf. Thorburn, 1976, and Gray and Schucany, 1972). Furthermore, if $\hat{\pi}_{(g)}$ is a consistent estimator, then $\hat{\pi}'_{.}$ as well

[1]) A prime is used in this chapter to indicate a jackknife estimate.

(Gray and Schucany, 1972). Secondly, inferences on π can be made in a way similar to the classical approach to the standard linear model. This will be described below.

Let

$$R\,\pi = r \tag{8.39}$$

be a set of k hypothesis with respect to π. In (8.37) R is a kxh matrix of full row rank and r is a k-vector, both containing known elements. (Recall from chapter 4 that h equals the number of independent parameters of π). Using the statistic

$$S'(R,r) = \frac{1}{k}\ (R\ \hat{\pi}_{\boldsymbol{\cdot}}' - r)^T\ (R\ \hat{D}'\ R^T)^{-1}\ (R\ \hat{\pi}_{\boldsymbol{\cdot}}' - r) \tag{8.40}$$

tests for the hypotheses (8.39) can be performed by means of the F-distribution. Moreover, a confidence region for R π can be constructed by means of:

$$S'(R,r) < F_{k,\ G-h}^{1-\alpha} \tag{8.41}$$

where $F_{k,\ G-h}^{1-\alpha}$ is the (1-α) th quantile of the F distribution, with k and G-h degrees of freedom. If k = 1 confidence region (8.41) reduces to the confidence interval

$$(q_\alpha,\ q_{1-\alpha}) \tag{8.42}$$

where

$$q_{\alpha'} = R^T\ \hat{\pi}_{\boldsymbol{\cdot}}' + t_{G-h,\alpha'}\ \sqrt{(R\ \hat{D}'\ R^T)} \tag{8.43}$$

with

$t_{G-h,\alpha'}$, the α'-th quantile of Student's t-distribution with G-h degrees of freedom.

It should be noted that the legitimacy of (8.39)-(8.41) can only be verified in the asymptotic case (see Miller, 1964). In Folmer (1985b) there is some evidence from crude computer simulations that the jackknife performs well with respect to some spatio-temporal LISREL models.

8.4. Model selection

In the preceding chapters the problem of model selection has been frequently touched upon. It has been especially pointed out that if the same data set is used for both model selection and testing purposes (which will be denoted as "data mining" here), the fit to the sample data is likely to be greater than the fit to the population. In particular, the variability of the estimators is likely to be under-estimated.

In this connection it is worthwhile to mention in brief the results obtained by Lovell (1983). He shows that the probalility of a Type I error for a data miner, who uncovers t-statistics that appear signiffcant at the 5% level by running a large number of alternative regressions on the same data, is actually much greater than the claimed 5%. Furthermore, by way of simulation experiments he investigates the problem whether data mining is likely to uncover those candidate variables that actually generated the data. Three strategies are considered; stepwise regression, maximizing $\bar{R}^2$ and maximizing minimum t-values in absolute value. Especialy the last two strategies are relevant here because a researcher using the LISREL or two-stage measurement approach might concentrate on statistics related to the $\bar{R}^2$ or to t-values in order to detect a satisfactory set of explanatory variables. Lovell's results show that the first two procedures are rather succesful in identifying the correct or related variables. The claims of signifiance a data-miner would usually make, however, are exaggerated. The third procedure of maximizing minimum t-values, which probably is the most important in practice, has a very poor performance. So, the author concludes:

> It is ironic that the data mining procedure that is most likely to produce regression results that appear impressive in terms of the customary criteria is also likely to be the most misleading in terms of what it asserts about the underlying process generating the data under study.

The purpose of this section is to describe how to proceed in the absence of a tightly structured theory. Before starting on this purpose we remark that the state of regional economic theory is such that the sets of impact variables, non-policy and policy variables and the relationships between these variables are usually known. In terms of the LISREL measurement approach this means that the structural and the latent variables measurement models can be specified a priori. The absence of theory refers in particular to the structure of the covariance matrices of the residuals and measurement errors and to spatio-temporal correlation. In the case of the two-stage time series measurement approach the absence of theory regards such matters as the number of time lags, the degrees of differencing, the orders of the autoregressive and/or moving average polynomials, etc. Finally, it should be observed that because of its complexity of structure, the LISREL approach is not suitable if no theoretical notions with regard to the structural and latent variables measurement models are available.

As an introduction to the various model selection procedures we mention the rough and ready rule of thumb given by Lovell (1983) for the case when a search is conducted for the best k of c candidate explanatory variables. This rule says that a regression coefficient that appears to be significant at the level α should be regarded as significant only at level

$$a = 1 - (1 - \alpha)^{c/k} \tag{8.44}$$

A more extensive way to take the consequences of data mining into account is by means of **cross-validation**. The key idea of cross-validation may be characterized as follows. The data set at hand is randomly divided into two subsets. One subset, the socalled **training set**, is used for model selection and model fitting purposes (i.e. the examination of outliers, looking for patterns, transforming the data, trying large numbers of different models, preliminary checking, etc.). Next, the model chosen and fitted to the training set is estimated using the second data set, which has not been exercised upon at the previous stage. This set is called the **validation set**. If the two sets of estimates (based on the training and validation set, respectively) do not differ substantially, one will usually have confidence in the selected model and conclude that it is close to the "true" model. The proximity of the two relevant sets of estimates, such as the parameter estimates and the various goodness of fit statistics, could be used as a criterion of correspondence. To be more specific, suppose for instance that in the training set a given variable has been found to be a significant explanatory variable. If this variable turns out to be insignificant in the validation set, its inclusion into the model is likely to be a consequence of data mining, in particular if there is no clear theoretical reason for its inclusion.

If a given model is rejected in the validation set, other model candidates which also performed well in the training set, are exercised on the validation set. This process is continued until a model has been found which performs well in both sets, i.e. a model for which the criterion of correspondence holds between both sets of estimates.

It is remarked here that the present kind of cross-validation requires the number of observations in both the training and the validation set to be such that adequate estimation is not hampered. (Applications of this kind of cross-validation can be found in Van Dijk and Folmer, 1986 and in Folmer and Van Dijk, 1985.)

The following remarks are in order here. First, the present kind of cross-validation requires the number of observations in both the training and the validation set to be such that adequate estimation is not hampered. Secondly, the validation set is often much more like the training set than is typical of the population, which forms a drawback of cross-validation. Thirdly, a variant of cross-validation, which requires even more data than the so called simple cross-validation variant discussed above, is double cross-validation. This variant requires different training sets for model identification and for estimation (see Mosteller and Tukey, 1977 for details).

Another form of cross-validation focuses on the prediction of the dependent variable in the validation set by means of the model estimated on the basis of the training set. In this version one data point is left out at a time (i.e. the validation set consists of one point only), the model under consideration is fitted to the remaining points and is taken to predict the excluded point (cf Stone, 1974, and Geiser, 1975). The model performance is measured by means of the estimated **excess error**. This kind of error is also used when the consequences of data mining are investigated by means of the bootstrap and the jackknife. Because of the similarities, these three approaches will be dealt with simultaneously below. The two-stage time series measurement method will be considered first. The pre-intervention model and the transformed n_t-intervention model (7.56) are simultaneously dealt with. The predetermined variables are denoted as x-variables.

Let $Q[y, \hat{y}]$ be a measure of error between an observed value y and a predicted value $\hat{y}$. Usually a quadratic error is chosen:

$$Q[y, \hat{y}] = (y - \hat{y})^2 \tag{8.45}$$

The expected excess error is defined as:

$$R((y|X), F) = E_F Q[y, \hat{y}] - E_{\hat{F}} Q[y, \hat{y}] \tag{8.46}$$

where E_F indicates expectation over a single new data point from the population with distribution F:

$$[y | x^T] \sim F \tag{8.47}$$

and $E_{\hat{F}}$ the expectation over:

$$[y | x^T] \sim \hat{F} \tag{8.48}$$

The first term om (8.46) gives the error with respect to new population data points, whereas the second term gives the error in the observed data set. So, the latter will typically be smaller than the former.

The **cross-validation** estimate of expected excess error is defined as:

$$\frac{1}{T} [\Sigma_t Q[y_t, \hat{y}_{(t)t}] - \Sigma_t Q[y_t, \hat{y}_t]] \tag{8.49}$$

The second term in (8.49) denotes the observed error if $[y_t|x_t^T]$ is included in the data set on the basis of which the model to predict y_t is estimeted. The first term is the observed error with the data point $[y_t|x_t^T]$ excluded from the data set used to estimate the prediction model of y_t.

The **jackknife** estimate of expected excess error is rather similar to (8.49). It is defined as:

$$\frac{1}{T} \sum_t [Q[y_t, \hat{y}'_{(t)t}] - \frac{1}{T} \sum_s Q[y_t, \hat{y}'_{(s)t}]] \qquad (8.50)$$

where

$$\hat{y}'_{(s)t} = y(x_t^T, \hat{\pi}_{V(s)}) \qquad (8.51)$$

(8.51) is the prediction of y_t based on the datapoint x_t^T and the parameter vector $\hat{\pi}_{V(s)}$ where $V(s)$ is the data matrix with the s-th observation deleted. So, $\hat{\pi}_{V(s)}$ is the parameter vector estimated on the basis of $V(s)$.

Finally, the **bootstrap** estimate of expected excess error is calculated as: [1]

$$\frac{1}{B} \sum_b \sum_t (p_{bt}^o - p_{bt}^*) Q [y_{bt}, y^* (x_{bt}^T, \hat{\pi}_b^*)] \qquad (8.52)$$

where

$$p_{bt}^o = \frac{1}{T}, \ b = 1, 2, \ldots, B; \ t = 1, 2, \ldots, T \qquad (8.53)$$

[1] The data points $[y_t | x_t^T]$ are thought of as independent random variables from an unknown distribution F.

with

$$P^*_{bs} = {}^{\#}\frac{\{[\ y^*_{bs}\ |\ x^*{}^T_{bs}] = [y_t\ |\ x^T_t\ ]\}}{T} \qquad \begin{array}{l} b = 1,\ 2,\ ...,\ B; \\ t = 1,\ 2,...\ T \end{array} \qquad (8.54)$$

The following remark is in order here. From some simulation experiments by Efron (1982) it follows that neither of the three kinds of estimates of expected excess error correlates well with the actual excess error. Therefore, these estimates are not well suited for bias correction. The only purpose for which the estimates of expected excess might probably be used is model selection, if the number of observations is too small to allow of the estimation of a model on both the training and the validation set. In that situation the selection out of a set of competitive model candidates could be made by using the smallest estimated excess error as the criterion of selection. It is obvious that in order to obtain an insight into the under-lying cause of difference in performance the candidate models should only differ in one respect.

It should be observed that there is still much uncertainty about model selection by means of the estimated excess error. Moreover, it is less in-formative than the cross-validation method outlined above. In particular, it only focusses on the predictive ability of model candidates and does not give an insight into the variability of the parameter estimates and of the various estimated goodness of statistics. This problem, however, could be mitigated by combining this approach with the rule of thum (8.44). Finally, from these remarks it follows that this approach should only be applied if simple cross-validation is not applicable.

8.5 Conclusions

Three issues have been discussed in this chapter. First, the bootstrap and jackknife estimation procedure have been dealt with. Next, attention has been paid to model selection.

The computer-based bootstrap and jackknife are distribution free statistical approaches. Though both approaches are conceptually rather simple, their consequences are rather far-reaching, since they provide freedom from the constraints of traditional parametric theory with its over-reliance on a limited number of standard approaches. The key idea of both approaches is to mimic the process of selecting many samples from the population so as to gain an insight into the variability of the estimators. The actual variability is assessed from the variability over the "fake" data. Non-parametric measures of variability, confidence intervals and estimates of bias may be calculated. The jackknife and the bootstrap are closely related. The main reason why the former has been introduced here is that it is more efficient from a computational point of view than the bootstrap. From various experiences with the bootstrap and the jackknife it is clear that a necessary condition for the legitimate application of both approaches is that a well-specified model is available and that an appropriate estimator is applied.

With respect to model selection two kinds of approaches have been described: simple cross-validation and comparison of expected excess errors estimated by means of the bootstrap, the jackknife and cross-validation. It has been pointed out that the latter approach should only be applied in case of a small number of observations. Moreover, the rule of thumb (8.44) may provide an insight into the significanse level of a parameter, which has been selected by means of trial and error.

This chapter is brought to an end with the remark that there is much uncertainty with respect to both the bootstrap, the jackknife and model selection. Many aspects are still rather speculative and much further research in these areas has still to be done. If, however, one has serious doubts about the adequacy of traditional estimation procedures and if there is no sound theoretical basis for model selection, the approaches described here may form possible devices of research, provided they are carefully applied.

Part III: **CASE STUDIES**

9. EFFECTS OF REGIONAL INDUSTRIALIZATION POLICY

9.1   Introduction

In this chapter the LISREL approach will be applied to measure effects
of two instruments of Dutch regional industrialisation policy, i.e., investment premiums and accelerated fiscal depreciation, on investments in
the sector of industry during the period 1973 - 1976.

It would be natural to start this chapter with a comprehensive overview of Dutch regional economic policy, in particular industrialization
policy, since, for instance, World War II. However, this is an issue
extensively described. (For comprehensive overviews of Dutch regional
policy the reader is referred to Hendriks, 1972; Zoon, 1974; Cremers,
1975;   Lambooy, 1975; de Smidt 1978; Tamsma 1980 and Oosterhaven and
Folmer, 1983). Therefore, only a framework needed for the analysis of the
effects of the instruments under consideration will be presented here.
This framework consists of the history of the investment premiums and
accelerated fiscal depreciation arrangements (section 9.2) and an overview
of additional instruments of Dutch regional industrialization policy (section 9.3).

In the other sections of this chapter the following subjects will be
dealt with. In section 9.4 the measurement model will be designed on the
basis of theoretical and intuitive considerations. Finally, estimation and
validation of the theoretical model is the subject of section 9.5.

This section ends with the following remarks. First, from the overviews of Dutch regional policy it follows that the investment premiums and
accelerated fiscal depreciation arrangements are the most important and
most widely applied instruments of Dutch regional policy. Secondly, as
described in section 2.3, these instruments are of the influencing kind.
In section 3.5 it has been argued that the LISREL approach is appropriate
to measure effects of this kind of instruments. Thirdly, the application
given in this chapter refers to a relatively short and remote period.
This is a consequence of the scarceness of the data available. The application requires data from **Regionale Economische Jaarcijfers** (see

Appendix 9.IV). When the model presented in section 9.5 was estimated, this source was only available for the years 1971 and 1973 - 1976 because of an incidental delay. Because of the data deficiencies the results presented below should be interpreted carefully.

9.2 History and main features of the investment premiums and fiscal accelerated deprecation arrangements

In 1953 the first investment premiums arrangement was introduced. The arrangement was called "Bevordering Industrievestiging Kerngemeenten" (Stimulating Industrial Enterprises to locate in Industrialization Nuclei) and abbreviated as "BIK-arrangement". It provided a 25% premium on the building costs connected with setting up or enlarging industrial enterprises in the so-called industrialization nuclei. The nuclei were characterized by an acute, structural shortage of employment combined with an outmigration insufficient to solve the prevailing unemployment. The premium was given under the condition, that for each $50m^2$ of useful floor area, one local unemployed male was given work. The BIK-arrangement was designed to be temporary only.

In 1959 the BIK-arrangement was replaced. The new arrangement was called "Bevordering Industrialisatie Ontwikkelingskernen" (Stimulating Industrialization in Development Centers) and abbreviated as the "BIO-arrangement". Its most important characteristic was that the employment condition no longer referred to locally unemployed persons but to the provision of jobs as such. Furthermore, the premiums available were raised. Finally the spatial operation was changed. Some of the original nuclei were replaced by some larger towns. This replacement was a consequence of the experience that the newly located industries had shown a very strong preference for the largest nuclei. Ultimately, this led to the policy of 'grouped deconcentration'. Like the BIK-arrangement the BIO-arrangement was temporary.

In 1969 the BIO-arrangement was revised. The new arrangement was called "Stimulering Industrievestiging Ontwikkelingskernen" (Stimulating Industrial Enterprises to locate in Development Centers) and abbreviated as the "SIO-arrangement". The main difference with the BIO-arrangement was that it had no employment condition at all. It was terminated in 1970.

Next to the SIO-arrangement the Investeringspremieregeling (Investment Premiums Arrangement), abbreviated as the "IPR-arrangement", was introduced. It is inter alia this arrangement of which the effects are analyzed here. Therefore, it is described in greater detail.

The IPR-arrangement provided a 25% subsidy on all investments in fixed assets, i.e., land, buildings and machinery, of new industrial establishments in the stimulation areas. IPR-premiums were given under the following conditions:
- The investments in fixed assets should be at least as large as Dfl. 400,000;
- The maximum of the subsidy was Dfl. 3 million;[1]
- At least 40% of the capital expenditures should be financed by the entrepreneur;
- The shareholder's equities should be at least 40% of the total investment.

In 1969 the IPR-arrangement was widened to include **enlargements** of industrial fixed assets under the following conditions:
- In the North, encompassing the provinces Groningen, Friesland and Drente (see Appendix 9.I), the premium was 15% with a maximum of Dfl. 1,800,000 and in other stimulation areas the premium was 10% with a maximum of Dfl. 1,200,000;
- The new investments should be at least as large as Dfl. 500,000.
- At least 40% of the new investments should be financed by the entrepreneur;
- The shareholder's equities should be at least 40% of the total investment.

The IPR-arrangement has been changed several time since its introduction. For the present study the spatial enlargement by 18 centres outside the North and Southern Limburg is of importance. The premiums, however, were differentiated so as to retain a preferential position for

1) The Minister of Economic Affairs was allowed to exceed the maximum in particular circumstances.

the North and Southern Limburg.[1] The percentages per province for the period under investigation, 1973-1976, are given in Appendix 9.II. Furthermore, it should be observed that investment premiums could be combined with labor subsidies since 1975.

Concerning the history succeeding the period of investigation only the "Wet Investeringsrekening" (Investment Account Act) is mentioned here. The act was introduced in 1977. It has both a general macro-economic and a regional economic aspect. It intends to stimulate the investments at the macro level and simultaneously to influence the spatial distribution in such a way that the stimulation areas are favored. Because the original proposal was not approved by the European Economic Community it was combined with the "Selectieve Investeringsregeling" (Selective Investement Regulation) in 1978. (For further details on this arrangement see section 9.3.)

In the recent past the IPR-arrangement was continued, enlarged and the premiums were changed and differentiated according to the seriousness of the problems in the regions and cities concerned. (For further details the reader is referred to the references given in section 9.1, and to Ministerie van Economische Zaken (1981, 1985) for the period since 1980.)

The main characteristic of the **fiscal accelerated depreciation-arrangement** is that, depending on the profits earned, a given percentage of the investments can be fiscally depreciated with acceleration. The history of this arrangement consists mainly of changes of the percentages. The percentages for the period under investigation are given in Appendix 9.II. The arrangement was terminated at the introduction of the Wet Investeringsrekening.

---

1) The North has been a stimulating area ever since the Dutch regional economic policy was put into effect in 1950. This region has been characterized by structural unemployment because of its high dependence on agriculture and agricultural industries.
The closing of the coal mines led to a substantial increase in structural umemployment in the southern part of the province of Limburg (see Appendix 9.I) Therefore, in 1966 it became the second area at which Dutch regional policy was aimed (For further details see the references mentioned in 9.1.)

9.3   Overview of additional instruments of Dutch regional industrializa-
      tion policy

As mentioned above, investment premiums and fiscal accelerated depreciation were the most important instruments of Dutch regional industrialisation policy during the period 1973-1976. However, these instruments were
not the only ones used for regional industrialization purposes during this
period. The following additional instruments can be mentioned (see also
Oosterhaven and Folmer, 1983).
- For unemployed people who leave the Randstad[1] for a job outside it and
for employed people who are permanently needed in the North, migration
subsidies were introduced in 1971 (see Van Dijk and Folmer (1985) about
the importance of this instrument).
- Labor subsidies, consisting of wage supplements of 35% for elderly
people who were difficult to place, were introduced for Eastern Groningen
in 1970 and extended to the entire North in 1972. However, its restrictive
conditions prevented its use on a large scale. In 1975 another type of
labor subsidy was introduced in combination with the IPR-arrangement.
Instead of a 25% premium on investments in fixed assets a 15% premium
could be chosen in combination with a fixed subsidy per new job. This
mixed version has hardly been used.
- State-owned development companies were established from 1973 onwards.
The first and largest works for the North and is able to establish joint
ventures as well as completely state-owned enterprises. Similar companies
can be found in Limburg, Overijssel and Gelderland. The latter, however,
are much less important than the NOM, the Northern Development Company.
- During the period 1972-1976 the relocations of government offices was
handled very activily. Within 4 of 5 years from 1972, over 6000 working
places were planned to be relocated from The Hague (in the province of
Zuid-Holland) to the North and to Southern Limburg. As mentioned in
chapter 2, one of the purposes of the relocations is the improvement of
the locational profiles, which may stimulate industrial enterprises to

1) The Randstad is formed by the Western metropolitan Netherlands (cf.
   Riley and Ashworth, 1975).

locate in these regions.[1)]

- In 1974 the "Selectieve Investeringsregeling" law (abbreviated as SIR-law) was passed. It aimed at a selective slowing down of private invest-ments in the Randstad, which has had a high concentration of population and activities. The SIR-law consisted of three elements: (1) levies on investments in buildings and installations in the open air; (2) a duty to report large projects of this type; (3) an obligatory allowance for very large projects.

Due to economic problems that also influenced the western provinces, the working of the SIR was restricted. The levies were only applied in the years 1975-1976 and were restricted, just like the allowances, to the Rotterdam harbor area (Rijnmond). Hence this law was hardly used in its original design.

- All types of industries which had to face 'necessary' employment cuts and which had a minimum scale necessary for political support, got direct financial aid from the Ministery of Economic Affairs. This aid was also regionally differentiated.

This short overview clearly shows that the additional instruments were used rather incidentally. Furthermore, with the exception of the develop-ment companies, these instruments were not primarily aimed at stimulating new investments. Finally, the only important development company was the northern, so that the spatial operation of this instruments was limited. Therefore, it is legitimate to restrict regional industrialization policy, the main purpose of which was to stimulate investments of industrial en-terprises in the stimulation areas, to the instruments of investment pre-miums and accelerated fiscal depreciation.

9.4 The conceptual measurement model

The purpose of this section is to design the conceptual measurement

---

1) The plans have been only partially realized. In particular, the reloca-tion of the Headquarters of the Dutch Postal Services will take place at a much smaller scale and at a later stage than originally planned.

model on theoretical and/or intuitive considerations. As mentioned in chapter 1, the conceptual model consists of a set of variables and a set of relationships between these variables which are expected to describe and explain the problem under investigation, i.e., the effects of regional industrialization policy on industrial investments. Furthermore, for each explanatory variable the expected sign of its effect is indicated. In section 9.4.1 the conceptual model is outlined in general terms. A formal presentation is given in section 9.4.2.

It should be noted that various variables, in particular the endogenous investment variables, which will be described below, have been measured in absolute units (see section 9.4.2). An alternative would have been to consider growth rates. As both aspects are of interest and because the results in terms of growth rates (of an analysis on an extended data base) will be published in Folmer and Nijkamp (1986), the absolute measurement scales are used here.

9.4.1 General structure

We will start this section with a discussion of the **endogenous** variables. As mentioned in section 9.2, the purpose of Dutch regional industrialization policy was to stimulate investments, both in **buildings** and in equipments, i.e. **machinery**. Therefore, a distinction will be made in the model between investments in buildings (IB) and investments in machinery (IM).[1] It should be observed that it would be desirable to distinguish new investments, enlargements and replacements in the case of buildings, and new investments and replacements in the case of machinery. The main reason for this is that the reactions of each kind to the various policy and non-policy variables may differ (see also section 9.6). The data, however, does not allow disaggregation along these lines.

As pointed out in chapter 6, an adequate representation of the interaction between the regional economic system and regional policy requires the policy instruments to be endogenous. Therefore, the model contains a

1) In order to facilitate recognition a two-letter abbreviation for each variable is used here instead of the notation introduced in chapter 4.

third endogenous variable: **regional industrialization policy** (RI). As described in section 9.2, the main instruments of Dutch regional industrialization policy were investments premiums (IP) and fiscal accelerated depreciation (FA). Both instruments were usually applied in a combined way so as to reinforce each other's effects. This can be seen in Appendix 9.II and is also reflected in their relatively high correlation coefficient (r=.6). Therefore, the instruments are viewed here as a policy **package**. The policy package is represented by the latent variable "regional industrialization policy". The two instruments (IP and FA) are viewed as the observable indicators.

Let us now turn to the **explanatory** variables of both investment equations. As was pointed out in the chapters 2, 3 and 6, one of the main requirements of measuring effects of policy is to establish to what extent the impact variables have been affected by policy and to what extent by autonomous developments. In order to meet this requirement of adequate measurement, both the relevant policy variables and the relevant non-policy variables have to be included in the set of explanatory variables of each investment equation.

Concerning the first category, both current and lagged policy variables are included in each investment equation. This is because the investments consist of aggregates of both 'short-term' realizations, affected by current policy, and 'long-term' realizations, affected by lagged policy. Because of the scarcity of data only one time lag will be considered. It is obvious that the effect of regional industrialization policy must be either positive or zero.

The following explanatory variables of the non-policy kind are included into the investment equations:
- In each equation the dependent variable lagged for one period is included. This variable is incorporated because investments started up in a given period may be terminated in a following period, i.e. there may be some continuity of investments throughout time. It should be observed that longer lags were not possible because of the scarcity of data. The sign of the effect of the lagged variable is uncertain. Because of the simple follow-up nature one would expect a positive sign. However, in situations where large investments in one period lead to relatively modest investments in the next period, or vice versa, a negative sign may occur.

- In each equation changes in current and lagged regional products (RP) are included. These variables provide information on the basis of which expectations about the development of the regional economy can be formed. It is well-known that these expectations play an important role in invest- ment decisions. It should be noted that changes instead of the absolute levels are used because the former reflect the development of the economy more adequately. Both lagged and current variables are considered in order to take the various degrees of inertia into account (see also section 6.2). The changes of the variables concerned are defined as first-order differences. The sign of the effect of this variable is expected to be positive.

It should be noted that it would have been more appropriate to use current and lagged sales instead of current and lagged regional products. Unfortunately, data on this variable was not available. However, the vari- ables sales and regional product are usually highly correlated.

- According to location theory the socio-cultural and the physical envi- ronment are important explanatory variables with regard to investments in buildings. The latent variable socio-cultural environment (SE) will be operationalized by population density (PD) and degree of urbanization (DU). The sign of the socio-cultural environment is expected to be positi- ve.[1]

The only observable indicators available for the physical environment are distance by road from the economic centre of The Netherlands (the Randstad) (DR), and available sites for industrial activities in hectares (SH). Because each of these two variables represents a quite different aspect of the physical environment, they will not be combined into a sing- le latent variable but will be separately treated as observables. On the basis of location theory the distance variable is expected to have a nega- tive effect. The availability of sites for industrial locations is likely to have a positive impact in the case of scarcity and to be neutral in situations of abundance.

1) The following remarks are in order here. First, the expected effects of the socio-cultural environment formed the basis of the "grouped decon- centration" policy. Secondly, when certain tresholds are passed the negative disaggregation effects may outweight the positive agglomera- tion effects.

It should be observed that the four last-mentioned variables will be treated as time-invariant background variables. For the variable DR this is
obvious. For the other variables it is a consequence of the availability
of one observation only. However, these variables usually change slightly
over as short a period as the one under investigation, so that they may
well be considered as time-invariant here.

- Changes in labor volume (LV) is included in the investments in machinery
equation. The reason to include this variable is that production costs can
usually be depressed by exchanging labor for capital. For the same reason
this variable is expected to have a positive impact on investments in
machines.

- Investments in buildings is incorporated into the investments in machinery equation. The sign of this effect is uncertain. On the one hand, one
would expect a positive sign because the new buildings have to be equipped
as soon as possible after their construction has been terminated. On the
other hand, during the process of construction there is no need for investments in machinery for the new buildings.[1] Furthermore, investments
in buildings may lead to a shortage of funds for investments in machines.
This may in particular be the case in periods of slow or negative growth
of the regional economy. In the latter two cases the sign of the effect is
negative.

- Variables representing spatial auto- and cross-correlation effects will
be included in each equation. The variables for which spatial correlation
has to be taken into account and the orders of contiguity and time lags
are unknown. Because of the limited number of observations (see section
9.5.1) only time lags of the Moran coefficients (5.7) and (5.11) of orders
zero and one (i.e. $\ell=0$ and $\ell=1$) will be considered. Furthermore, only
three orders of contiguity will be investigated because fourth-order contiguity does not exist for several provinces (see Appendix 9.III). The
procedure described in section 5.3.2 will be applied to detect spatial
correlation.

- A time-specific variable is included in each investment equation. The

---

1) In this situation we can not speak of an "effect" as defined in chapter
   2, but only of covariation.

first two approaches described in section 5.4.2 gave rise to identification problems. Therefore, a variant of the covariance analytical approach
will be used. As mentioned in section 5.4.2, the use of dummy variables,
which are applied in the original covariance analytical approach to represent time-specific characteristics, should be avoided. Hence, an alternative will be used. It consists of including the variable "total national
investments" (NI) in the investments equations. This procedure can be
rationalized in the following way. Maddala (1971) states that the dummy
variables represent some ignorance, just like the residuals. In the present regional case, however, this ignorance can be partially prevented by
using existing knowledge of the national trend, because the national trend
is the aggregate of the regional trend. Because it is the aggregate of the
regional variables, the sign of the national investment variable is expected to be positive or zero. The latter will be the case when the explanatory power of the other explanatory variables is high and temporal correlation is not relevant.

Next, attention is paid to the explanatory variables in the **policy
equation**. The variables included are the following:
- Lagged regional industrialization policy. This variable is included
because regional industrialization in a given period is usually continued
in subsequent periods, inter alia, for political reasons, such as the
promotion of regional interests at the national level by regional governments. For the same reason the sign of this variable is expected to be
positive.
- Changes in the official total unemployment percentage because the major
ultimate goal of Dutch regional industrialisation policy was to stimulate
employment (see, among others, Oosterhaven and Folmer, 1983). As data on
this variable can easily and frequently be obtained (in contrast to information about investments at the regional level), policy-makers usually
base their decisions (partly) on the development of the unemployment percentage. For reasons of inertia of regional policy a time lag of one period will be assumed. It is obvious that the sign of the effect is expected to be negative.
- A time-specific variable, which is decided to be the change in total
national investments. It should be noted that the variable national investments and not national unemployment has been chosen because policy-

makers usually base their decisions with respect to regional investment policy also on this variable rather than on the development of unemployment solely (cf. Oosterhaven and Folmer, 1983). From the discussion in section 9.2 it follows that the sign of this variable is likely to be negative.

- From a theoretical point of view there is **no** reason to take spatial correlation into account in the policy equation. Regional policy or unemployment in a given region is usually no reason to intensify regional policy in another region.

This section ends with the following remarks. First, various variables, which are usually included in macro investment equations, such as the prevailing interest rate, have not been considered above. The reason for this is that the variables concerned are the same in all regions and therefore have no explanatory power at the regional level. Secondly, the model described above will be presented more formally in the next section.

9.4.2 Formal representation

This section starts with an overview of the set of variables which appear in the model.[1] Furthermore, their measurement scales are enumerated.

The directly **observable** variables mentioned above are:

IB : investments in buildings, measured in millions of guilders;

IM : investments in machines, measured in millions of guilders;

NI : total national investments measured in millions of guilders;

IP : the prevailing percentage of investment premiums;

FA : the prevailing percentage of accelerated fiscal depreciation;

RP : change of regional product, measured in millions of guilders;

PD : population density;

DU : degree of urbanization;

DR : distance by road in kilometers from the Randstad;

SH : available sites for industrial activities in hectares;

1) The sources of the variables can be found in Appendix 9.IV.

LV : change in labour volume, measured in thousands of man-years;

UE : change of the official total unemployment percentage;

A( ) : variable representing first-order spatial correlation (indicated by the letter "A") of the variable between brackets. Similarly, B( ) and C( ) denote second – and third – order spatial correlation, repsectively.

The **latent** variables are:

RI : regional industrialisation policy, measured in the scale of investment premiums;

SE : the socio-cultural environment, measured in the scale of the population density.

Next, the various equations of the model are presented. In order to facilitate notation the index r is dropped. In section 9.4.1 two latent variables measurement models have been implicitly described: one for the endogenous policy variable (RI) and one for the exogenous variable socio-cultural environment (SE). In formal terms these models read as follows:

Latent variables measurement models

$$IP(t) = RI(t) + \varepsilon_1(t) \qquad (9.1)^{1)}$$
$$FA(t) = \lambda_{2,1} RI(t) + \varepsilon_2(t) \qquad (9.2)$$

$$PD = SE + \varepsilon_3 \qquad (9.3)$$
$$DU = \lambda_{4,2} SE + \varepsilon_4 \qquad (9.4)$$

Three structural equations have been described above: two investment equations (IB and IM, respectively) and a policy equation (RI). These equations are formally represented in the following structural model:

1) The lagged policy variables are not combined to a latent policy variable so as to have both kinds of representations in the model.

Structural model

$$IB(t) = \beta_{1,3} \, RI(t) + \beta_{1,4} SE + \gamma_{1,1} RP(t) + \gamma_{1,2} RP(t-1) + \gamma_{1,3} \, FA(t-1) +$$

$$\gamma_{1,4} \, IP(t-1) + \gamma_{1,5} IB(t-1) + \gamma_{1,6} SC(t) + \gamma_{1,7} DR + \gamma_{1,8} SH +$$

$$\gamma_{1,13} NI(t) + \zeta_1(t) \qquad\qquad (9.5)^{1)}$$

$$IM(t) = \beta_{2,1} IB(t) + \beta_{2,3} \, RI(t) + \gamma_{2,1} RP(t) + \gamma_{2,2} RP(t-1) + \gamma_{2,3} FA(t-1) +$$

$$+ \gamma_{2,4} IP(t-1) + \gamma_{2,5} IB(t-1) + \gamma_{2,9} IM(t-1) + \gamma_{2,10} LV(t) +$$

$$\gamma_{2,11} SC'(t) + \gamma_{2,13} NI(t) + \zeta_2(t) \qquad\qquad (9.6)^{1)}$$

$$RI(t) = \gamma_{3,3} FA(t-1) + \gamma_{3,4} IP(t-1) + \gamma_{3,12} UE(t-1) + \gamma_{3,13} NI(t) + \zeta_3(t)$$
$$(9.7)$$

A path diagram of model (8.1) - (8.7) is given in Figure 8.1. For the sake of clarity, a set of explanatory variables, which influence the same set of endogenous variables has been grouped in a rectangle. (For further details about the symbols used see section 6.1.)

In addition to the theoretical selection of the endogenous and exo-genous variables and the description of the causal relationships (i.e. of the matrices Λ_y, Λ_x, B and Γ), various other specifications have to be made before estimating the model. These specifications regard the struc-ture of the other model parameter matrices, i.e. the matrices Φ, Ψ, Θ_ε and Θ_δ. The matrix Φ is discussed below; the a priori structure of the other matrices can be found in Appendix 9.V.

This section ends with the following remarks:
- First, for estimation purposes data is available for eleven provinces

---

1) SC(t) and SC'(t) denote sets of spatial correlation variables which will be identified in the next section.

207

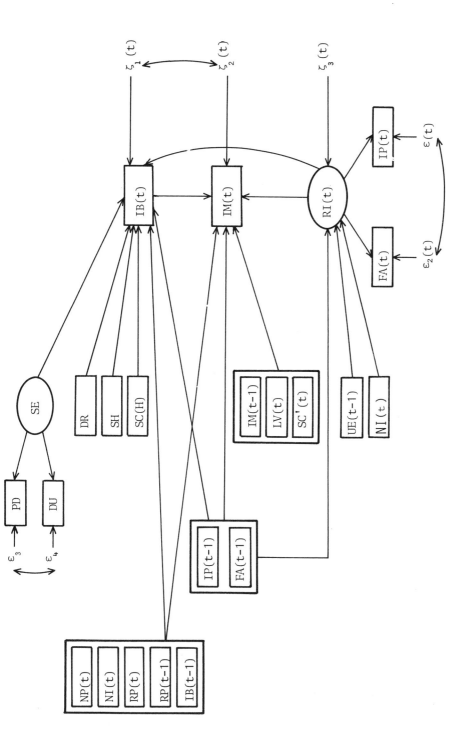

FIGURE 9.1. Path diagram of model (9.1)–(9.7).

over a period of four years (1973-1976). Because the variables are lagged for one year, the number of observations for the time series is equal to three and the total number of observations to thirty-three.

- Secondly, we will be concerned in the sequel with the conditional distribution of the endogenous variables (the fixed-x option mentioned in section 4.2), so that no distributional assumptions are required with respect to the exogenous variables. Furthermore, in this way the number of parameters to be estimated can be kept relatively small because if the x-variables are fixed, Φ is automatically equal to the sample covariance or sample correlation matrix of the x-variables (Jöreskog and Sörbom, 1981). This is desirable, given the small number of observations. The consequence of the fixed-x option is that the effects assessed are only valid for the x-variables in the period under investigation. Statistical inferences for values of the x-variables other than the ones under consideration do not hold. Given the short period under investigation this limitation of statistical inference is self-evident.

- Thirdly, for reasons of identification the measurement scale for each latent variable has to be fixed. This is be done by fixing one λ-coefficient for each latent variable at 1 (see also section 4.3 and (9.1) and (9.3)).

- Finally, because of the different measurement scales of various variables a correlation matrix will be analyzed so that every variable is expressed in its standard deviation (see also section 4.4).

9.5. The empirical measurement model

9.5.1 Introduction

In this section the conceptual model described above is estimated and evaluated. Moreover, it will be interpreted in the light of the empirical findings. Before going into detail, the following remarks are made.

- First, the model will be estimated by the LISREL IV computer-program (Jöreskog and Sörbom, 1978). The reason for this is that the LISREL V program was not yet available at the moment of estimation. The main difference between both programs is that the LISREL IV program only contains the maximum likelihood estimation procedure. Furthermore, several of the judgement statistics mentioned in section 4.6, especially (4.42), (4.43), (4.46) - (4.50) are not given by the LISREL IV program. However, these limitations do not hamper adequate estimation and judgement of model (9.1)-(9.7), as will be shown below.

- Secondly, estimation will be done by means of the jackknife procedure (see sectin 8.3). This is because a correlation matrix will be analyzed and because there is evidence that the distribution of the endogenous observable variables deviates from normality. An indication of the latter can be found in Appendix 9.VI where the coefficients of kurtosis and of skewness of the endogenous observable variables are given.

It should be noted that the main reason for choosing the jackknife instead of the bootstrap is the time-consuming nature of the LISREL IV program, which only contains the relatively slow maximum likelihood estimation procedure. From chapter 8 it follows that the bootstrap would have required this estimation procedure to be applied at least a hundred times. Application of the jackknife is much less time consuming because only 11 sets of pseudo-values will be calculated. This number arises because the group of observations to be deleted is taken to consist of all three observations over time on one province. The reason to construct this group in this way is to preserve the temporal structure for the provinces not deleted, i.e. to have both the current and the lagged variables of these provinces included in the data set.

The remainder of this section consists of two subsections. In the first attention is paid to spatial correlation and in the second to the main results of the actual measurement model.

9.5.2 Spatial correlation

As described in section 5.3.2, the first step to detect spatial correlation is to estimate the model without specifications for spatial correlation. Next, the residuals are calculated by means of (4.32) - (4.38) and checked for spatial autocorrelation by means of (5.7). For the calculation of the Moran coefficients of spatial autocorrelation the weights $w_{r,s}^s$ (5.9) have to be specified. In the present case these weights have been chosen as (see also Hordijk and Nijkamp, 1978):

$$w_{r,i}^{s} = \frac{1}{\sum\limits_{i \in A_{s,r}} \delta_{i}} \qquad \forall \; r,s,\ell \tag{9.8}$$

where $\delta_{i} = 1$ if $i \in A_{s,r}$ and $\delta_{i} = 0$ if $i \notin A_{s,r}$

It should be noted that (9.8) in combination with (5.9) implies that for each region r an unweighted average over all the regions contiguous with region r for a given order is considered.

With respect to the residuals of the relevant equations of model (9.1)-(9.7), which had been estimated by maximum likelihood without normality, the 95% confidence intervals were obtained by means of the bootstrap. The hypothesis of spatially uncorrelated residuals was rejected in the cases of the equations (9.5) and (9.6). The 95% confidence intervals were (-.711,-.497) and (-.639,-.382), respectively.[1] Therefore, the procedure described in Figure 5.1 was continued by calculating the matrix of Moran coefficients of spatial auto- and cross-correlations for the relevant variables in model (9.1) - (9.7). The same weights $w_{r,i}^{s}$ as in (9.8) are used. The Moran coefficients for the various variables investigated can be found in Appendix 9.VII.

The variable having the highest spatial correlation with IB(t) is $C(IB(t))$ (M_{0}^{3} (IB,IB) = -.614) and with IM(t) is $C(IM(t))$ (M_{0}^{3} (IM,IM) = -.56). As mentioned in section 9.4.2, $C(IB(t))$ and $C(IM(t))$ refer to third-order spatial correlation. From the Appendices 9.I an 9.III it follows that third-order contiguity exists especially between the "strong" western provinces (Noord-Holland, Zuid-Holland and Utrecht) and the peripheral "problem" provinces (Groningen, Friesland, Drenthe, Limburg). The negative Moran coefficients indicate opposite development trends in the western and in the peripheral provinces.

1) Because of space limitations the bootstrap distibutions of the Moran coefficients of spatial autocorrelation of the residuals and errors of the various structural and latent variables measurement equations are not given here.

The next steps in procedure described in Figure 5.1 are:

- To incorporate the variables $C(IB(t))$ and $C(IM(t)$ into the equations (9.5) and (9.6), respectively;[1]
- To estimate the enlarged model;
- To check whether the coefficients of $C(IB(t))$ and $C(IM(t))$ are significantly different from zero.

The procedure was slightly modified in the sense that the checks on the coefficients of $C(IB(t)$ and $C(IM(t))$ were postponed until all possible spatial correlation variables had been identified. The reason for this is that the jackknife procedure, which is computationally burdensome, is to be used for judgement purposes. The enlarged model was provisionally estimated by maximum likelihood without the assumption of normality and the residuals of the model estimated in this way were calculated by means of (4.32) - (4.38) and tested for spatial autocorrelation by means of (5.7) and the bootstrap. The null hypotheses of no spatial autocorrelation for three orders of contiguity and for $\ell=0$ and $\ell=1$ were accepted for the residuals of both $IM(t)$ and of $IB(t)$ (probability level[2] > 0.65). So, it may be concluded that spatial correlation has been adequately taken into account by incorporating $C(IB(t))$ and $C(IM(t))$ into the model. Therefore, we may proceed to the next phase: the ultimate estimation of the model (9.1) - (9.7).

9.5.3 The main estimation results

Before presenting the estimated measurement model the following remarks are in order.

- First, the exogenous latent variable 'socio-cultural environment' is included in the model as a quasi-endogenous latent variable (see section

---

1) It should be noted that $C(IB(t))$ and $C(IM(t))$ will replace the unspecified variables $SC(t)$ and $SC'(t)$ in (9.5) and (9.6), respectively.

2) The probability level is defined as the probability of obtaining a sample value as extreme as the one actually obtained if H_0 is true.

5.4.1.2), because the fixed-x option, which does not allow for exogenous latent variables, is used.

- Secondly, the estimated errors of the measurement equations and the estimated residuals of the structural equations, including the spatial correlation variables, obtained via (4.32) - (4.38) have been tested for heteroscedasticity. Because no a priori notions about how the variances of the residuals and errors might change are available and because of the evidence of non-normality, the non-parametric check based on the number of peaks in the residuals has been applied (cf. Goldfeld and Quandt, 1972). The hypotheses of homoscedasticity were not rejected.

- Thirdly, the first step in the evaluation of the empirical model is to judge how well it corresponds to the conceptual model. In particular, the various estimated coefficients are investigated in order to detect whether their **signs** correspond with the a priori expectations. As mentioned in section 4.6.3, a wrong sign is usually an indication of a parameter incorrectly specified as free, provided the other specification errors (a, b, c, e, f) discussed in section 4.6.3, are absent. Estimation of model (9.1) - (9.7) gave the following results. The coefficients of the latent variables postulated in the latent variables measurement model (9.1) - (9.4) had correct signs. The same applied to the variables in equation (9.7). However, in equation (9.5) the coefficients of RP(t), FA(t-1), IP(t-1) and in equation (9.6) the coefficients of RI(t), RP(t-1) and IP(t-1) had wrong (negative) signs.

As described in section 4.6.3, the variables with coefficients with wrong signs are to be deleted and then the modified model is to be re-estimated. This procedure has been applied here. The various judgement statistics, such as the R^2's and chi-square value, of the modified model did not show any decrease in quality compared with the primarily estimated model which was based on the specifications (9.1) -(9.7). So we may conclude that the deletion of the variables mentioned above is correct.

The most important results of the re-estimated model are given in the equations (9.9) - (9.15).[1] The values in parentheses are t-values, i.e., estimated coefficients divided by their standard errors. The main results are:

1) The model has also been estimated with the time-specific variable NI(t) replaced by a set of dummy variables. The results differed only slightly.

The latent variables measurement models[1,2,3]

$$IP(t) = RI(t) + E_1(t) \tag{9.9}$$
$$R^2 = .71$$

$$FA(t) = 1.49 \; RI(t) + E_2(t) \tag{9.10}$$
$$\quad\quad (6.48)$$
$$R^2 = .60$$

$$PD = SE + E_3 \tag{9.11}$$
$$R^2 = .90$$

$$DU = 0.94 \; SE + E_4 \tag{9.12}$$
$$\quad\quad (31.3)$$
$$R^2 = .89$$

The structural model[2,4]

$$IB(t) = 0.01 \; RI(t) + 0.12 \; SE + 0.26 \; RP(t-1) + 0.95 \; IB(t-1) - 0.15 \; C(IB(t))$$
$$\quad\quad (0.02) \quad\quad\quad (0.24) \quad\quad (4.33) \quad\quad\quad\quad (3.17) \quad\quad\quad\quad (-2.67)$$

$$\quad\quad + 0.03 \; DR - 0.06 \; NI(t) + I_1(t)$$
$$\quad\quad\quad (0.12) \quad\quad (-0.43)$$
$$\tag{9.13}$$
$$R^2 = 0.91$$

$$IM(t) = 0.03 \; IB(t) + 0.18 \; RP(t) + 0.28 \; FA(t-1) - 0.47 \; IB(t-1) +$$
$$\quad\quad (0.11) \quad\quad\quad (2.03) \quad\quad\quad (1.12) \quad\quad\quad\quad (-1.96)$$

$$\quad\quad + 1.22 \; IM(t-1) - 0.07 \; LV(t) - 0.11 \; C(IM(t)) - 0.06 \; NI(t) + I_2(t)$$
$$\quad\quad\quad (4.36) \quad\quad\quad\quad (-0.54) \quad\quad\quad (-2.22) \quad\quad\quad\quad (-0.86)$$

$$R^2 = 0.82 \tag{9.14}$$

1) The matrices $\hat{\theta}_\varepsilon$ and $\hat{\Psi}$ are given in Appendix 9.VIII. Other, less important information such as the matrix $S-\hat{\Sigma}$ and the matrix of first-order
derivatives are not given because of space limitations.

2) In order to test at, say, the 5% level whether a given estimate is
significantly different from zero, these t-values should be compared
with the critical values $|t_{10}| = 2.23$ in the case of a two-sided test
and with $|t_{10}| = 1.81$ in the case of a one-sided test.

3) $E(t)$ denotes the measurement error of the estimated equation.

4) $I(t)$ denotes the residual of the equation of the estimated equation.

$$RI(t) = 0.67 \; FA(t-1) + 0.42 \; IP(t-1) + 0.01 \; UE \; (t-1) - 0.14 \; NI \; (t) + I_3(t)$$
$$ (3.53) (2.84) (2.25) (2.81)$$

$$R^2 = 0.96 \hspace{6cm} (9.15)$$

Before paying attention to the judgement of model (9.9) – (9.15) we want to remark that the model has a data-instigated nature (see section 4.6), because several specifications (i.e., the spatial correlation varia-bles $C(IB(t))$ and $C(IM(t))$, various elements of the matrices $\hat{\Psi}$ and $\hat{O}_\varepsilon$, and the variables deleted from the original model), were found by trial and error. Because of the limited number of observations cross-validation as described in section 8.4 was not possible. It should be noted, however, that the jackknife estimate of expected excess error of the ultimate model was the smallest of the various models entertained. In spite of that, the judgement statistics (in particular t-values), which slightly exceed their critical values, should be interpreted cautiously.

Let us now pay attention to the **overall** fit of model (9.9) – (9.15). As mentioned in section 4.6, the chi-square test is inappropriate to testing purposes in the present case, because of deviations from norma-lity. Therefore, we have to rely on other judgement procedures. The fol-lowing judgement statistics for the overall fit have been investigated:[1]
– Several alternative specifications have been tried out. The chi-square value of the present model could not be improved substantially.
– The matrix $S-\hat{\Sigma}$, and the matrix of first-order derivatives contain no substantial elements. The largest element in absolute value in the first matrix is smaller than 0.1 and in the second smaller than 0.3.[2]
– The various individual equations do not show substantial inadequacies (see below).

1) As mentioned above, the judgement statistics (4.42), (4.43), (4.46) – (4.50) are not given by the LISREL IV program.

2) Because of space limitations these matrices are not given here.

In addition to the statistical considerations mentioned above the estimated model (9.9) – (9.15) is also acceptable from a **theoretical** point of view. This follows from the close correspondence between the conceptual and the empirical models.

On the basis of the statistical and theoretical considerations it may be concluded that the overall fit of the model is acceptable.

Next the **individual** equations are considered. From the following two facts it may be concluded that the **operationalization** of the latent variables is quite satisfactory. First, from the t-values one can derive that the observable variables are highly significant indicators of the underlying latent variables. Secondly, in the estimated variance – covariance matrix of the measurement errors, $\hat{\Theta}_\varepsilon$, the only substantial element is the variance of accelerated fiscal deprecation, which has a value of 0.40 (see Appendix VIII).

Turning to the **structural** equations, it should first be noted that all three equations have high R^2 values. With respect to the investment equations (9.13) and (9.14) the following aspects need to be mentioned. First, in both equations the lagged investments are by far the most important variables. Furthermore, the lagged and current changes in regional product in (9.13) and (9.14), respectively, are important explanatory variables. In both investments equations the negative spatial autocorrelation variable should be mentioned, and in equation (9.14) the negative effect of lagged investments in buildings on investments in machinery. Secondly, the location variables (SE and DR) in equation (9.13) have coefficients which are not significantly different from zero. However, according to location theory, the location variables apply in particular to investments in buildings of **new** establishments. The data used in the present case refers to investments in new establishments, to enlargements and to replacements of existing investments. Therefore, aggregation could have blurred the effects of location variables'. Thirdly, the most interesting variables, i.e. current and lagged regional industrialization policy, have effects **not** significantly different from zero at the 5% level. (This result will be discussed further in section 9.6).

In the third structural equation it is striking that regional industrialization policy is primarily influenced by accelerated fiscal deprecation and investment premiums in the previous period. Furthermore, national

change in investments, which is the time-specific variable, has a significant effect and has the correct sign. Finally, the change in the official
unemployment percentage is insignificant. So, we may conclude, that during
the period of investigation regional industralization policy had a very
strong self-sustaining tendency and was rather insensitive to changes in
the unemployment percentage.

9.6 Conclusions

In this chapter the spatio-temporal LISREL measurement approach has
been applied to measure effects of regional industrialisation policy on
investments in buildings and and in machinery in the eleven Dutch provinces during the period 1973-1976. Dutch regional industrialization policy
primarily consisted of two instruments during this period: investment
premiums and accelerated fiscal depreciation. These instruments were usually applied in a combined way and therefore formed a policy package. The
package was represented by a latent variable in the LISREL measurement
model. Not only has the effect of policy on investments been investigated,
but also the sensitivity of policy to changes in unemployment and to lagged policy.

The LISREL measurement method turned out to be applicable here, because data on various variables that went to describe the regional systems
of the provinces was available. The modified covariance analysis approach
had to be used due to identification problems. Furthermore, the jackknife
procedure was employed because of deviations from normality of various
endogenous variables and because a correlation matrix was analyzed.

The main results of this case study are:
- Current third-order spatial autocorrelation for both investment equations had to be taken into account.
- No significant effects of the investment premium and accelerated fiscal
deprecation arrangements on investments could be discerned.
- Regional industrialization policy is mainly determined by lagged policy
and is rather insensitive to changes in unemployment.
The second finding, i.e. that no significant effects of regional industrialisation policy on either type of investments could be discerned will
be considered in greater detail below.

In the first place it should be recalled that the investments considered here consist of enlargements, replacements and new investments. It
is obvious that the **locations** of enlargements cannot be influenced by
policy, though their sizes and periods of realization could. It is well-
known, however, that enlargements are very sensitive to economic expectations, operationalized by regional product here. Therefore, it may be
concluded that only slight spatial effects of policy are likely to be
found with respect to enlargements. On the other hand, the location of new
investments could in principle be influenced by policy. For these reasons, it could be possible that disaggregation of investments along the
lines indicated above would reveal significant effects of policy, in particular for new investments.

From this discussion it follows that the **efficiency** of regional
industrialization policy in the form it had during the period of investigation (and still has) is questionable, because it is a priori clear that
its applicability to enlargements can hardly change the spatial pattern of
investments in the Netherlands.

Secondly, the sector of industry was studied here as a **whole**. The
aggregate nature may have blurred significant effects in certain sub-sectors. Some sectors of industry must (e.g. for technical reasons) be located in particular regions, such as harbors, close to agricultural areas,
etc. It is obvious that industries, which are tied to particular locations, will not be affected by policy, unless their specific location
requirements are met in regions where subsidies can be obtained. Other
sectors, however, may not be tied to a particular type of location. Therefore, disaggration with respect to location-dependent and location-independent industries might reveal positive effects of policy in the latter
kind of sectors.

From this discussion it follows that the efficiency of subsidizing
both location-dependent and location-independent industries is questionable because the choice of location of the former is given a priori and
can not be influenced by policy.

Thirdly, only a relatively short period has been studied here. Furthermore, this period was the beginning of a severe, world-wide recession
during which relatively few investments were realized. There are some
indications in the literature that regional industrialization policy is

likely to be more effective during periods of economic growth than during recessions (cf. Folmer and Oosterhaven, 1983). Therefore, a necessary condition to come to a final conclusion about the efficiency of regional industrialization policy is to extend the period of investigation.

Finally, the insignificant effects found here are in agreement with various other studies into the effects of Dutch regional industrialisation policy (see Folmer and Oosterhaven, 1983, for an overview). The main conclusion of these studies is that investments are primarily determined by economic variables and location facilities and that subsidies only play a minor role or no role at all.

This chapter ends with the overall conclusion that the usefullness of regional industrialisation policy as a global instrument, which applies to the sector of industry as a whole and to new investments, to enlargements and replacements, may be doubted. In order to find out what sectors and what kind of investments can be influenced further research is required.

Appendix 9.I <u>The Dutch provinces</u>

Appendix 9.II Percentages for investment premiums (IP) and fiscal accelerated depreciations (FA), 1973-1976[1]

Province	1973		1974		1975		1976	
	IPR	AFD	IPR	AFD	IPR	AFD	IPR	AFD
Groningen	25	33	25	34.5	30	47.5	30	50
Friesland	25	33	25	34.5	30	47.5	30	50
Drente	25	33	25	34.5	30	47.5	30	50
Overijssel	3	33	3	34.5	15	47.5	15	50
Gelderland	0	33	0	34.5	3	47.5	3	50
Utrecht	0	0	0	0	0	0	0	0
Noord-Holland	0	3.3	0	3.5	0	4.8	0	5
Zuid-Holland[2]	0	0	0	0	-3	0	-2	0
Zeeland	0	33	0	34.5	8	47.5	8	50
Noord Brabant	0	33	0	34.5	6	47.5	6	50
Limburg	15	33	15	34.5	19	47.5	19	50

1) The data on investment premiums and accelerated depreciations is derived from Folmer and Oosterhaven (1983). For those provinces that only
partially benefit from these regulations, the data is derived by means
of weighting the percentages with the populations shares of the areas
concerned.

2) The negative values for investment premiums for Zuid-Holland are consequences of SIR levies.

Appendix 9.III <u>Matrix of orders of contiguity of the Dutch provinces</u>[1]

	Gron.	Frl.	Dr.	Ov.	Gld.	Utr.	N.H.	Z.H.	Zeeland	N.B.	Limburg
Groningen	-										
Friesland[2]	A	-									
Drente	A	A	-								
Overijssel	B	A	A								
Gelderland	C	B	B	A	-						
Utrecht	D	C	C	B	A	-					
Noord-Holland	C	B	C	C	B	A	-				
Zuid-Holland[2]	D	C	D	C	B	A	A	-			
Zeeland	E	D	D	C	B	B	B	A	-		
Noord Brabant	D	C	C	B	A	A	B	A	A	-	
Limburg	D	C	C	B	A	B	C	B	B	A	-

1) A, B, C, D, E denote first-, second-, third-, fourth- and fifth-order contiguity, respectively.

2) Friesland and Noord-Holland, separated by the IJsselmeer and connected by the Afsluitdijk, are treated here as second-order contiguous.

Appendix 9.IV Sources of the variables of model (9.9) - (9.15)

- The data on labor volume and regional product comes from **Regionale Economische Jaarcijfers, 1971** and **1973-1976**, Centraal Bureau voor de Statistiek; Den Haag.

Industry is defined as the total of the sectors 4 (food industry) to 20 (remaining industry). It does not include mining and quarrying (sectors 2-3) and public utility.

The data for 1972 is not available and therefore only effects of policy for the period 1973-1976 have been estimated. In order to obtain the lags for 1973 the data for 1972 is calculated as the unweighted average of 1971 and 1973.

- The data on investments in buildings and in machinery comes from **Statistiek van de Investeringen in Vaste Activa in de Nijverheid, 1973-1976**, Centraal Bureau voor de Statistiek, Den Haag.

- The data on investment premiums and fiscal accelerated depreciations is derived from Folmer and Oosterhaven (1983). See also Appendix 9.II.

- The data on unemployment comes from **Sociale Maandstatistiek, 1972-1976**, Centraal Bureau voor de Statistiek, Den Haag.

- The data on distance by road, sites available for industrial activities, population density and degree of urbanization comes from **Central Economisch Plan 1978**, Centraal Planbureau, Den Haag.

Appendix 9.V A priori structure of the matrices Θ_δ, Θ_ε and Ψ

- The matrix Θ_δ is the zero matrix because of the fixed-x option.
- The matrix Θ_ε is a 6×6 symmetric matrix. Indicating the lower triangle and explicitly mentioning non-zero elements only, it reads as:

$$
\begin{array}{l}
(IB) \\
(IM) \\
(IP) \\
(FA) \\
(PD) \\
DU)
\end{array}
\left[
\begin{array}{cccccc}
 & & & & & \\
 & & & & & \\
 & & \theta_{33} & & & \\
 & & \theta_{43} & \theta_{44} & & \\
 & & & & \theta_{55} & \\
 & & & & \theta_{65} & \theta_{66}
\end{array}
\right]
$$

where the variables between brackets in the margin are those whose error variances are given on the diagonal.

The variances of $\varepsilon_1(t)$ and $\varepsilon_2(t)$ are fixed at zero because of identification problems as a consequence of the availability of only one observable indicator for each of these latent variables.

The errors $\varepsilon_3(t)$ an $\varepsilon_4(t)$ are assummed to be correlated because of the high correlation between the variables determining IP and FA. For the same reason ε_5 and ε_6 are assummed to be correlated.

It should be noted that no specifications for temporal autocorrelation are made with respect to the policy variables in the measurement model (9.1)-(9.4). In the first instance, however, the national investment variable was treated as an endogenous observable so as to correct for temporal auto correlation. It was incorporated into the measurement model of the latent policy variable in the following way:

$$
\begin{bmatrix} IP(t) \\ FA(t) \\ NI(t) \end{bmatrix} = \begin{bmatrix} 1 & \lambda_{1,2} \\ \lambda_{2,1} & \lambda_{1,2} \\ 0 & 1 \end{bmatrix} \begin{bmatrix} RI(t) \\ NI(t) \end{bmatrix} + \begin{bmatrix} \varepsilon_1(t) \\ \varepsilon_2(t) \\ 0 \end{bmatrix}
$$

Estimation gave an insignificant result for $\lambda_{1,2}$. Therefore, the investment variable was deleted from the measurement model and was treated as an exogenous observable. The resulting structure is given in section 9.4.2 and above.

- The matrix Ψ is a 4×4 symmetric matrix. Using the same conventions as in the case of O_ε it reads as:

$$
\begin{array}{l} (IB) \\ (IM) \\ (RI) \\ (SE) \end{array}
\begin{bmatrix} \Psi_{11} & & & \\ \Psi_{12} & \Psi_{22} & & \\ & & \Psi_{33} & \\ & & & \Psi_{44} \end{bmatrix}
$$

Because of the high correlation of both types of investments, omitted explanatory variables in both investment equations are assumed to be correlated and thus Ψ_{21} is expected to be different from zero.

Appendix 9.VI <u>Coefficients of kurtosis and skewness of the endogenous</u>
<u>observable variables of model (9.9)-(9.15)</u>[1]

	IP	FA	PD	DU	IM	IB	normally distributed variable
kurtosis	-1.421	-1.056	.166	- .394	.048	- .505	0
skewness	.497	- .053	1.234	.915	.972	.897	3

[1] The coefficients of kurtosis and skewness are defined as $\dfrac{m_4}{m_2^2}$ and $\dfrac{m_3}{m_2^{3/2}}$, respectively, with m_j as the j-th moment about zero.

Appendix 9.VII <u>Moran coefficients of spatial auto- and cross correlations</u>
<u>of the relevant observables of model (9.1) - (9.7)</u> [2]

	A(IB(t))	A(IM(t))	A(IB(t-1))	A(IM(t-1))	A(RP(t))
IB(t)	.164	.200	.203	.165	-.018
IM(t)	.248	.261	.350	.253	.049

	A(RP(t-1))	B(IB(t))	B(IM(t))	B(IB(t-1))	B(IM(t-1))
IB(t)	.163	.166	.307	.158	.324
IM(t)	.010	.107	.327	.130	.295

	B(RP(t))	B(RP(t-1))	C(IB(t))	C(IM(t))	C(IB(t-1))
IB(t)	-.111	-.000	-.644	-.378	-.407
IM(t)	-.014	-.079	-.357	-.560	-.432

	C(IM(t-1))	C(RP(t))	C(RP(t-1))	A(PD)	A(DU)
IB(t)	-.336	-.249	-.121	.357	.380
IM(t)	-.356	-.267	-.185	.375	.325

[2] A, B and C refer to first-, second- and third-order contiguity. For instance, the (1,3)th element .203 gives the first-order Moran coefficient of IB(t) and IB(t-1).

Appendix 9.VIII The matrices $\hat{\Theta}_\varepsilon$ and $\hat{\Psi}$ of model (9.9) – (9.15)

$$\hat{\Theta}_\varepsilon$$

(IB)				
(IM)				
(IP)	.29			
	(3.7)			
(FA)	.18	.42		
	(2.21)	(1.62)		
(PD)			.10	
			(3.03)	
(DU)			.01	.11
			(.96)	(2.8)

$$\hat{\Psi}$$

(IB)	.09			
	(3.81)			
(IM)	-.01	.18		
	(-.67	(.95)		
(RI)			.04	
			(2.1)	
(SE)				1.00
				(3.68)

The matrices $\hat{\Theta}_\varepsilon$ and $\hat{\Psi}$ are jacknife estimates. The figures between brackets are t-values.

10.   EFFECTS OF EXTRA EMPLOYMENT PROGRAMS

10.1 Introduction

In this chapter the two-stage time series measurement approach is applied to measure the total effect of extra employment programs on
unemployment in the public infrastructure sector in the province of
Groningen (the Netherlands) during the period 1972-1976. The extra employment programs were initiated in several provinces in 1972. Their main aim
was to combat short-term unemployment. These programs were made up by such
projects such as the construction of socio-cultural and recreational
facilities and investments in public infrastructure. The latter kind of
projects consisted of the construction of roads, bridges, etc. In this chapter attention is only paid to the effect on unemployment in the public
infrastructure sector because this is the only sector for which suitable
data on the impact variable could be obtained.

Now the variables of the measurement model and their data bases are
discussed. The **impact** variable y is measured as the number of officially
registered unemployed building trade workers in the sector of public
infrastructure. The time series of the impact variable over both the pre-
intervention and intervention periods is made up by monthly data during the
period 1965-1976 [1]. So, the number of observations for the pre-intervention
series is 84.

The amounts spent on extra employment programs form the data on the
policy variable x. Only annual data is available for the period 1972-1976
(Ministerie van Economische Zaken, 1977) which gives a total of 5 observations only. Furthermore, it should be noted that this data on the policy
variable not only contains expenditures on public infrastructure, but

[1] The data comes from an unofficial source of the Centraal Bureau voor de
Statistiek, Den Haag. It is given in Appendix 10.I and graphed in Figure
10.1.

also on such projects as the building of schools, medical-, cultural- and sporting facilities. Because of the limited number of observations, and the mixed nature of the data on the policy variable this application should primarily be seen as an illustration of the measurement procedure described in chapter 7.

This section ends with the following remarks. First, instead of unemployment decline employment growth might have been an equally adequate or perhaps even more adequate impact variable. It should be observed that effects on unemployment may differ from effects on employment. This is because the persons set to work may not have been unemployed previously. This is the case if e.g. hidden unemploymed or schoolleavers are set to work in extra employment projects. Secondly, effects on employment (instead of unemployment) could not only be obtained by means of two-stage time series analysis but also by other measurement procedures discussed in chapter 3. Because of the absence of effects of non-policy variables, a non-experimental micro approach or a spatial model with policy variables only could be applied to estimate direct employment effects. The present problem had been best analyzed, however, by means of the interregional input-output model available for the province of Groningen and the remainder of the Netherlands (cf. FNEI, 1983). Then not only direct effects in the public infrastructure sector could be obtained, but also indirect, second and higher order effects in this and other sectors in the province of Groningen and in the remainder of the Netherlands. It should be marked that no input-ouput tables for various other Dutch provinces are available.

Summarizing, the present case study with respect to effects of extra employment programs on unemployment in the province of Groningen should primarily be seen as an illustration of the two-stage time series measurement approach. Because an appropriate time series on employment in the public infrastructure sector in Groningen is not available, the effect on unemployment is analyzed. The province of Groningen has been chosen as the study area so as to allow of (crude) comparison with the input-output

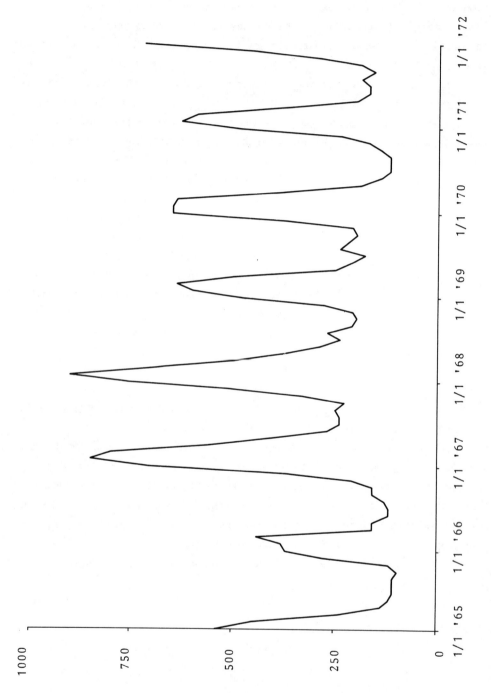

FIGURE 10.1. Officially registered unemployed persons in the public infrastructure sector in Groningen, 1965-1971.

approach. Because of the illustrative nature of the case study only the in-traregional effect is estimated.

The organization of this chapter is as follows. In section 10.2 iden-tification, estimation and checking of the pre-intervention model is discussed. The transfer model is paid attention to in section 10.3.

10.2 Identification, estimation and checking of the pre-intervention model [1])

The first step in the identification process is to investigate whether the original series is white noise or not, i.e. whether the observations originate from a series of independently and normally distributed random variables with zero mean and constant variance. If that is the case, one can immediately proceed to the stage of estimating the intervention model (7.57). The chi-square value under the null-hypothesis that the original series originates from a white noise process is 353.4 with 27 degrees of freedom. Therefore, the null-hypothesis is rejected (probability level < 0.001).

As mentioned in section 7.4.1., the next step in the indentification process is to determine the period s. For this purpose the original series is graphed in Figure 10.1. Furthermore, its auto- and partial autocorrela-tions functions are estimated (Tables 10.1 and 10.2).

Visual inspection of Figure 10.1 reveals seasonal characteristics with period s=12. The peaks occur yearly during the period November-February. Further evidence of non-stationarity can be derived from the autocorrelation function given in Table 10.1. In the case of stationarity the autocorrela-tions at higher lags die out. In the present case the autocorrelations fail to do so. They oscillate with a period of 12. In order to remove seasonal non-stationarity the original series is differenced by $(1-B^{12})$.

[1]) The calculations at all stages were performed by the computer program by Pack (1974).

Table 10.1 Estimated autocorrelations (r_k) and their standard errors (se_k) of the original series.

k	1	2	3	4	5	6	7	8	9
r_k	.78	.40	.02	-.25	-.37	-.42	-.40	-.30	-.05
se_k	.11	.16	.17	.17	.18	.19	.20	.21	.21

k	10	11	12	13	14	15	16	17	18
r_k	.30	.59	.68	.52	.21	-.11	-.34	-.45	-.49
se_k	.21	.22	.24	.26	.27	.27	.27	.28	.29

k	19	20	21	22	23	24	25	26	27
r_k	-.48	-.39	-.18	.12	.40	.50	.27	.12	-.11
se_k	.30	.31	.31	.31	.31	.32	.33	.33	.33

Table 10.2 Estimated partial autocorrelations ($\hat{\phi}_{kk}$) of the original series.[a)]

k	1	2	3	4	5	6	7	8	9
$\hat{\phi}_{kk}$	.78	-.55	-.14	.00	-.09	-.23	-.05	.11	.33

k	10	11	12	13	14	15	16	17	18
$\hat{\phi}_{kk}$	.28	.11	.01	-.20	-.12	-.10	-.06	.01	-.06

k	19	20	21	22	23	24	25	26	27
$\hat{\phi}_{kk}$	-.12	-.19	-.06	.06	.04	-.05	-.07	.03	-.03

[a)] The standard errors are approximately equal to $84^{-1/2}$ = .11 (see (7.35)).

The chi-square value of the seasonally differenced series is 175.8 with 27 degrees of freedom. The null-hypothesis that this series is white noise has to be rejected (probability level < 0.001). In order to detect further non-stationarities, autoregressive and moving average aspects, the auto- and partial autocorrelation functions of the seasonally differenced series are calculated in Tables 10.3 and 10.4.

Table 10.3 Estimated autocorrelations (r_k) and their standard errors (se_k) of the original series differenced by $(1-B^{12})$.

k	1	2	3	4	5	6	7	8	9
r_k	.82	.65	.50	.39	.31	.23	.17	.13	.09
se_k	.12	.18	.21	.23	.24	.24	.24	.25	.25

k	10	11	12	13	14	15	16	17	18
r_k	.00	-.15	-.26	-.23	-.18	-.12	-.07	-.08	-.08
se_k	.25	.25	.25	.25	.25	.26	.26	.26	.26

k	19	20	21	22	23	24	25	26	27
r_k	-.12	-.18	-.24	-.23	-.15	-.13	-.07	-.07	-.09
se_k	.26	.26	.26	.26	.27	.27	.27	.27	.27

Table 10.4 Estimated partial autocorrelations $(\hat{\phi}_{kk})$ of the original series differenced by $(1-B^{12})$.[a]

k	1	2	3	4	5	6	7	8	9
$\hat{\phi}_{kk}$	.82	-.04	-.06	.02	-.02	-.04	-.03	.05	-.04

k	10	11	12	13	14	15	16	17	18
$\hat{\phi}_{kk}$	-.18	-.27	-.06	.35	.05	.00	-.01	-.11	-.08

k	19	20	21	22	23	24	25	26	27
$\hat{\phi}_{kk}$	-.09	-.06	-.03	.04	.07	-.21	.26	-.01	-.08

[a] The standard errors are approximately equal to $72^{-1/2} = 0.12$ (see (7.3 5)).

The linear decline of the autocorrelation function and the value of $\hat{\phi}_{11}$ = .82 indicate the non-stationarity character of the seasonally differenced series. Therefore further differencing was undertaken. The results are given in Table 10.5.

Table 10.5 Standard deviations of successively differenced series.

D \ d	0	1	2
0	2267.1	1397.2	1306.2
1	151.4	85.2	119.3
2	2541.3	1443.5	1921.1

From table 10.5 it may be concluded that the values for both d and D are 1 (see (7.32)).

The chi-square value of the series differenced by $(1-B)(1-B^{12})$ is 34.1 with 27 degrees of freedom. The probability level of the null-hypothesis of white noise is between 10% and 25%. So, the null-hypothsis cannot be rejected at the 10% level. The auto- and partial autocorrelation functions of the series differenced by $(1-B)(1-B^{12})$ are given in the Tables 10.6 and 10.7.

Tables 10.6 and 10.7 suggest a $(0,1,0)$ $(0,1,1)_{12}$ model for the following reasons. First, $\phi_{12,12}$ and $\phi_{24,24}$ are found to be significantly different from zero, which indicates a decaying partial autocorrelation function and thus a seasonal moving average structure. Secondly, on the basis of Table 10.6 ρ_{12} is found to be significantly different from zero and ρ_{24} is not, which indicates an autocorrelation function which cuts off. The latter suggests $q_2 = 1$.

Table 10.6 Estimated autocorrelations (r_k) and their standard errors (se_k) of the series differenced by $(1-B)$ $(1-B^{12})$.

k	1	2	3	4	5	6	7	8	9
r_k	.01	-.04	-.05	-.11	-.02	.00	-.09	.03	.17
se_k	.12	.12	.12	.12	.12	.12	.12	.12	.12

k	10	11	12	13	14	15	16	17	18
r_k	.22	-.01	-.36	-.11	-.05	.02	.12	.01	.05
se_k	.13	.13	.13	.14	.15	.15	.15	.15	.15

k	19	20	21	22	23	24	25	26	27
r_k	.11	-.04	-.17	-.29	.13	-.16	.13	.15	-.02
se_k	.15	.15	.15	.15	.16	.16	.16	.16	.17

Table 10.7 Estimated partial autocorrelation ($\hat{\phi}_{kk}$) of the series differenced by $(1-B)$ $(1-B^{12})$. a)

k	1	2	3	4	5	6	7	8	9
$\hat{\phi}_{kk}$	.01	-.04	-.05	-.11	-.02	-.02	-.10	.02	.16

k	10	11	12	13	14	15	16	17	18
$\hat{\phi}_{kk}$	.22	.00	-.36	-.11	-.02	.02	.10	.03	.00

k	19	20	21	22	23	24	25	26	27
$\hat{\phi}_{kk}$	-.03	-.10	-.09	-.15	.26	-.33	.26	-.01	-.08

a) The standard errors are approximately equal to $71^{-1/2}$ = 0.12 (see (7.35)).

Subsequent estimation of the tentative $(0,1,0)(0,1,1)_{12}$ model gave:

$$(1-B) (1-B^{12})n_t = (1-.65 B^{12})a_t \qquad (10.1)$$

with .49 and .85 as lower and upper limits of the 95% confidence interval.

The chi square value of the residuals of model (10.1) is 14.9 with 26 degrees of freedom, which gives a probability level between 90% and 95% for the hypothesis of white noise. This probability level is quite acceptable.

The auto- and partial autocorrelation functions of the residuals of model (10.1) are given in the Tables 10.8 and 10.9.

Table 10.8 Estimated autocorrelations (r_k) and their standard errors (se_k) of the residuals of model (10.1).

k	1	2	3	4	5	6	7	8	9
r_k	.00	.02	-.02	-.14	-.06	-.01	-.10	-.06	.10
se_k	.12	.12	.12	.12	.12	.12	.12	.12	.12

k	10	11	12	13	14	15	16	17	18
r_k	.12	.07	.03	-.08	.02	-.01	-.01	.00	.01
se_k	.12	.13	.13	.13	.13	.13	.13	.13	.13

k	19	20	21	22	23	24	25	26	27
r_k	.05	-.05	-.14	-.21	.18	-.11	.07	.13	-.04
se_k	.13	.13	.13	.13	.13	.14	.14	.14	.14

Investigation of the Tables 10.8 and 10.9 gives no reason to change model (21.1).

To summarize, we have found a model for the pre-intervention series with a regular $(1-B)$ and a seasonal $(1-B^{12})$ component. Furthermore, the disturbances are seasonally related.

As shown above, model (10.1) is acceptable from a statistical point

Table 10.9 Estimated partial autocorrelations $\hat{\phi}_{kk}$ of the residuals of model (10.1).[a]

k	1	2	3	4	5	6	7	8	9
$\hat{\phi}_{kk}$	.00	.02	-.02	-.14	-.06	-.01	-.11	-.09	.09

k	10	11	12	13	14	15	16	17	18
$\hat{\phi}_{kk}$	.12	.04	.00	-.06	.06	.01	.01	.03	.04

k	19	20	21	22	23	24	25	26	27
$\hat{\phi}_{kk}$	.05	-.09	-.17	-.21	.22	-.12	.00	.09	.00

a) The standard errors are approximately $71^{-1/2}$ = .12 ((see 7.3.5))

of view. Moreover, it is also acceptable from a theoretical - economical point of view for the following reasons:

- First, the regular shift represented by (1-B) follows from the recession which had the highest unemployment rates in 1967 and 1968 (see also Oosterhaven and Folmer, 1980);

- Secondly, economic activities in infrastructural projects such as ground works, the construction of roads and bridges, etc., is highly sensitive to weather conditions. This means that unemployment in the present sector tends to be relatively high during the winter season and low during the summer period. This phenomenon explains the seasonal component $(1-B^{12})$ and the seasonal relationship between the disturbances.

This section ends with the following remarks. First, as mentioned in section 7.2, useful estimates of the cross-correlations require in general that the number of observations should be larger than 50. As the total number of observations of the original time series is only 84 cross-validation as described in section 8.4 has not been applied. Moreover, there is no urgent need for cross-validation because the model is plausible from a theoretical point. Secondly, for the sake of illustration of the selection procedure outlined in section 8.4 the following alternative, though less plausible, model was also entertained:

$$(1-\Phi B^{24})(1-B)(1-B^{12}) \; n_t = (1-\Theta B^{12}) \; a_t \qquad (10.2)$$

Subsequent estimation gave $\Phi = -0.25$ and $\Theta = 0.69$. According to the procedures of chapter 7 both estimates are significantly different from zero. In order to select between both model candidates the bootstrap estimates of expected excess error were calculated. The estimate for model (10.2) was twice as large as that for model (10.1). On the basis of these findings it follows once more that model (10.1) is preferable. Thirdly, the point estimate and confidence interval of Θ in (10.1) were obtained by conventional methods. In addition estimates by means of the bootstrap have been obtained. The point estimate of Θ obtained by means of the algorithm outlined in section 8.2.2. on the basis of 1000 replications equals .63. In the Figures 10.2 and 10.3 the histogram and the cumulative distribution of $\hat{\Theta}^*$ are given.

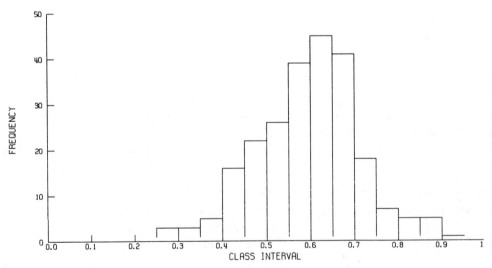

FIGURE 10.2 Bootstrap histogram of the parameter $\hat{\Theta}^*$ of model (10.1)

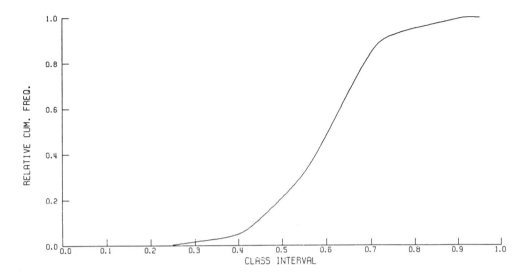

FIGURE 10.3 Cumulative bootstrap distribution of the parameter $\hat{\theta}^*$ of model
(10.1).

Because $P(\hat{\theta}^* < \hat{\theta}) \approx 0.5$ the percentile method without bias correction is
applied. The 95% confidence interval with equal tail probabilities thus ob-
tained is (.398, .821) which is slightly smaller than the interval obtained
by the conventional method.

With the aid of model (10.1) we can proceed to the transfer model in
the next section.

10.3. The intervention model

As described in section 7.4, the multivariate intervention series is
transformed by the estimated pre-intervention model. In section 7.3.1.,
however, various conditions for the application of this procedure have been
mentioned. Before proceeding we will briefly investigate whether these conditions may be assumed to be met here.

The first condition is that in both the pre-intervention and the intervention periods the same relationships hold between the impact variable and the non-policy variables. The most important factors, which could disturb this constant relationship, are technological changes, changes of economic trend and of the business cycle. Because of the short intervention period, which immediately follows the pre-intervention period there is no reason to assume the occurence of essential technological changes or basic alterations of trend. Furthermore, the pre-intervention series was characterized by an economic decline with peak in 1968. Therefore, the series was transformed by (1-B) in order to take the shift of level into account. The intervention period also shows a shift of level with an unemployment peak in 1977, which can also be accounted for by the term (1-B). Finally, the seasonal pattern of the impact variable may be assumed to hold for both periods. So, the first condition mentioned in section 7.3.1 may be assumed to be satisfied.

The second condition relates to the independence of the instruments of policy of the non-policy variables. As mentioned in section 10.1, the extra employment programs were initiated in order to combat short-term unemployment. That is, the programs were mainly influenced by the development of unemployment, which is not an explanatory non-policy varable. In other words, the independence of the instrument of policy of the explanatory non-policy variables may be assumed.

The third condition requires an additive model structure of the form (7.18). Because the extra employment programs for the period under investigation can be viewed as independent additions to the existing stock of infrastructural projects under execution this third condition may also be assumed to be met.

Before applying the procedure described in section 7.4.2 we want to repeat that only annual data for the policy variable for the period 1972-1973 is available. The small number of observations on the policy variable hampers the adequate estimation of the transfer model. Therefore, monthly figures were derived from the annual data by means of a method developed by Boot et.al. (1967.) As was expected in advance, the data thus obtained concealed the variation in the interventions which was known to exist. Therefore, the annual totals had to be used anyway. (The data on the policy variable are given in Appendix 10.II).

The first step in the estimation procedure of the effects is to transform the intervention time series of the impact and policy variables by

$$\frac{(1-B)\ (1-B^{12})}{1-.63\ B^{12}} \qquad (10.3)^{1)}$$

Because the date on the policy variable consisted of annual observation, the transformed monthly figures on the impact variable were summed to yearly totals. Furthermore, the first-order differences of the annual data on the policy variable were calculated according to the non-seasonal component of model (10.1).

The fitted transfer model is:

$$\tilde{y}_t^{(2)} = \underset{(-3.6)}{-\ 8.9}\ \tilde{x}_t + a_t \qquad R^2 = .72 \qquad (10.4)$$

where $\tilde{y}$ and $\tilde{x}$ are the transformed impact and policy variable and the t-value, obtained by conventional methods, is written in brackets.[2]

With respect to model (10.4) we can draw the following conclusions:
- The estimated coefficient has the correct sign because it may be assumed on theoritical considerations that extra employment programmes have a negative effect on unemployment. Furthermore, a one-sided t-test of level 5% with 4 degrees of freedom reveals that the effect of policy is significantly different from zero.

- Ignoring estimation errors, the deficiency of the data base and possible

[1] It should be noted that (10.3) derives from (10.1) with the conventional estimate of θ replaced by the bootstrap estimate. Furthermore, estimation errors in the estimated n_t model (10.1) are ignored (see also the note corresponding to (7.54) - (7.55)).

[2] Because of the data deficiencies no attempts have been made to create exactitude by applying the bootstrap.

specification errors, such as omitted lagged varables [1], one can derive from
model (10.4) that a policy intervention of one million guilders leads to a
reduction of unemployment of 8.9 persons in the current period. It should be
marked that this reduction of unemployment is in close confirmity with the
direct effect of the stimulation of **employment** in the public infrastructure
by the same amount. From the interregional input-ouput table for the
province of Groningen (FNEI, 1983) it follows that this effect equals 9.5
persons.

10.4 Conclusions

In this chapter two-stage time series analysis has been used (for illustrative purposes) to measures effects of extra employment programs on
unemployment in the sector of public infrastructure in the province of
Groningen (the Netherlands) during the period 1972-1976. For the present
measurement problem a pre-intervention series, consisting of monthly observations on unemployment for the period 1965-1971, is avalable. For the
intervention period 1972-1976, the multivariate time series on the impact
variable and the instrument of regional policy consists of yearly
observations.

The pre-intervention model found was acceptable both from a statistical
and from a theoretical - economical point of view. Furthermore, the conditions to transform the intervention series by the pre-intervention model
could be assumed to be satisfied.

The data for the policy instrument did not only contain expenditures on
public infrastructure, but also on other kinds of extra employment projects.
Furthermore, the number of observations for the intervention series is very
small. These deficiencies of the data base hampered adequate estimation of
the transfer model. Therefore, the point estimate of the effect, consisting
of a reduction of unemployment by 8.9 persons caused by a policy input of

---

[1] Lagged variables have been omitted because of the small number of
observations.

one million guilders, has to be interpreted cautiously. Finally, we want to remark that the negative effect of extra employment programs on unemployment is not only plausible from a theoretical point of view but has also been confirmed by other measurement approaches (cf. FNEI, 1983).

Appendix 10.I. Number of officially registered unemployed building trade
workers in the sector of public infrastructure in Groningen,
1965-1971.

	Jan.	Febr.	Mar.	Apr.	May	June	July	Aug.	Sept.	Oct.	Nov.	Dec.
1965	503	407	175	67	47	34	31	34	23	44	219	319
1966	333	410	86	69	40	44	60	84	87	142	322	694
1967	850	791	526	360	209	172	174	186	167	280	474	744
1968	900	664	461	333	231	177	206	145	134	149	224	445
1969	573	611	459	190	148	113	174	157	136	145	315	626
1970	625	613	335	118	62	46	49	42	70	95	178	456
1971	609	555	321	128	101	95	119	84	124	234	407	706

Appendix 10.II. Expenditures on extra employment programs in Groningen,
1972-1976 (millions of guilders)

1972	188,8
1973	98,5
1974	135,9
1975	59,9
1976	62

EPILOGUE

11.   SOME ISSUES FOR FURTHER RESEARCH

11.1   Introduction

The purpose of this chapter is to formulate some issues which could be of interest for further research. Two main areas are distinguished. In section 11.2 directions for further research **within** the framework of the methodological and econometric methods, which have been dealt with in this study, are discussed. Particular attention is paid to changing behavioral econometric relationships under alternative policy scenarios. In section 11.3 it is argued that important topics for further research can be found in the **extension** of assessment of effects of policy into the direction of more comprehensive forms of impact assessment and policy evaluation.

11.2 Inclusion of rational expectations in the measurement model

In an interesting article Lucas (1976) analyzed the uses and especially abuses of econometric approaches to policy evaluation. He came to the conclusion that current practice is to estimate an econometric relationship and to use this relationship to analyze behavior under alternative scenarios. This kind of analysis rests on the assumption that the relations will remain stable under the different scenarios. Lucas argued that this assumption is false because behavior is likely to change as the scenarios change. The reason for this is that agents usually change their expectations and forecasting schemes in changing economic environments. This point can be made more specific by considering the following example of the econometric relationships applied in the preceding chapters :

$$y_{t+1} = f (y_t, x_t, \pi, \varepsilon_t) \tag{11.1}$$

where:

y_{t+1} is the policy objective at t + 1 ;
x_t denotes the exogenous variables, including the policy variables ;

ε_t is the disturbance term ;

π denotes the parameters of the relationship.

The basic assumption of tradional econometric impact analysis is that the parameters π will remain unchanged as the x-varaibles are systematically varied. In Lucas' view the parameters π are likely to change under different scenarios. (For an example with respect to investment theory see Lucas, 1976.)[1]

  From this exposition it follows that it is of great importance to account for changing parameters in a measurement model. This can be achieved by including rational expectations into the measurement model. The econometric work along these lines is in its infancy. (For some attemps in macro economics see Taylor, 1979, Wallis, 1980, Hansen and Sargent, 1980 and Sargent, 1981). Therefore, it is an inportant topic for further research.

11.3 <u>Towards more comprehensive forms of impact assessment and policy</u>
      <u>evaluation</u>

  In the chapters 1 and 2 the main purpose of this study has been described as the adaptation of the methodology of economics and of some econometric methods to the specific conditions of ex post assessment of regional effects of regional economic policy. Moreover, it was decided to leave the cost aspect of policy out of consideration. In section 2.3. it has been shown that this limited kind of ex post impact assessment is only part of the comprehensive process of policy evaluation. So, possible topics for further research are immediately revealed by widening the scope to aspects of policy evaluation other than this limited kind of assessment of regional effects. The following issues immediately present themselves.

[1] It should be observed that in the case study presented in chapter 9 the variation in industrialization policy is not very large so that the equation may be assumed to be invariant. (Further details about invariance of behavioral equations can be found in Mishkin, 1979, and Sums, 1980)

- Estimation of effects at the national and international levels, e.g. national and international environmental, employment, income and investment effects. It should be observed that effects which can less easily be defined and measured than the above-mentioned should also be taken into account. Examples of such effects are efficiency losses for firms that have located in assisted areas, the exploitation of resources that might have remained idle, etc (see for further details Moore and Rhodes, 1974, 1977 and Schofield, 1979).

- Costs of economic policy. It is obvious that efficient policymaking is only possible if both the effects and the public costs are taken into account. Therefore, an obvious issue for further research is the development of methods to assess costs so that effects could be weighed by the costs. The following types of costs should be taken into account. First, **budget** costs at both the national and the regional level, such as public expenditures on investment premiums, employment programs, etc. In order to arrive at as complete a financial overview as possible the financial yields should also be taken into account. That is, increases in tax payments, savings in unemployment benefits, etc., should be deducted from the expenditures. Secondly, **opportunity** costs which are made up by the alternative uses that could have been made of the funds spent on regional economic policy. In this regard two aspects have to be distinguished. In the first place, identification of restrictions on the regional and the national economy because of the expenditures on regional economic policy. Secondly, assessment of the effects of the possible relaxation of the restrictions.

- Determination of policy interventions. This step in the process of policymaking consists of the choice for the policy variable to maximize a function that describes the preferences of the policymakers. In this function should be included the expectation of the private sector of the policy instruments and the policy objectives. Traditionnally, the expectations of the private sector are assumed to be predetermined and to be based on the past history of the economy. This assumption, however, negates that expectations are responsive to current and future choices of policy variables. Consequently, inconsistent policy plans may arise (see, among others Kydland and

Prescott, 1977, Prescott, 1977 and Fischer, 1980). An important topic for further research is the development of methods which allow of adequate handling of expectations and of developing consistent policy plans.

So far attention has only briefly been paid to some steps in the process of policy evaluation which are directly related to impact assessment. It is obvious that various aspects of the other steps described in section 2.3. also need further investigation. These problems, however, are not considered here.

REFERENCES

Aigner, D.J. and Goldberger, A.S. (Eds), (1977). Latent Variables in Socio-
    Economic Models. North-Holland, Amsterdam.

Anderson, O.D. (1976). Times Series Analysis and Forecasting. Butterworths,
    London and Boston.

Armstrong, H. and Taylor, J. (1978). Regional Economic Policy and its
    Analysis. Allen, London.

Ashcroft, B. (1979). The evaluation of the regional economic policy: The
    case of the United Kingdom. In: Allen, K. (Ed). Balanced National
    Growth. Lexington Books, Lexington, MA.

Ashcroft, B. and Taylor, J. (1977). The movement of manufacturing industry
    and the effect of regional policy. Oxford Economic Papers; 29, 84-101.

Ashcroft, B. and Taylor, J. (1979). The effect of regional policy on the
    movement of industry in Great Britain. In: MacLennan, D and Parr, J.B.
    (Eds) Regional Policy: Past Experiences and New Directions. Robertson,
    Oxford, UK.

Ballard, K.P.; Glickman, N.J. and Windling, R.M. (1980) Using a multi-
    regional econometric model to measure the spatial impacts of federal
    polices. In: Glickman, N.J. (Ed) The Urban Impacts of Federal Policies,
    John Hopkins University Press, Baltimore.

Bartels, C.P.A. and Duyn, J.J. van (1980). Regionaal Economisch Beleid in
    Nederland. Van Gorcum, Assen.

Bartels, C.P.A., Nicol, W.R. and Duyn, J.J. van (1982). Estimating t h e
    impacts of regional policies: A review of applied research methods.
    Regional Science and Urban Economics, 12;4-41.

Bartlett, M.S. (1946). On the theoretical specification of sampling
    properties of autocorrelated time series. Journal of the Royal
    Statistical Society B, 8; 22-41.

Bartlett, M.S. (1955). Stochastic Processes. Cambridge University Press,
    Cambridge, UK.

Basman, R.L. (1963). The causal interpretation of non-triangular systems of
    economic relations. Econometrica, 31; 439-448.

Batey, P.W.J. (1985) Input-output models for regional demographic-economic
    analysis: Some structural comparisons. Environment and Planning A, 17;
    73-100.

Batey, P.W.J. and Madden, M (1983) The modelling of demographic-economic change within the context of regional decline: Analytical procedures and empirical results. Socio-Economic Planning Sciences. 17; 315-328

Beaumont, P.B. (1979) An examination of assisted labour mobility policy. In: MacLennan, D and Parr, J.B. (Eds) Regional Policy: Past Experiences and New Directions. Robertson, Oxford, UK.

Begg, H.M., Lythe, C.M. and MacDonald, D.R. (1976). The impact of regional-policy on investment in manufacturing industry: Scotland 1960-71. Urban Studies, 13; 171-179

Bennett, R.J. (1979). Spatial Time Series. Pion, London.

Bentler, P.M. (1982). Linear Systems with multiple levels and types of latent variables. In: Jöreskog, K.G. and Wold, H.O.A. (Eds) Proceedings of the Conference "Systems under Indirect Observation. Causality-Structure-Prediction". North-Holland, Amsterdam.

Bentzel, R. and Hansen, B. (1955). On recursiveness and interdependency in economic models. The Review of Economic Studies, 22; 153-168.

Berentsen, W.H. (1978). Austrian regional development policy: The impact of policy on the achievement of planning goals. Economic Geography, 54; 115-134.

Bickel, P.J. and Freedman, D.A. (1981) Some asymptotic theory for the bootstrap. Annals of Statistics, 9; 1196-1217.

Bishop, Y.M.M., Fienberg, S.E. and Holland, P.W. (1975). Discrete Multivariate Analysis: Theory and Practice. MIT Press, Cambridge, Mass.

Blalock, H.M. Jr. (1971). Theory building and causal influences. In: Blalock, H.M. Jr. and Blalock, A.B. (Eds) Methodology in Social Research. McGraw-Hill, London et al.

Bolton, R (1980) Multiregional models: Introduction to a symposium. Journal of Regional Science, 20; 131-142.

Boot, J.C.J., Feibes, W. and Lisman, J.H.C. (1967). Further methods of derivation of quarterly figures from annual data. Applied Statistics, 16; 65-75.

Boudeville, J.R. (1966). Problems of Regional Economic Planning. Edinburgh University Press, Edinburgh.

Bowers, J.K. and Gunawardena, A. (1978). Industrial development certificates and regional policy, Part 2. Bulletin of Economic Research, 30; 3-13.

Box, G.E.P. and Jenkins, G.M. (1976). **Time Series Analysis: Forecasting and Control.** Holden-Day, San Francisco et al.

Box, G.E.P. and Tiao, G.C. (1975). Intervention analysis with applications to economic and environmental problems. **Journal of the American Statistical Association,** 70; 70-79.

Buck, T.W. and Atkins, M.H. (1976). The impact of British regional policies on employment growth. **Oxford Economic Papers,** 28; 118-132.

Buiter, W.H. and Owen R.F. (1970). Stabilization policy in The Netherlands. **De Economist,** 127; 88-102.

Calame, A (1980). Impacts and costs of wage subsidy programmes: experiences in Great Britain, Sweden and the USA. Paper of the International Institute of Management, Berlin.

Campbell, D.T. (1963). From description to experimentation: Interpreting trends as quasi-experiments. In: Harris, C.W. (Ed) **Problems in Measuring Change.** University of Wisconsin Press, Madison, Wisc.

Campbell, D.T. (1969). Reforms as experiments. **American Psychologist,** 24; 118-131.

Campbell, D.T. and Stanley, J.C. (1966). **Experimental and Quasi-experimental Designs for Research,** Rand MacNally, Chicago.

Cannell, C.F. and Kahn, R.L. (1953). The collection of data by interviewing. In: Festinger, L. and Katz, D. (Eds) **Research Methods in the Social Sciences.** The Dryden Press, New York.

Cannell, C.F. and Kahn, R.L. (1968). Interviewing. In: Lindzey, G. and Aronson, E. (Eds) **The Handbook of Social Psychology,** Vol. II. Addison-Wesley, Reading, Mass.

Carnap, R. (1936). Testability and meaning. **Philosophy and Science,** 3; 420-468.

Carnap, R. (1937). Testability and meaning. **Philosophy and Science,** 4; 1-40.

Carnap, R. (1956). The methodological character of theoretical concepts. In: Feigl, H. and Scriven, M. (Eds) **Minnesota Studies in the Philosophy of Science I.** University of Minnesota Press, Minneapolis.

Carter, R.A.L. and Nagar, A.L. (1977). Coefficients of correlation for simultaneous equation systems. **Journal of Econometrics,** 6; 65-76.

Centraal Planbureau (1973). Een regionaal arbeidsmarktmodel. Paper of the Centraal Planbureau, Den Haag, Netherlands.

Chernoff, H. and Rubin, H. (1953) Asymptotic properties of limited information estimates under generalized conditions. In: Koopmans, T.C. and
Hood, W.C. (Eds) **Studies in Econometric Method.** Wiley, New York.

Cliff, A.D. and Ord, J.K. (1969) The problem of spatial autocorrelation. In:
Scott, A.J. (Ed) **Studies in Regional Science.** Pion, London.

Cliff, A.D. and Ord, J.K. (1973). **Spatial Autocorrelation.** Pion, London.

Cliff, A.D. and Ord, J.K. (1981) **Spatial Processes. Models and Applications.**
Pion, London.

Courbis, R. (1979). The Regina Model. A regional-national model for French
planning. **Regional Science and Urban Economics,** 9; 117-139

Cremers, W.J.M. (1975). Een kwart eeuw regionaal overheidsbeleid:
Machteloosheid van de regio's door nevenvestingen. Department of
Sociology, University of Groningen, Groningen, Netherlands.

Danziger, S., Haveman, R., Smolensky, E. and Tauber, K (1980). The urban
impacts of the program for better jobs and income. In: Glickman, N.J.
(Ed). **The Urban Impacts of Federal Policies.** John Hopkins University
Press, Baltimore.

Delft, A. van, Hamel, B.A. van, and Hetsen, H. (1977). Een multi-regionaal
model voor Nederland. Occasional Papers no. 13, Centraal Planbureau,
Den Haag, Netherlands.

Dessant, J.W. and Smart, R. (1977). Evaluating the effects of regional
economic policy: A Critique. **Regional Studies,** 11; 147-152.

Dhrymes, Ph, J. (1971). **Distributed Lags: Problems of Estimation and
Formulation.** Holden-Day, San Francisco.

Dhrymes, Ph, J. (1978). **Introductory Econometrics.** Springer Verlag, New York
et al.

Diaconis, P. and Efron, B. (1983) Computer-intensive methods in statistics.
Scientific American. Vol. 83; 96-107.

Dijk, J van and Folmer, H. (1985). Entry of umemployed into employment:
Theory, Methodology and Dutch experience. **Regional Studies,** Special
Issue on Information in Labor Markets. (Forthcoming).

Dijk, J van and Folmer, H (1986). The consequences of interregional migration for the regional labor market: Theory, methodology and
Dutchexperience. **Review of Economics and Statistics.** (Forthcoming).

Dijkstra, T.K. (1981). Latent Variables in Linear Stochastic Models.
Reflections on `Maximum Likelihood` and `Partial Least Squares`
Methods. Unpublished Ph.D. Thesis, Department of Econometrics,
University of Groningen, Groningen, Netherlands.

Dijkstra, T.K. (1983). Some comments on maximum likelihood and partial least
squares methods. **Journal of Econometrics,** 14; 67-91.

Dijkstra, T.K. (Ed) (1984) **Misspecification Analysis**. Springer, Heidelberg.

Droth, W. and Fischer, M.M. (1981). Zur Theoriebildung und Theorie-testung. Eine Diskussion von Grundlagen Problemen am Beispiel der Sozialraum-analyse. In: Ostheider, M. and Steiner, D. (Eds) **Theorie und Quantitative Methodik in der Geographie**. Geographischer Institut, ETH-Zürich, Zürich.

Duncan, O.D. (1975). **Introduction to Structural Equation Models**. Academic Press, New York.

Durbin, J. (1970) Testing for serial correlation in least-squares regression when some of the regressors are lagged dependent variables. **Econometrica**, 38; 410-421.

Durbin, J. and Watson, G.S. (1950). Testing for serial correlation in least squares regression, I. **Biometrika**, 37; 409-428.

Durbin, J. and Watson, G.S. (1951). Testing for serial correlation in least squares regression, II. **Biometrika**, 38; 159-178.

Duyn, J.J. van (1975). De doelmatigheid van het regionaal-economisch beleid in Nederland in de jaren zestig. **Tijdschrift voor Economische en Sociale Geografie**, 66; 258-271.

Efron, B. (1979) Bootstrap methods: Another look at the jackknife. **Annals of Statistics**, 7; 1-26.

Efron, B. (1982) **The Jackknife, the Bootstrap and other Resampling Plans**. SIAM, Philadelphia.

Efron, B. and Gong, G. (1983). A leisurely look at the bootstrap, the jack-knife and cross-validation. **The American Statistician**, 37; 36-48.

Eliasson, G (1980). Experiments with fiscal policy parameters on a micro to macro model of the Swedish economy. In: Haveman, R.H. and Hollenbeck, K. (Eds) **Micro-economic Simulation Models for Public Analysis**. Volume II. Sectoral, Regional and General Equilibrium Models. Academic Press, New York.

Engström, M.G. (1970). **Regional Arbetsfordelning. Nya Drag i Forvärvs-arbetets Geografiska Organisation i Sverige**. Gleerup, Lund, Sweden.

Feigl, H. (1956). Some major issues and developments in the philosophy of science of logical empiricism. In: Feigl, H. and Scriven, M. (Eds) **Minnesota Studies in the Philosophy of Science I**. University of Minnesota Press, Minneapolis.

Ferguson, T.S. (1967). **Mathematical Statistics: A Decision Theoretic Approach**. Academic Press, New York.

Festinger, L and Katz, D (Eds) (1954). **Research Methods in the Behavioural Sciences**. Staples Press, London.

Fischer, M.M. (1982). Theory and testing in empirical sciences. Paper of the Department of Geography, University of Vienna, Austria.

Fischer, M.M. and Folmer, H. (1982). Measurement of effects of regional policy by means of time series analysis. **Papers of the Regional Science Association**, 49; 133-151.

Fischer, M.M. and Folmer, H. (1983). Progress and problems in the methodology of regional science. Summary report of the 22nd European RSA conference. **Papers of the Regional Science Association**, 52; 214-218.

Fisher, F.M. (1966). **The Identification Problem in Econometrics**. McGraw-Hill, New York.

Fisher, F.M. (1970). A correspondence principle for simultaneous equation models. **Econometrica**, 38; 73-92.

Fischer, S. (1980). Dynamic inconsistency, cooperation and the benevolent dissembling government. **Journal of Economic Dynamics and Control**, 2; 93-107.

Fisher, W.D. (1971). Econometric estimation with spatial dependence. **Regional and Urban Economics**, 1; 19-40.

FNEI (1981). Arbeidsmarktvooruitzichten. FNEI, Assen, Netherlands.

FNEI (1983). De constructie van de Input-Output- tabel Noorden 1972. FNEI, Assen, Netherlands.

Folmer, H. (1980). Measurement of the effects of regional policy instruments. **Environment and Planning A**, 12; 1191-1202.

Folmer, H. (1981). Measurement of the effects of regional policy instruments by means of linear structural equation models and panel data. **Environment and Planning A**, 13, 1435-1448.

Folmer, H (1985). Bootstrapping ARIMA models: some simulation results. Research Memorandum. Faculty of Economics, University of Groningen, Netherlands.

Folmer, H (1985b). Jackknife estimation of a spatio-temporal LISREL model. Some evidence from computer simulation. Research Memorandum. Department of Economics. University of Groningen, Netherlands.

Folmer, H. and Dijk, J. van (1985). Differences in labour market characteristics between unemployed with different spells of unemployment. Research Memorandum. Faculty of Economics. University of Groningen, Groningen, Netherlands.

Folmer, H and Fischer, M.M. (1984). Bootstrap estimation in spatial analysis. Research Memorandum. Faculty of Economics, University of Groningen, Netherlands.

Folmer, H. and Knaap, G.A. van der (1981). A linear structural equation approach to cross-sectional models with lagged variables. **Environment and Planning A**, 13; 1529-1537.

Folmer, H. and Nijkamp, P. (1984). Linear structural equation models with spatio-temporal autocorrelation. In: Bahrenberg G. and Fischer M.M. (Eds) **Models in Geography and Planning**. Bremer Beitrage zur Geographie und Raumplannung, University of Bremen, Bremen, FRG.

Folmer, H. and Nijkamp P. (1986) Effects of Dutch regional industrialisation policy, 1972-1980. Research Memorandum. Faculty of Economics. University of Groningen. Groningen, The Netherlands.

Folmer, H. and Oosterhaven J. (1983). Measurement of employment effects of Dutch regional socio-economic policy. In: Kuklinski, A. and Lambooy, J.G. (Eds.) **Dilemmas in Regional Policy**, Mouton, Berlin.

Folmer, H and Oosterhaven, J. (1985). An interregional labour market model incorporating vacancy chains and social security. **Papers of the Regional Science Association**. (Forthcoming)

Freedman, D.A. (1981) Bootstrapping regression models. **Annals of Statistics**, 9; 1218-1228.

Freedman, D.A. and Peeters, S.C. (1984). Bootstrapping a regression equation: Some empirical results. **Journal of the American Statistical Association**, 97; 97-106.

Friedmann, J. (1979). On the contradictions between city and countryside. In: Folmer, H. and Oosterhaven, J. (Eds) **Spatial Inequalities and Regional Development**. Martinus Nijhoff, Boston et al.

Frost, M.E. (1975). The impact of regional policy: A case study of manufacturing employment in the Northern Region. **Progress in Planning**, 4; 169-237.

Fuller, W.A. (1976) **Introduction to Statistical Time Series**. Wiley, New York.

Gabrielsen, A. (1978) Consistency and identifiability. **Journal of Econometrics**, 8; 261-265.

Gaver, K.M. and Geisel, M.S. (1974). Discriminating among alternative models: Bayesian and non-Bayesian methods. In: Zarembka, P. (Ed). **Economic Theory and Mathematical Economics**. Academic Press, New York.

Geary, R.C. (1954). The contiguity ratio and statistical mapping. **The Incorporated Statistician**, 5; 115-145.

Geiser, S. (1974). A predictive approach to the random effect model. **Biometrika**, 61; 101-107.

Geiser, S. (1975). The predictive sample re-use method with applications. **Journal of the American Statistical Association**, 70, 320-328.

Geweke J. (1977). The dynamic factor analysis of economic time series models. In: Aigner, D.J. and Goldberger, A.S. (Eds) Latent Variables in Socio-Economic Models. North-Holland, Amsterdam.

Glickman, N.J. (Ed) (1980). The Urban Impacts of Federal Policies. John Hopkins University Press, Baltimore.

Gnadadesikan, R. (1977). Methods for Statistical Data Analysis of Multivariate Observations. Wiley, New York.

Goldberger, A.S., Nagar, A.L. and Odeh, M.S. (1961). The covariance matrices of reduced-form coefficients and of forecasts for a structural econometric model. Econometrica, 29; 556-573.

Goldberger, A.S. (1972). Structural equation methods in the social sciences. Econometrica, 40; 979-1002.

Goldberger, A.S. (1973). Structural equation models. In: Goldberger, A.S. and Duncan, O.P. (Eds) Structural Equation Models in the Social Sciences. Seminar Press, New York.

Goldberger, A.S. and Duncan, O.P. (Eds) (1973). Structural Equation Models in the Social Sciences. Seminar Press, New York.

Goldfeld, S.M. and Quandt, R.E. (1972). Nonlinear Methods in Econometrics. North-Holland, Amsterdam.

Graff, M.A. and Schmidt, P. (1982). On decomposition of effects in causal models. In: Jöreskog, K.G. and Wold, H.A.O. (Eds) Proceedings of the Conference `Systems under Indirect Observation. Causality-Structure-Prediction`. North-Holland, Amsterdam.

Gray, M.L. and Schucany, W.R. (1972). The Generalized Jackknife Statistic. Dekker, New York.

Griliches, Z. (1967). Distributed Lags: A Survey. Econometrica, 35; 16-49.

Haavelmo, T. (1944). The probability approach in econometrics. Econometrica, 12, Supplement.

Haggett, P., Cliff, A.D. and Frey, A. (1977). Locational Methods. Arnold, London.

Hahn, F.M. (1980). Money and Inflation. Blackwell, Oxford.

Hahn, F.M. (1982). Monetarism and economic theory. Economica, 47; 1-17.

Hailstones, J (Ed) (1982). Viewpoints on Supply-Side Economics. R.F. Dame, Richmond.

Hall, R.E., (1975). Effects of the experimental negative income tax on labor supply. In: Peckman, J.A. and Timparrel, J. (Eds). Work Incentives and Income Garantees. Brookings Institute, Washington, D.C.

Hanssen, L.P. and Sargent, T.J. (1980). Formulating and estimating dynamic lineair rational expectations models. Journal of Economic Dynamics and Control, 1 ; 7-46

Hart, R.A. (1971). The distribution of new industrial buildings in the 1960's. Scottish Journal of Political Economy, 18;181-197.

Hartigan, J.A. (1969) Using subsample values as typical values. Journal of the American Statistical Association, 64; 1303-1317.

Haveman, R.H, and Hollenbeck, K. (Eds) (1980). Micro economic Simulation Models for Public Policy Analysis. Volume I. Distributional Impacts. Volume II. Sectoral, Regional and General Equilibrium Models. Academic Press, New York.

Hempel, C.G. (1958). The theoretician's dilemma. A study in the logic of theory construction. In: Feigl, M., Scriven, M., Maxwell, G. (Eds) Minnesota Studies in the Philosophy of Science. University of Minnesota Press, Minneapolis.

Hempel, C.G. (1970). On the 'standard conception' of scientific theories. In: Radner, M., Winokur, S. (Eds) Minnesota Studies in the Philosophy of Science. University of Minnesota Press, Minneapolis.

Hendriks, A.J. (1972). Economie en regionale politiek. In: Klaassen, L.H. (Ed) Regionale Economie: Het Ruimtelijk Element in de Economie. Wolters-Noordhoff, Groningen, Netherlands.

Hirschman, A.O. (1958). The Strategy of Economic Development. Yale University Press, New Haven.

Holland, S. (1976). Capital versus The Regions. MacMillan, London.

Holland, S. (1979). Capital, labor and the regions. In: Folmer, H. and Oosterhaven, J. (Eds) Spatial Inequalities and Regional Development. Martinus Nijhoff, Boston.

Hoover, E.M. (1975). An Introduction to Regional Economics. Second Edition. Knopf, New York.

Hordijk, L. (1974). Spatial correlation in the disturbances of a linear interregional model. Regional and Urban Economics, 4; 117-140.

Hordijk, L. and Nijkamp, P. (1977). Dynamic models of spatial autocorrelation. Environment and Planning A, 9; 505-519.

Hordijk, L. and Nijkamp, P. (1978). Estimation of spatio-temporal models. In: Karlqvist A., Lundquist, L. and Snickars, F. (Eds) Spatial Interaction Theory and Planning Models. North-Holland, Amsterdam.

Insée (1978). Annales de l'Insee. The Econometrics of Panel Data, Issue 30-31 (April-September), Paris.

Johnston, J. (1972). Econometric Methods. McGraw-Hill, New York.

Jöreskog, K.G. (1973a). A general method for estimating a linear structural equation system. In: Goldberger, A.S. and Duncan, O.D. (Eds) **Structural Equation Models in the Social Sciences.** Seminar Press, New York.

Jöreskog, K.G. (1973b). Analysis of covariance structures. In: Krishnaiah (Ed) **Multivariate Analysis.** III. Academic Press, New York.

Jöreskog, K.G. (1977a). Structural equation models in the social sciences: Specification, estimation and testing. Paper of the Department of Statistics, University of Uppsala, Uppsala, Sweden.

Jöreskog, K.G. (1977). An econometric model for multivariate data. In: **Annales de l'Insee.** Issue 30-31.

Jöreskog, K.G. (1981). Basic issues in the application of LISREL, **Data,** 1; 1-6.

Jöreskog, K.G. and Sörbom, D. (1978). Lisrel IV-a general computer program for estimating of linear structural equation systems by maximum likelihood methods. Department of Statistics, University of Uppsala, Uppsala, Sweden.

Jöreskog, K.G. and Sörbom, D. (1981). LISREL V. Analysis of linear structural relationships by maximum likelihood and least squares methods. Research Report 81-8. Department of Statistics, University of Uppsala, Uppsala, Sweden.

Jöreskog, K.G. and Sörbom (1984). LISREL VI. Analysis of linear structural relationships by the method of maximum likelihood. Users Guide. Department of Statistics, University of Uppsala, Uppsala, Sweden.

Judge, G.G., Griffiths, W.E., Hill, R.C. and Lee, T.C. (1980) **The Theory and Practice of Econometrics.** Wiley, New York et al.

Kish, L. and Frankel, M.R. (1974). Inference from complex samples. **Journal of the Royal Statistical Society** A, 143; 141-165.

Kirschen, E.S., Blackaby, F., Csapo, L., Karnecki, Z., Kestens, P. (1974). **Economic Policies Compared. West and East. General Theory.** Vol. 1. North-Holland, Amsterdam.

Kiviet, J.F. (1984). Bootstrap inference in lagged-dependent variable models. Report AE 18/84. Faculty of Acturial Science and Econometrics. University of Amsterdam, Amsterdam.

Klein, L.R. (1977). Economic policy formation through the medium of economic models. In: Intrilligator, M. (Ed). **Frontiers of Quantative Economics.** North-Holland, Amsterdam.

Koyck, L.M. (1954). **Distributed Lags and Investment Analysis.** North-Holland, Amsterdam.

Krist, H. (1980). An appreciation of regional policy evaluation studies: The case of the Federal Republic of Germany. Paper of the International Institute of Management, Berlin.

Kydland, F.E. and Prescott, E.C. (1977). Rules rather than discretion: The inconsistency of optimal plans. Journal of Political Economy. 85; 473-491.

Lambooy, J.G. (1975). Ekonomie en Ruimte: Inleiding in de Economische Geografie en de Regionale Economie. Van Gorcum, Assen.

Lawley, D.N. and Maxwell, A.E. (1963). Factor Analysis as a Statistical Method. Butterworth, London.

Leamer, E.E. (1978). Specification Searches. Ad hoc Inference with Nonexperimental Data. Wiley, New York.

Lehman, E.L. (1959). Testing Statistical Hypotheses. Wiley, New York.

Leontief, W.; Morgan, A.; Polenske, K.; Simpson, D. and Tower, E (1965). The economic impact - industrial and regional - of an arms cut. Review of Economics and Statistics. 47; 217-241.

Lloyd, P.E. and Dicken, P. (1979). Location in Space. Harper and Row, New York.

Lovell, M.C. (1983) Data mining. Review of Economics and Statistics, 65; 1-12.

Lucas, R.E. Jr. and Prescott, E. (1971). Investment under uncertainty. Econometrica; 39; 659-681.

Lucas, R.E. Jr. (1976). Econometric policy evaluation: A critique. In: Brunner, K. and Meltzer, A.H. (Eds). The Phillips Curve and Labor Markets; North-Holland, Amsterdam.

MacKay (1979). The death of regional policy- or resurrection squared? Regional Studies, 13; 281-296.

Maddala, G.S. (1971). The use of variance component models in pooling cross section and time series data. Econometrica, 39; 341-358.

Maddala, G.S. (1977) Econometrics, McGraw-Hill, New York.

Madden, M. and Batey, P.W.J. (1983). Linked population and economic models : Some methodological issues in forecasting, analysis and policy optimization. Journal of Regional Science, 23; 144-164.

Malinvaud, E. (1970). Statistical Methods of Econometrics. North-Holland, Amsterdam.

Marquand, J. (1980). Measuring the effects and costs of regional incentives. Working Paper, No. 32, Department of Industry, London.

Marschak, J. (1969). On econometric tools. Synthese, 20; 483-488.

Martin, R.L. and Oepen, J.E. (1975). The identification of regional forecasting models using space-time correlation functions. Transactions of the Institute of British Geographers, 66; 465-474.

260

McCarthy, Ph.J. (1976) The use of balanced half-sample replication in cross-validation studies. Journal of the American Statistical Association, 71; 596-604.

McCorquodale, K. and Weehl, P.E. (1956). Operational validity of intervening constructs. In: Marx, M.H. (Ed). Psycological Theory. MacMillan, New York.

Miernyk, W.H., Bonner, E.R., Chapman, J.H. and Shellhammer, K. (1967). Impact of the Space Progran on a Local Economy: An Input-Output Analysis. West Virginia University Library, Morgantown, W.V..

Miller, R.G. (1964). A trustworthy jackknife. Annals of Mathematical Statistics, 39; 1594-1605.

Ministerie van Economische Zaken (1977). Nota regionaal sociaal-economisch beleid 1977 t/m 1980. Tweede Kamer, Den Haag, Netherlands.

Ministerie van Economische Zaken (1982). Nota regionaal sociaal-economisch beleid 1981/1985. Tweede Kamer, Den Haag, Netherlands.

Ministerie van Economische Zaken (1985) Nota regionaal sociaal-economisch beleid 1986-1990. Tweede Kamer, Den Haag, Netherlands.

Mishkin, F.S. (1979). Simulation methodology in macro economics: An innovation technique. Journal of Political Economy 87; 816-836.

Mood, A.E., Graybill, F.A., and Boes, D.C. (1974). Introduction to the Therory of Statistics. McGraw-Hill, London.

Moore, B. and Rhodes, J. (1973). Evaluating the effects of British regional economic policy. Economic Journal, 83; 87-110.

Moore, B. and Rhodes, J. (1974). The effects of regional economic policy in the United Kingdom. In: Sant, M. (Ed) Regional Policy and Planning for Europe. Saxon House, Farnborough.

Moore, B. and Rhodes, J. (1976). Regional economic policy and the movement of manufacturing firms to development areas. Economica, 43; 17-31.

Moore, B. and Rhodes, J. (1976b). A quantative analysis of effects of the Regional Employment Premium and other regional policy instruments. In: Whiting, A. (Ed). The Economics of Industrial Subsidies. Department of Industry, London.

Moore, B. and Rhodes, J. (1977). Evaluating the economic effects of regional policy. In: Report on Methods of Measuring the Effects of Regional Policy. OECD, Paris.

Moran, P.A.P. (1950). Notes on continuous stochastic phenomena. Biometrika, 37; 17-23.

Mosteller, F. and Tukey, J.W. (1977). Data Analysis and Regression. A Second Course in Statistics. Addison-Wesley, Reading, Mass.

Muthén, B. (1978) Contributions to factor analysis of dichotomous variables. **Psychometrika**, 43; 551-560.

Muthén, B. (1979) A structural brobit model with latent variables. **Journal of the American Statistical Association**, 74; 807-811.

Muthén, B. (1981) Some categorical response models with continuous latent variables. In: Jöreskog, K.G. and Wold, H. (Eds) **Procedings of the Conference " Systems under Indirect Observation: Causality, Structure and Prediction"**. North-Holland, Amsterdam.

Myrdal, G. (1957). **Rich Lands and Poor**. Harper and Row, New York.

Naylor, T.H. (1971). Policy simulation experiments with macro-econometric models: The state of the art. In: Intrilligator, M. (Ed). **Frontiers of Quantative Economics**, North-Holland, Amsterdam.

NEI (1972). Zwolle en Kampen na tien jaar stimulering. Paper of the Netherlands Economic Institute, Rotterdam, Netherlands.

Nelson, C.R. (1973). **Applied Time Series Analysis**. Holden Day, San Francisco.

Nerlove, M. and Wallis, K.F. (1966) Use of the Durbin-Watson statistic in inappropriate situations. **Econometrica**, 34; 235-238.

Nicholls, D.E., Pagan, A.R. and Tenell, R.D. (1975) The estimation and use of models with moving average disturbance term: A survey. **International Economic Review**, 16; 113-134.

Nijkamp, P. (1977). **Theory and Applications of Environmental Economics**. North-Holland, Amsterdam.

Nijkamp, P. (1979). **Multidimensional Spatial Data and Decision Analysis**. Wiley, New York.

Nijkamp, P. and Rietveld, P. (1981). Measurement of effectiveness of regional policies by means of multi-regional economic models. Paper of the Department of Economics, Free University, Amsterdam.

OECD (1978). **Public Expenditure Trends**. OECD, Paris.

Ohlsson, L. (1980). Regional industrial policies in a small open economy: A retrospective study of means, effects and limitations of Swedish regional policies 1965-75. Paper of ERU, Department of Industry, Stockholm, Sweden.

Olsson, U. (1979). Maximum likelihood estimation of the polychoric correlation coefficient. **Psychometrika**, 44; 443-460.

Olsson, U., Drasgow, F. and Dorans, N.I. (1981). The polyserial correlation coefficient. Paper of the Department of Statistics, University of Uppsala, Uppsala, Sweden.

Oosterhaven, J. (1981). **Interregional Input-Output Analysis and Dutch Regional Policy Problems.** Gower, Hampshire, England.

Oosterhaven, J. and Folmer, H. (1983). Review and evaluation of Dutch regional socio-economic policy. In: Kuklinski, A. and Lambooy, J.G. (Eds) **Dilemmas in Regional Policy,** Mouton, Berlin.

Oppenheim, A.M. (1966). **Questionnaire Design and Attitude Measurement,** Butterworth, London.

Orcutt, G.H., Glazer, A., Harris, R. and Wertheimer, R. (1980). Micro analytic modeling and the analysis of public transfer policies. In: Haveman, R.H. and Hollenbeck, K. (Eds). **Micro Economic Simulation Models for Public Policy Analysis,** Volume I, **Distrubutional Impacts.** Academic Press, New York.

Pack, D.J. (1974). Computer programs for the analysis of univariate time series models and single input transfer function models using the methods of Box and Jenkins. Paper of the Ohio State University, Columbus, Ohio.

Paelinck, J.M.P. (1971). Techniques of regional plan formulation: Problems of interregional consistency. In: Dunham, D.M. and Hilhorst, J.G.M. (Eds). **Issues in Regional Planning,** Den Haag, Netherlands.

Paelinck, J.M.P. (1973). **Hoe Doelmatig kan Regionaal en Sectoraal Beleid zijn?** Stenfert Kroese, Leiden, Netherlands.

Paelinck, J.H.P. and P. Nijkamp (1976). **Operational Theory and Method in Regional Economics.** Saxon House. Farnborough.

Perroux, F. (1955). Note sur la notion de pole de croissance. **Economie Applique,** 7; 307-320.

Pindyck, R. (1973). **Optimal Planning for Economic Stabilization.** North-Holland, Amsterdam.

Poolman, F.S. and Wever, E. (1978). Vestigingspremies en lokale arbeidsmarkt. Paper no. 4 of the Institute for Geography and Planning, University of Nijmegen, Nijmegen, Netherlands.

Pred, A. (1967a). **Behaviour and Location, Part I and Part II.** Lund Studies in Geography, Series B, 27 and 29. University of Lund, Sweden.

Prescott, E.C. (1977). Should control theory be used for economic stabilization? In: Brunner, K. and Meltzer, A.H. (Eds). **Optimal Policies, Control Theory and Technology Exports.** Carnegie-Rochester Conference Series on Public Policy. North-Holland, Amsterdam.

Quenouille, M.M. (1949). Approximate tests of correlation in time series. **Journal of the Royal Statistical Society,** B, 11; 68-84.

Rao, R. (1965). **Linear Statistical Inference and its Applications.** Wiley, New York.

Rasmussen, D.W. (1980). The urban impacts of the Section 8 existing housing assistence program. In: Glickman, N.J. (Ed) The Urban Impacts of Federal Policies. John Hopkins University Press, Baltimore.

Recker, E. (1977). Erfolgskontrolle regionaler Aktionsprogramme durch Indikatoren. Forschung zur Raumentwicklung, Vol. 6, Bonn, FRG.

Richardson, H.W. (1978). Regional and Urban Economics. Penguin Books. Harmondsworth, UK.

Richardson, H.W. (1979). Aggregate efficiency and interregional equity. In: Folmer, H. and Oosterhaven, J. (Eds) Spatial Inequalities and Regional Development. Martinus Nijhoff, Boston.

Riley, M.W. (1963). Sociological Research. I.A Case Approach. Harcourt, Brace and World, New York.

Riley, R.C. and Ashworth, G.J. (1975). Benelux. An Economic Geography of Belgium, The Netherlands and Luxembourg. Chatto and Windus, London.

Rindskopf, D. (1983). Parameterizing inequality constraints on unique variances in linear structural models. Psychometrika, 48; 73-83.

Rindskopf, D. (1984). Using phantom and imaginary latent variables to parameterize contraints in linear structural models. Psychometrika, 49; 37-47.

Rothenberg, T.J. (1971). Identification in parametric models. Econometrica, 39; 577-591.

Sant, M. (1974). Industrial movement and regional development: The British case. In: Sant, M. (Ed) Regional Policy and Planning for Europe. Saxon House, Farnborough, UK.

Sargent, T.J. (1981) Interpreting ecomomic time series. Journal of Political Economy, 89; 213-248.

Schofield, J.A. (1979). Macro evaluations of the impact of regional policy in Britain: A review of recent research. Urban Studies, 16; 251-271.

Segers, J.H.G. (1977). Sociologische Onderzoeksmethoden. Van Gorcum, Assen.

Shaffer, R. (1979). Determinants of the competetive share in Wisconsin countries, 1962-1972: The role of government policy. Annals of Regional Science, 13; 67-80.

Silvey, S.D. (1970). Statistical Inference. Penguin Books, Harmondsworth, Middx.

Simon, M.A. (1954). Spurious correlation: A causal interpretation. Journal of the American Statistical Association, 49; 467-479.

Singh, K. (1981) On the asymptotic accuracy of Efron's bootstrap. **Annals of Statistics**, 9; 1187-1195.

Smidt, M. de (1978). Ruimtelijke spreiding en regionale ontwikkeling. In: Borchert, J.G., Egbers, G.J.J. and Smidt, M. de (Eds). **Ruimtelijk Beleid in Nederland**. Romen, Bussum, Netherlands.

Smith, V.L. (1979). **Research in Experimental Economics**, Vol. 1. JAI Press, Greenwich, Conn.

Sörbom, D. (1978). An alternative to the methodology for analysis of covariance. **Psychometrika**, 43; 381-396.

Sörbom, D. (1981). The use of structural equation models in evaluation research. Research Report 81-6. Department of Statistics, University of Uppsala, Uppsala, Sweden.

Spector, M. (1966). Theory and observation. **The British Journal for the Philosophy of Science**, 17; 1-20 and 89-104.

Stegmüller, W. (1970). **Probleme und Resultate der Wissenschaftstheorie und Analytischen Philosophie** 2. Springer, Berlin.

Stilwell, F.J.B. (1972). **Regional Economic Policy**. MacMillan, London.

Stone, M. (1974). Cross-validitory choice and assessment of statistical predictions. **Journal of the Royal Statistical Association B**, 36; 111-147.

Streitberg, B. (1979). Multivariate models of dependent spatial data. In: Bartels, C.P.A. and Ketellapper, R.M. (Eds). **Exploratory and Explanatory Statistical Analysis of Spatial Data**. Martinus Nijhoff, Boston.

Strotz, R.H. and Wold, H.O.A. (1960). Recursive versus nonrecursive systems: An attempt at synthesis. **Econometrica**, 28; 417-427.

Strotz, R.H. and Wold, H.O.A. (1963). The causality interpretability of structural parameters: A reply. **Econometrica**, 31; 449-450.

Sums, C.A. (1980). Macro-economics and reality. **Econometrica**, 48; 1-48.

Tamsma, R. (1981). Three decades of regional policy in the Netherlands, 1950-1980. Sociaal-Geografische Reeks, Department of Geography, University of Groningen, Groningen, Netherlands.

Taylor, J.B. (1981). Stabilization, accomodation and monetary rules. **American Economic Review Papers and Proceedings**, 71; 145-149.

Terlouw, J. (1982). Address by the Minister of Economic Affairs at the opening of the 22nd European Congress of the Regional Science Association at Groningen on August 24, 1982. Mimeographed paper of the Department of Economics, University of Groningen, Netherlands.

Theil, H. (1957). Specification errors and the estimation of economic relationships. **Review of the International Statistical Institute**, 25; 41-51.

Theil, H. (1971). Principles of Econometrics. Wiley, New York.

Theil, H. (1975). **Theory and Measurement of Consumer Demand**. Vol. 1. North-Holland, Amsterdam.

Theil, H. (1976). **Theory and Measurement of Consumer Demand**. Vol. 2. North-Holland, Amsterdam.

Thorburn, D. (1976). Some asymptotic properties of jackknife statistics. **Biometrika**, 63; 305-313.

Tiebout, C.M. (1969). An empirical regional input-output projection model: the State of Washington 1980. **Review of Economics and Statistics**, 51; 334-40.

Tinbergen, J. (1956). Economic Policy: Principles and Design. North-Holland, Amsterdam.

Tinbergen, J. (1977). **On the Theory of Economic Policy**. North-Holland, Amsterdam.

Tuppen, J. (1979). New towns in the Paris region: An appraisal. **Town Planning Review**, 50; 55-70.

Vanhove, N. (1962). De doelmatigheid van het Regionaal Economische Beleid in Nederland. Ph.D. Dissertation, Nederlandse Economische Hogeschool, Rotterdam.

Wallis, K.F. (1980) Econometric implication of the rational expectations hypothesis. **Econometrica**, 48; 49-73.

Whittle, P. (1954). On stationary processes in the plane. **Biometrika**, 41; 434-449.

Wold, H.O.A. (1954). Causality and econometrics. **Econometrica**, 22; 162-177.

Zellner, A. (1978). Causality and econometrics. Paper of the Department of Econometrics, University of Wisconsin, USA.

Zoon, J.H. (1974), Regionaal-Economisch beleid. Beleid en Maatschappij, 1; 216-223.

SUBJECT INDEX